STEPHEN HAY is Lecturer in Audio-Visual Production at the Institute of Communication Studies, University of Leeds and continues to direct independent film and video programmes as part of his work. He is currently completing a historical documentary, casting a short drama set in Leeds and working with writer Heather Wallis on a feature-length drama set in both France and Scotland.

THELMA SCHOONMAKER is Martin Scorsese's regular film editor and has edited his major works since *Raging Bull* (1980), for which she won the Academy Award for Best Editing.

*This book is respectfully dedicated
to the memory of
Eugène Pons
1886–1945*

Bertrand Tavernier

THE FILM-MAKER OF LYON

Stephen Hay

FOREWORD BY
Thelma Schoonmaker

I.B.Tauris *Publishers*
LONDON · NEW YORK

Published in 2000 by I.B.Tauris & Co Ltd
Victoria House, Bloomsbury Square, London WC1B 4DZ
175 Fifth Avenue, New York NY 10010
Website: http://www.ibtauris.com

In the United States and Canada distributed by St. Martin's Press
175 Fifth Avenue, New York NY 10010

Copyright © Stephen Hay, 2000

All rights reserved. Except for brief quotations in a review, this book, or any part thereof, may not be reproduced, stored in or introduced into a retrieval system, or transmitted, in any form or by any means, electronic, mechanical, photocopying, recording or otherwise, without the prior written permission of the publisher.

ISBN 1 86064 462 7

A full CIP record for this book is available from the British Library
A full CIP record for this book is available from the Library of Congress

Library of Congress catalog card: available

Typeset in Caslon by Dexter Haven, London
Printed and bound in Great Britain

CONTENTS

		page
	Foreword	vii
	List of Illustrations	xi
	Author's Note	xv
	Acknowledgements	xvii
1	Introduction	1
2	Bertrand Tavernier	4
3	Political Film-maker	13
4	Humanist Film-maker	25
	THE DRAMAS	37
5	*L'Horloger de Saint-Paul* (1973)	39
6	*Que La Fête Commence...* (1975)	48
7	*Le Juge et l'Assassin* (1976)	57
8	*Des Enfants Gâtés* (1977)	66
9	*Death Watch* (1979)	75
10	*Une Semaine de Vacances* (1980)	84
11	*Coup de Torchon* (1981)	94
12	*Un Dimanche à la Campagne* (1984)	103
13	*'Round Midnight* (1986)	112
14	*La Passion Béatrice* (1987)	121
15	*La Vie et Rien d'Autre* (1989)	131
16	*Daddy Nostalgie* (1991)	141
17	*L.627* (1992)	151
18	*La Fille de D'Artagnan* (1994)	161
19	*L'Appât* (1995)	169
20	*Capitaine Conan* (1996)	179
21	*Ça Commence Aujourd'hui* (1999)	189
22	Directing	201
23	The Film-maker of Lyon	217
	Filmography	225
	Bibliography	233
	Index	235

FOREWORD

As well as having his place in the world of cinema as a successful film-maker, Bertrand Tavernier is a devoted film historian. A complete cinema enthusiast, he has been working diligently over the years to educate people about film history, touring festivals incessantly, talking to critics, students and general audiences about his passion for the film-makers who have gone before him. Like my closest colleague, Martin Scorsese, Bertrand has an insatiable desire to share his love of movies with others, and I know that his tremendous enthusiasm has prompted many people to go and search out the films and the film-makers he admires. It was because of Bertrand's devotion to the work of my husband, Michael Powell, and his partner, Emeric Pressburger, that I came to know him.

Gradually, through excited letters and telephone calls from Bertrand to Michael, and finally, as his guest at an excellent meal in a Parisian restaurant (Bertrand's love of food rivals his love for movies), I became aware of how special his friendship with Michael was, and how it began. It turned out that Bertrand had given precious support to Michael back in the sixties when his film *Peeping Tom* was savagely attacked by critics in England. Although Michael felt the distributor should have stood behind the film with ads saying, 'Look, the critics hate this movie – but come and see for yourself,' the film was pulled from theatres, and died. But Bertrand Tavernier, then a young press agent and critic in France, and immensely struck with the power and quality of the film, actively defended and promoted *Peeping Tom*, at a time when Michael's career and reputation had been destroyed. *Peeping Tom* is now considered a masterpiece by many people, including Martin Scorsese, who was later responsible for reviving it in America, but Bertrand was among the first to recognise the astonishing quality of the film when it came out, and this meant so much to Michael Powell, whose career had been literally ruined by the devastating critical reaction in England. In the late sixties, Bertrand sought out Michael, and although I wasn't there, I can imagine how refreshing it was for Michael, who loved France and French movies, to be talking to someone whose encyclopaedic knowledge of film equalled his own. Bertrand began stirring up interest in France about Powell and Pressburger. He got French festivals to show their films, and brought Michael and Emeric to France to speak at these showings. He inspired students to do their PhD theses on the films of 'The Archers', at a time when British cinema was in disrepute in France because of Truffaut's famous remark that had dismissed it completely. More recently, Bertrand has given another gift to Michael Powell. Along with Thierry Frémaux at L'Institut Lumière in Lyon, he arranged for volume one of Michael's autobiography *A Life in Movies* to be translated and published in France. It was so well received that these indefatigable champions of film history are now embarking on the translation and publication of volume two, *Million Dollar Movie*. For Michael Powell, whose career in film began in the South of France, and who spoke French fluently (with a strong English accent), and who read French literature eagerly, this may be the greatest gift of all.

Bertrand Tavernier and Martin Scorsese could hardly be more different as directors, but in the support they gave Michael Powell and in their voracious appetite for film, they are startlingly similar. Over the years they have bombarded each other with videotapes of hard-to-find films they think the other will enjoy, and if they ever get into a room together (which they are too busy to do anymore), we all know that many hours later they will have to be prised apart, or they will go on until dawn, agreeing, disagreeing, exclaiming over some minute detail in an obscure film they both relish, their brains exploding with a vast knowledge of world cinema. Separately they have helped to restore the reputation of many film-makers. But their great triumph together is the way Bertrand in France, and Marty in America and around the world, gave back to Michael Powell and Emeric Pressburger the recognition their work deserved.

I only wish they could have been there to observe Michael as we travelled to retrospectives of The Archers films all over the world: Russia, Finland, England, Scotland, Wales, Holland, France, Spain and to maybe ten cities in the United States. In the beginning, the audiences were mainly people who remembered seeing the films when they were first released. But gradually, the audiences started getting younger and younger, until at the last retrospective Michael attended, they were eighteen years old, and riveted to their seats by the films. It was so moving to watch Michael slowly awake from the oblivion he had existed in for decades, and to see him finally allow himself to believe that his films were alive again and loved. He was fascinating in front of an audience, fully aware of how to entertain them, but also how to shock and arouse them. I learned something new each time he spoke. When the audience would erupt into prolonged applause after he finished speaking, he would cover his face with his hands for a long time and blush – overcome by what was at long last happening to him.

Bertrand's desire to right the wrongs of cinema history has a direct connection to the themes of justice that pervade his own films. *Life and Nothing But, L.627, The Undeclared War, Capitaine Conan, It All Starts Today* – his later films reflect increasingly his deep-rooted conviction that the people we are indebted to, one way or another, should not be forgotten. Read on about the film-maker of Lyon, and you will discover that there is little difference between Tavernier, cinema historian and Bertrand Tavernier, film director.

Thelma Schoonmaker Powell
New York City
July 2000

LIST OF ILLUSTRATIONS

	PAGE
L'Horloger de Saint-Paul	
'Your son has killed a man.' Inspecteur Guibou gives Michel Descombes the news, going on to court and gain his friendship, though it is to be short-lived.	41
Distance between the generations – Michel listens to his son Bernard's confession on tape.	45
Que La Fête Commence…	
'Let the party begin…!' – orgies as Philippe's only means of escape from failure.	50
An anguished regent's confidante – Émilie the prostitute and Philippe d'Orléans.	54
Le Juge et l'Assassin	
'He doesn't listen to me!' – Bouvier comes across Christ in the wilderness.	59
'… Judas!' – Judge now accused by Assassin, Rousseau tries to block Bouvier's words of sympathy to Rose.	62
Des Enfants Gâtés	
Tension and uncertainty – Rougerie and his neighbour and Anne edge towards an impossible love.	70
'I'm just a film director' – Bernard Rougerie, the reluctant campaigner.	72
Death Watch	
A selfish child heads blindly towards tragedy – Roddy Farrar plays the caring companion, while secretly transmitting Katherine Mortenhoe's 'escape' direct to NTV.	78
The pain of truth – Katherine tells stories and Roddy's deception starts to falter.	80
Une Semaine de Vacances	
'Your life is finished' – superficial taunts find Laurence Cuers's Achilles heel: doubt.	87
The repose of undemanding love, the fear of ageing – Laurence visits her sick father.	90

Coup de Torchon
    Rose is led unwittingly into becoming part of Cordier's murderous scheming.   97

    The confident killer – Cordier now happy to threaten Nono openly with the worst.   101

Un Dimanche à la Campagne
    Bitterness momentarily swept aside – Marie-Thérèse, Gonzague and Monsieur Ladmiral delight in Irène's 'splendid' symbol of modernity and success.   106

    '… and if I didn't achieve more, at least I glimpsed what I could have done' – Monsieur Ladmiral opens up his sharpest critic, Irène: sharing a dream about Moses, and intimate doubts about his past choices.   110

'Round Midnight
    Francis watches over his alcoholic jazz hero in utter despair, fearful that he has no power to prevent Dale Turner from drinking himself to death.   114

    Brief respite from the pressures of Paris – Francis shares a few final idyllic moments in Lyon with Dale, just before the maestro expresses his need to return to New York City.   117

La Passion Béatrice
    Enlightened child – Béatrice shares with Our Lady her joy over François's impending return.   124

    Deliberate destruction of love itself – François de Cortemart intent on dragging Béatrice into the Hell to which he has consigned himself.   128

La Vie et Rien d'Autre
    Mme de Courtil searches for clues about her missing husband, whom Major Dellaplane has agreed to completely devote exactly 'one 350,000th' of his 'stunning incompetence'.   133

    'We've done nothing *but* keep quiet!' – after the Grézancourt tunnel explosion, Major Dellaplane refuses to hide his men's suffering in order to make Mme de Courtil feel at ease.   138

Daddy Nostalgie
    Insistent memories – thoughts of the past drag Daddy back yet again to question his life.   143

    Past the hardest truth – following Caroline's bitter accusations over his past selfishness, Daddy suppresses his own hurt for a moment in order to comfort his injured daughter.   148

L.627
 Totally committed, surviving in chaos – Looping, Lulu, Vincent and Marie, all making do within a corrupt system, and inside squalid, prefabicated offices.   154

 Displaced anger – Lulu's frustration with state bureaucracy and his own professional impotence finally explodes, finding only Miloud, a petty drug dealer.   158

La Fille de D'Artagnan
 Beautiful, feisty heroine – Élöise D'Artagnan in full flow, true to the cape-and-sword genre.   163

 Élöise's stubbornness confronts D'Artagnan with the rebellious energy that he has lost.   166

L'Appât
 Seduced by instant gratification and by Hollywood – Eric enjoys posing in front of Bruno with their newly-acquired 'passport' to quitting France for guaranteed quick riches in America.   171

 Forever waiting for life to get better – Nathalie sits in the hall outside the lawyer Jousse's living-room, about to scramble for her earphones.   176

Capitaine Conan
 Courage, but with eyes open – Conan assesses the risks ahead around Mount Skopol.   182

 Blind loyalty – Conan threatens Norbert if he crosses him by prosecuting his comrades.   185

Ça Commence Aujourd'hui
 'There was once a little man…' – Daniel Lefèvre soaks up his small triumph that brings a ray of light into a community burdened by relentless problems and endemic poverty.   191

 Ready to throw in the towel – Valéria struggles to help Daniel after the death of Mme Henry, Laetitia and her baby brother.   196

AUTHOR'S NOTE

French and English usage

Bertrand Tavernier has made films in both the French and English languages. The French and English title of each film is provided at the beginning of each film's respective chapter. In the main text, in the case of his French-language films, the French title is used; in the case of his English-language films, the English title is used.

Technical Terms Used

A few technical terms relating to film-making are used in the main text. These are explained in the endnotes to each chapter.

Author's Interviews

All quotes included in the text which are unmarked with references were taken from the following interviews conducted by the author:

Bertrand Tavernier	22 July 1998	Ciné-Rencontres, Prades
	9 April 1999	TGV Paris–Lyon
		Hotel Mercure, Lyon
Frédéric Bourboulon	29 July 1998	Little Bear, Paris
Pierre-William Glenn	23 July 1998	Ciné-Rencontres, Prades
Bruno de Keyzer	2 December 1998	Kensington, London
Alain Choquart	18 March 1999	Montparnasse, Paris
Jean Cosmos	22nd July 1998	Ciné-Rencontres, Prades
Tiffany Tavernier	18 June 1998	Anzin, Valenciennes

ACKNOWLEDGEMENTS

Early on during the planning for this book, I decided against writing large, thematically-grouped chapters, and chose a structure based on a chronological examination of Bertrand Tavernier's major works. I am grateful to Philippa Brewster at I.B.Tauris for having faith in this approach. For me, it became very important, offering a sense of open journey that helped me to shape this book with an understanding of Tavernier's own development as a director, infinitely curious, continually learning. It helped me to avoid pre-judgement of my subject. For me, this paid off – I learned more about Tavernier since beginning writing than I could have imagined; much that made immediate sense, some that was surprising. Maybe my own justification can best be expressed with words similar to Tavernier's own explanation for the creative principles he adopted to make *L.627* and *Ça Commence Aujourd'hui*: 'For me, it was the only way to be true to my subject'. I hope that my book reflects aptly the element of discovery which is a very real aspect of Tavernier's film-making.

The number of people who deserve thanks for their generous help, encouragement and support in the conception, research and production of this book goes beyond those listed here. All the same, I shall try to mention all those kind people assisted me who would probably be too polite to reprimand me to my face for missing them out. As for the rest, I apologise – and no doubt you will let me know.

I owe a great deal to everyone who nurtured my interest while I was just starting to discover Tavernier's work, including Barry Callaghan, John Edmonds, Dean Jones, Jean Stewart and Liz Wainwright of the Northern School of Film and Television. Kind practical assistance also came from: Colin H. Evans, University of Wales; Barbara Fiorato, University of Salford; Kathleen Hay, FH Associés, Paris; Jill Henderson, Birmingham Film Festival; Claire Holterman, Service Culturel de L'Ambassade de France en Grande-Bretagne; Christine Jimack, University of Glasgow; Aline Kandalaft, French Embassy Cultural

Attaché; Professor Brent MacGregor, Edinburgh College of Art; Dr Francine Wetherill, UMIST.

I am very grateful for the advice of my eternally patient colleagues at the Institute of Communications Studies, University of Leeds, who placed their faith in my idea long before I was brave enough to talk to publishers, and who answered the silliest questions of a novice without any visible eye-rolling: Professor Nicholas Pronay and Professor Philip Taylor. Dr Richard Howells and Dr David Gauntlett are the right people to accept thanks on behalf of all those whose enthusiasm gave me a boost when confidence was flagging; Dr Graham Roberts for practical assistance, moral support and for discussing the work of Bertrand Tavernier during lunch-breaks endlessly – when he could just as easily have been talking about the work of Nicholas Roeg.

I am indebted to the following people, connected with Little Bear and Tavernier, who gave me more of their precious time than I could ever have expected: Agnès Le Pont for her hard work on illustrations, Frédéric Bourboulon, Audrey Brasseur, Sophie Brunet, Anne-Laure Farges, Alain Choquart, Jean Cosmos, Michel Desrois, Thierry Frémaux (Institut Lumière, Lyon), Pierre-William Glenn, Bruno de Keyzer, Florence Loubeau, Tiffany Tavernier, Philippe Torreton, and finally to Bertrand Tavernier himself, for all his generosity, and especially his warm welcome during the last few days shooting of *Ça Commence Aujourd'hui*. I must thank Sigma Photo Agency and Gamma Photo Agency for giving their kind permission to use the stills in this book, and to those at the Roland Grant Archive for their assistance in acquiring images. I am also grateful to Robert Doisneau's daughter, Françine Deroudille, for giving me permission to use his photographs of *Un Dimanche à la Campagne*. I remain truly touched and grateful to Thelma Schoonmaker, for agreeing to write the Foreword to this book while in the midst of the Herculean task of editing Martin Scorsese's documentary on Italian cinema.

A few names may slip past, but it would be both unthinkable and impossible to miss out the following members of my family whose assistance has gone way beyond the moral support that can be selfishly taken for granted under circumstances like the past year: James and Marguerite Hay; David and Margaret Hope; Madeleine Rose Hay, for putting up with the rainiest day imaginable in Lyon so cheerfully; Marie-Laure Hay for asking so often if she could watch 'the film about the grandad and the little girl stuck in the tree' again. Most of all, my greatest thanks to Suzanne, which could quite justifiably fill a text as long as this book.

Stephen Hay

Bertrand Tavernier:
The Film-maker of Lyon

CHAPTER 1

INTRODUCTION

In 1991, while at the Northern School of Film and Television, part of my studies involved writing a dissertation based around the subject of directing fiction film. After several weeks research on my proposal to write about directing drama for television, I changed my mind completely and threw away everything that I had written, having decided to write a piece about directing drama, centred around an examination of the films of Bertrand Tavernier. I no longer remember exactly how I came to my decision, but can recall certain details. At the time, I had seen only five of the 11 feature-films he had made: *Death Watch*, *Un Dimanche à la Campagne* and *'Round Midnight* in the cinema, plus television transmissions of *Le Juge et l'Assassin* and *Une Semaine de Vacances*. I also recall a long conversation with an actor, who told me with great enthusiasm all about *Coup de Torchon*, which he had seen and I had not. So, why write about Tavernier? The first part of my answer is inevitably clichéd…

   I was immensely struck by films that were in such contrast with each other. In terms of atmosphere, visual tone and construction, I almost found it hard to accept that they were directed by the same person. Yet, they were clearly connected: a powerful feeling of reflection; an essentially cinematic dialogue between the past and the present, and one in which the past could suddenly intrude, without announcement; a striking absence of any obviously systematic approach to mise-en-scène and the frame; mise-en-scène in which the camera could disengage completely from simply framing action; camera movements that did not follow characters so much as connect people to each other, and to places; always a hidden side to the characters, intrinsic ambiguity; maybe most of all, loneliness as an inescapable aspect of the human condition, a feeling from which there can be respite but never escape, as the characters try to work out how their past is shaping their present, sometimes trying to work out if things could have been different; many questions, fewer answers. I was sure of little, other than the certainty that Tavernier's films reflected the feelings of someone with a profound curiosity about humanity, and the meaning of all the uncertainty and fragility of people's choices and lives.

So, I set out with the genuine desire to learn about Tavernier's work as a director – to find out how he actually created these films. With help, I started gathering pieces of the jigsaw, filling in the gaps in my viewing, and reading what has been written both about and by Tavernier – there is no shortage of either. I am infinitely more familiar with Tavernier's work now that I was in 1991. I have spoken to many of the fascinating people who have worked with him, some of whom know him very well. I have even got to know him myself – a little. I got the chance to watch him, at very close quarters, directing several scenes of his latest film (at the time of publishing), *Ça Commence Aujourd'hui*. However, I have to admit that elements of the mystery which existed in my mind when I first took notice of his work have not all disappeared. That is hardly surprising. Directing drama is complex and even mysterious in its very nature, and Tavernier's organic approach – at its centre wary of the limiting nature of formal pre-judgement – is not easy to pin down in a neat encapsulation. I was struck by how often those who work closely with him, both in front and behind the camera, said that the way he directs and communicates is hard to explain. Never mind – I do not believe in tidy definitions for everything, and certainly not when it comes to cinema. Alongside the intriguingly intangible, I did succeed in gathering plenty of solid material, which I have included in this book.

From the outset, I wanted to write a book on Tavernier that was centred on cinematic expression, but also about the film-making itself. For me, it seemed the right way in, to discover more about the work of a man whose entire life is saturated in his love of films, film-makers and film-making. This book is about directing films – especially drama, the largest part of Tavernier's work. I do not suggest for a moment that Tavernier's way of directing and constructing films represents any kind of ideal. His is no more than one approach among an endless number of others, some similar, some nearly opposite. The only thing I can safely assert about Tavernier's approach is that, as a relatively successful director, it works for him, his crew and his cast. What I have tried to do is provide some insight into the relationship between Tavernier's films, his practical approach to directing and his philosphical attitude to film-making, in the hope that it may stimulate thinking about the virtually endless possibilities that exist when creating drama, committing it to film, and shaping it into something which will make contact with an audience.

One of my aims has been to draw together the intriguing connections that run through Tavernier's deceptively eclectic body of work, thematically and stylistically. I hope to attract the attention of some people who might not be familiar with his films, as well as encouraging those who already are to seek out some of Tavernier's films that are harder to find. If I have succeeded at all, this book will appeal most of all to people interested in the medium of film itself, especially cinema, whether they be cinema-goers, students or film-makers, present and future. If this book takes anyone with a place, characters and a story in their head just a step or so closer to finding a small crew and a camera, and their first taste of the indescribable experience of making a film, I will be happy.

Tavernier's cinema, like any other, is open to analysis from a variety of angles. The fruits of his prolific career as a politically committed film director continue to meet with scorn as well as admiration. However, no matter how his work is defined or judged, when experiencing his emotional orchestration of places, people and feelings into rich layers of images, voices, sounds, music, movement and time we can be sure of one thing: it is true cinema.

CHAPTER 2

BERTRAND TAVERNIER

April, 1943:

> This is what I should like to teach my son, but I'll never be able to communicate it to him because his life will not be mine: that there is no sin for noble souls, except abandon, habit, sleep, and that the very act of waking up chases the devil away; that there is no suffering that a little feeling for human beings cannot render tolerable; that it may be necessary, as Bonaparte would say, 'to be exclusive in the way you think and act and to consider that the heart is worth more than the mind,' but as the head is more difficult to control, you must continually strive to fill a lively, new and ordered mind with knowledge, without which the heart is like a mad animal, throwing itself against the bars of its cage; that we have very little time, that we must hurry, that time flies. I open my eyes on my youth... I close my eyes: someone else speaks in my place...
>
> I'll have another treasure to leave to my son, a heritage as important as all the habits, manias, traditions, photo albums and recipes, furniture and houses which are handed down from one generation to the next, getting richer and changing gradually with the passing of time. This heritage is manifold: it is the curiosity for all human activity, the thirst for knowledge, that of using it to form a lifestyle; a certain desire for elegance in thought and deed which gives life an irksome but ever useful constraint; and above all, the power to love and the charm of being loved.
>
> 'Sur Une Autre Vie', René Tavernier (text written for his son Bertrand's second birthday)[1]

October, 1995:

> Nils Tavernier: How many films does this come to?
> Bertrand Tavernier: I don't know. I don't count them.

NT: You don't know how many films you have made?
BT: No, I don't know exactly. I couldn't say. I don't know if it's 13, 14, 12 or 15 – I've no idea. No, no – I swear it. I swear, I have absolutely no idea. When you set off for a film, the only thing you can remember sometimes is maybe your date of birth, other than that...

> From the opening of *Un Film Sur Bertrand Tavernier*, television documentary about the making of *Capitaine Conan*, directed by Nils Tavernier

Bertrand Tavernier was born in Lyon on 25 April 1941, the son of Ginette and René. René was a writer and poet, and notably the founder of the literary magazine *Confluences*, named after the two great rivers whose merging influenced the design of Lyon's landscape: the Rhône and the Saône. *Confluences* ran into difficulties with the local censor under the Vichy régime during the occupation, but was nevertheless one of only a few magazines to remain in publication throughout the period, its contributors including the writers Louis Aragon and Georges Sadoul, and the poet Francis Ponge. René Tavernier ran the magazine office on the second floor of the Tavernier home in rue Chambovet, high above the Montchat district of the city, in which he also rented a flat to Aragon and Elsa Triolet. In Bertrand's television documentary *Lyon: Le Regard Intérieur* (1988), René recalls how Aragon wrote many poems, as well as his novel *Auriélien* while living there. René's own activities included helping to launch national committees of writers, doctors and teachers led by figures such as Professor Debré and Jean Cassou, and when asked by his son whether he considered *Confluences* to have been 'an act of resistance', he described his hopes for the publication:

> Yes, I think we wanted our magazine to be that from day one. I thought that very sincerely. I came from a family which took patriotism very seriously, where the sense of duty to the state was taken seriously. Within the general collapse of values, it seemed that there was something which had not been defeated; that yes, of course, the Panzer divisions had invaded the front, that the Republic had collapsed in a lamentable manner and everything was in ruins, but there was one thing which had not been defeated by the German tanks, and that was our culture. And this culture was holding up well, faced with the derision and the caricature of culture which they wanted to impose on us – the Nazis and the Fascists. As a consequence, we wanted that for our magazine. We didn't want it to be a combat weapon. We never thought that the act of publishing *Confluences* could replace a battalion of paratroopers, but we thought that it was a means for us young Frenchmen of that period – young and less young – a way of saying 'No!', of not resigning to what Vichy wanted to make us believe: Work, Family, Motherland. Each of these things seemed to us to

be respectable; but the Vichy trilogy seemed to me then, and continues to seem to me today, the most repugnant thing.

In *Lyon: Le Regard Intérieur*, Bertrand identifies his first memory of the city as that of being taken onto the terrace of the house in Monchat to watch luminous explosions in the sky on one evening in August 1944. The flashes of light were shell bombardments by the American troops who had at last entered the city in the final stage of its liberation from the occupation. Tavernier draws a connection between the emotional drama of the event and his own idea of cinema: 'Everyone around me was laughing, clapping. Since then, I've never been able to separate this notion of light from all these emotions, from all that tumult, from all that life that seemed to be just beginning again.'

This sensitivity to the concept of life as something characterised above all by a persistent ability to reform and renew itself out of all kinds of human darkness is the vision which seems to lie behind all of Tavernier's work, most explicit in the persuasive optimism of *La Vie et Rien d'Autre*, but also lying behind the small rays of light that offer some hint of hope within the fear and pessimism of *Death Watch* and *Coup de Torchon*. His inclusion of a reference to cinema within this description of his earliest memory is predictable in a man who would always choose to talk about cinema rather than himself, describing his inevitable tendency to lapse into a series of historical cinematic anecdotes as being his own defence against a shy nature.[2] Jean Cosmos[3] has referred to Tavernier's 'elephant memory', and his ability to recall the details of films, their makers and their making is certainly remarkable, staggering even. His sheer energy for talking about this art-form which seems to be the very stuff he breathes inevitably makes one think of other high-profile *cinéphiles* such as François Truffaut and, perhaps most of all, of Tavernier's American friend and occasional colleague Martin Scorsese, with whom he shares the formative influence of a Catholic background, common admiration for personal favourites like John Ford and Michael Powell, and the same voracious appetite and memory for the cinema, old and new, the classic and the overlooked, and including films from cultures all over the globe.

Tavernier's passion for cinema really began when he was around twelve. By the time he was fourteen, he had decided that he wanted to be a film director, and remembers sticking photos from films in a scrapbook, along with the names of those whose films he admired, the first three who merited this recognition being John Ford, Henry Hathaway and William Wellman. Such names fed his formative love for American cinema, which grew rapidly into the passion that took hold of him completely, and inspired the naturally curious adolescent in a way that his formal education had failed to. When he was five, Tavernier's parents moved him and his two younger sisters to live in Paris, although he remained emotionally attached to Lyon, where he always returned to spend holidays with his grandmother. Tavernier was educated at the Saint Martin *pension* in Pontoise near Paris. When asked once about his experience there, he chose to draw a veil over the period, making explanatory reference to the 'feelings of humiliation' and 'the sadism of the gym teachers' which coloured his memory of the time, as well as the death of a very young, close friend from leukaemia.[4]

Tavernier's unpleasant associations with school are most explicitly voiced by the character Mancheron in *Une Semaine de Vacances* (1980): the father of a rebellious and under-achieving boy, he relates anecdotes to his son's teacher Laurence Cuers about the tyranny and fear of his own school days. Curiously, teachers appearing in Tavernier's films are still generally portrayed sympathetically, sometimes as heroic, such as Anne in *Coup de Torchon* (1981), Alice in *La Vie et Rien d'Autre* (1990), and Daniel in *Ça Commence Aujourd'hui* (1999). One of Tavernier's contemporaries at the Lycée Henri IV was the young Volker Schlöndorff,[5] who shared a bench in his philosophy class. Schlöndorff, who would later become godfather to Tavernier's son Nils, used to be invited to the Tavernier apartment in the Avenue de l'Opéra every Sunday, and recalls in his preface to Daniel Bion's *Cinéaste de l'Émotion* the pleasures of 'the conviviality, the spirit, the knowledge and the curiosity' that distinguished his visits to their home, as well as 'the pleasure of words'.[6] Such pleasures did not extend into Tavernier's study of the law, for which he had enrolled at the Sorbonne. Tavernier remembers Schlöndorff joining him in his 'first cinéphilic experience': a triple bill comprising *Los Olvidados* (Luis Bunuel, 1950), *Das Blue Engel* (*The Blue Angel*, Joseph von Sternberg, 1930) and *Espoir* (*Days of Hope*, André Malraux, 1945),[7] and going on to spend all of his study time at a number of small 'arthouse' cinemas which widened his experience, taking in directors such as Fritz Lang, Jean-Pierre Melville, Kenji Mizoguchi and Jean Renoir. For the end-of-year law exam, he handed in a blank paper.

At this time, Tavernier's commitment to cinema was propelled further by two important ventures. First, along with some friends from the Sorbonne, including Frédéric Vitoux and Philippe Haudiquet, he founded *L'Étrave* (*The Stem*), a cinema journal of articles and interviews. It was an interview for *L'Étrave* that brought him into contact with Jean-Pierre Melville, following the release of *Deux Hommes Dans Manhattan* (1959). Melville and Tavernier became friends, with Melville giving Tavernier a job as trainee assistant director on *Léon Morin, Prêtre*

(1961), Tavernier describing himself as 'a very bad assistant'. He went on to work as press assistant on the film, and then on *Le Doulos* (1961), learning the craft of the film publicist which would keep him occupied throughout the 1960s, alongside regular work as a film critic and a life increasingly taken up with the discovery and advocacy of world cinema. Second was his founding of his own *ciné club* Le Nickel Odéon – started with the poet Yves Martin and Bernard Martinand – dedicated mainly to screening American films impossible to see elsewhere. The founders of Le Nickel Odéon adopted King Vidor and Delmer Daves as their Honorary Chairmen. The club's first screening was *The Bandwagon* (Vincente Minnelli, 1953), and the event was marked by the seemingly miraculous arrival of Minnelli himself, whom Tavernier and his comrades spotted leaving the theatre in Avenue Hoche after screening some tests there. Minnelli agreed to stay and present the film, remaining for the screening of the French-dubbed print. They also arranged a projection of Pierre Rissient's first short film *Les Genoux d'Ariane*.

Tavernier was also a member of another *cinéphile* group which called itself Les Neo-MacMahoniens, enthusiastic subscribers of the MacMahon cinema whose cinematic heroes were Fritz Lang, Joseph Losey, Otto Preminger and Raoul Walsh. Still on attachment to *Léon Morin, Prêtre*, Tavernier persuaded Melville to go and see *Moonfleet* (Fritz Lang, 1955), which they had managed to get screened at the MacMahon, after which Melville famously instructed his entire crew not to speak to Tavernier for three days as a punishment, such was his hatred of Lang's film. Despite his temper, Melville stayed friends with Tavernier, on one occasion going to visit Tavernier's parents – along with one of Tavernier's future cinematic contemporaries Claude Sautet – to persuade them to allow their son to continue his involvement with film when they became seriously concerned over whether cinema could really represent a viable future for him. It was also Melville who recommended Tavernier to Georges de Beauregard, with whom Tavernier worked as press agent between 1961 and 1964, a period when de Beauregard produced many films of the New Wave, allowing Tavernier to work on the publicity for projects such as *Adieu Philippine* (Jacques Rozier, 1963), *Les Carabiniers* (Jean-Luc Godard, 1963), *Cléo de 5 à 7* (Agnès Varda, 1961), *Le Mépris* (Jean-Luc Godard, 1963), *L'Oeuil du Malin* (Claude Chabrol, 1962), *Pierrot Le Fou* (Jean-Luc Godard, 1965), *La 317ᵉ Section* (Pierre Schoendorffer, 1964). It was during this time that Tavernier was able to soak up all the practical and economic aspects of film production, interviewing directors, producers and editors, and talking to various technicians. Then Georges de Beauregard gave him his first chance at directing, allowing him to

avernier describing himself as 'a very bad assistant'. He went
rk as press assistant on the film, and then on *Le Doulos* (1961),
the craft of the film publicist which would keep him occupied
out the 1960s, alongside regular work as a film critic and a life
ingly taken up with the discovery and advocacy of world cinema.
was his founding of his own *ciné club* Le Nickel Odéon – started
the poet Yves Martin and Bernard Martinand – dedicated mainly
creening American films impossible to see elsewhere. The founders
Le Nickel Odéon adopted King Vidor and Delmer Daves as their
Honorary Chairmen. The club's first screening was *The Bandwagon*
(Vincente Minnelli, 1953), and the event was marked by the seemingly
miraculous arrival of Minnelli himself, whom Tavernier and his comrades
spotted leaving the theatre in Avenue Hoche after screening some tests
there. Minnelli agreed to stay and present the film, remaining for the
screening of the French-dubbed print. They also arranged a projection
of Pierre Rissient's first short film *Les Genoux d'Ariane*.

Tavernier was also a member of another *cinéphile* group which called itself Les Neo-MacMahonienns, enthusiastic subscribers of the MacMahon cinema whose cinematic heroes were Fritz Lang, Joseph Losey, Otto Preminger and Raoul Walsh. Still on attachment to *Léon Morin, Prêtre*, Tavernier persuaded Melville to go and see *Moonfleet* (Fritz Lang, 1955), which they had managed to get screened at the MacMahon, after which Melville famously instructed his entire crew not to speak to Tavernier for three days as a punishment, such was his hatred of Lang's film. Despite his temper, Melville stayed friends with Tavernier, on one occasion going to visit Tavernier's parents – along with one of Tavernier's future cinematic contemporaries Claude Sautet – to persuade them to allow their son to continue his involvement with film when they became seriously concerned over whether cinema could really represent a viable future for him. It was also Melville who recommended Tavernier to Georges de Beauregard, with whom Tavernier worked as press agent between 1961 and 1964, a period when de Beauregard produced many films of the New Wave, allowing Tavernier to work on the publicity for projects such as *Adieu Philippine* (Jacques Rozier, 1963), *Les Carabiniers* (Jean-Luc Godard, 1963), *Cléo de 5 à 7* (Agnès Varda, 1961), *Le Mépris* (Jean-Luc Godard, 1963), *L'Oeuil du Malin* (Claude Chabrol, 1962), *Pierrot Le Fou* (Jean-Luc Godard, 1965), *La 317ᵉ Section* (Pierre Schoendorffer, 1964). It was during this time that Tavernier was able to soak up all the practical and economic aspects of film production, interviewing directors, producers and editors, and talking to various technicians. Then Georges de Beauregard gave him his first chance at directing, allowing him to direct two short thrillers, *Le Baiser de Judas* (1963)[8] and *Une Chance Explosive* (1964),[9] which de Beauregard produced. Both films received some favourable reviews, but Tavernier disliked them intensely, mainly for what he regarded as their immature emulation of American cinema. He was immediately offered the possibility of directing a full-length feature, but decided against the idea of going through another kind of exercise in style determined by an imposed subject. Instead he decided to continue his period of learning more about film-making, discovering what kind of cinema he really wanted to make, and finding a subject that really concerned him personally before trying to direct something more ambitious.

Following his 'apprenticeship' with de Beauregard, Tavernier teamed up with Pierre Rissient and an associate independent press agent, working to promote the films of directors who included Robert Altman, Herbert Biberman, Claude Chabrol, John Ford, John Frankenheimer, Samuel Fuller, Howard Hawks, John Huston, Elia Kazan, Fritz Lang, Ida Lupino, Leo McCarey, Jacques Ruffio, Claude Sautet, Jerry Schatzberg and Raoul Walsh. They also worked to champion the cause of blacklisted directors such as Joseph Losey and Abraham Polonsky, and promote the films of directors whose work was neglected, or had fallen from favour. Jean-Pierre Melville had introduced Tavernier to *Peeping Tom* (Michael Powell, 1960) on its first release in Paris, and in 1968 Tavernier managed to get the film re-released, persuading Powell to come to Paris for the film's opening. Powell's career was still in ruins as a result of the concerted vilification of him in Britain that had followed the film's release, and this screening and invitation, coming during the darkest period of his artistic career, started the process of his critical rehabilitation and rediscovery around the world. The meeting marked the beginning of a friendship which lasted until Powell's death in 1990.[10] Tavernier's dedication to Powell's cause as an artist is very revealing in that it clarifies his basic dispute with certain narrow 'doctrines' of the New Wave, disagreements which have been partly responsible for an exaggerated idea of his supposed opposition to their principles:

> [Powell], who had been a very important director between 1940 and 1950, was either forgotten or held up for vilification; forgotten in France, or rather totally misunderstood, principal victim of the excesses of the politics of the *auteur*. In order to better defend Hitchcock, François Truffaut denied all talent in other British film-makers... In England it was worse. Powell had been scored off the card, put on a blacklist since *Peeping Tom*, such was the violence and injury of its critical reception. It shattered his career... Within British cinema, Powell has a place apart. On the margins, within a system, he refused to follow fashion, did not follow any school...

> The films he made between 1937 and 1951[11] are testament to a staggering originality and freedom of tone. Profoundly rooted in a national culture, they refuse all spirit of insularity, serving as proof of an openness of spirit, a curiosity and almost unique breadth of vision... His intentions go beyond everyday naturalism, and lead to an irrational, metaphysical intensity which bears innumerable visions. You don't follow a plot, you dive into a universe...[12]

At the same time, Tavernier continued to write articles and film reviews for a variety of publications, including *Cinéma*, *Combat*, *Les Lettres Françaises* and the two huge rivals of film criticism, *Les Cahiers du Cinéma* and *Positif*, his first review for the latter being of Joseph Losey's *Time Without Pity* (1956). He took some delight in being able to defend the work of Delmer Daves in *Positif*, then go on to defend the films of Samuel Fuller in *Cahiers du Cinéma*. Tavernier consciously sought to write about films across various publications, avoiding the risk of always seeking to fit the mould of a particular viewpoint, but acknowledges that he did feel somewhat closer to *Positif* than to *Cahiers du Cinéma*, which he regarded as not being political enough. All the time, Tavernier kept in mind his ambition to go on to direct 'properly', with various encounters taking him closer to his goal with the opportunity for practical work in film. He encountered Riccardo Freda, master of the type of historical cape-and-sword adventures which Tavernier loved – for which he was often ribbed while working for *Cahiers du Cinéma* – and the Italian director gave him a couple of jobs as co-screenwriter. By this time, Tavernier felt ready to attempt his first feature-film, although the route was not a straightforward one:

> I did an adaptation of Robert Louis Stevenson's *The Beach of Falesa*, and it was accepted at that time by Jacques Brel and James Mason, who liked the script very much, but I could not do anything with it as I could not find a producer. Producers were frightened to start with [a director] who had done nothing before with such a film. And the second screenplay was an adaptation of a book by Alexandre Dumas *La Fille du Régent*, and that screenplay became the basis of *Que La Fête Commence*. It was in re-adapting that screenplay that in the process we decided with Jean Aurenche to throw away the book of Dumas and to start on a new basis, and we wrote an original screenplay. I had done two little films before – two shorts – and I thought they were bad. They were imitative of the American cinema, very childish, immature, although one of them had rather good reviews. My wife[13] was very severe about them, saying 'I mean it's cartoon-like; it has nothing to do with reality and it's second-hand'. So I started on a new basis – those two screenplays which I wrote alone. I found it very, very boring to write alone because I am full of doubts, full of fear. I had no money at that time. I had to work very, very hard in order to get some money, as a freelance press agent with my wonderful partner Pierre Rissient, and I

decided that if I was going to do a long feature I must work together with somebody on the screenplay. So I decided to go to them, not with the idea of *L'Horloger* first, but with the idea of a film about the French Gestapo – French gangsters who collaborated with the Gestapo – something which had not been done, and I had written a small treatment too. Aurenche was attracted, because he knew that I wanted them because they had written one of the best films about the Occupation which was *La Traversée de Paris* [1956], but Bost was against the project. He said, 'We should not do a film about those people who were the most abominable bastards. If we do the film, we will be forced to find them excuses, when they have no excuses'. He said that the people who torture, we must never excuse. In a way he was saying, strangely enough for people who were so opposed, the same thing as Truffaut, who once said that you 'don't have the right to film torture – it's immoral'.

Tavernier shelved the plan to make *Bonny et Lafont* about the French collaborating militia,[14] but was by now determined to make his first personal film, and gave the idea for *L'Horloger de Saint-Paul* to Aurenche and Bost. While they developed the screenplay, he obtained a solid commitment to the film from Philippe Noiret, and managed to gain the support of Gaumont (Denis Chateau) and Pathé (Pierre Vercel), but spent a year being turned down by producers until he met Raymond Danon. Danon was convinced that the film's subject was worthwhile, and decided to take a risk with the project, despite the fact that he actually disliked the screenplay intensely. After a failed attempt to persuade Tavernier to shoot somewhere other than in Lyon by offering to double his director's salary, Danon put *L'Horloger de Saint-Paul* into production. The result of Tavernier's inability to get his other ideas off the ground was his creation of a first film which was marked in its themes, setting and atmosphere by the personal feeling which he had waited to express. Tavernier had not thought out the principles of mise-en-scène which he would develop over the years, but he went into the production having established one firm principle already: to be eclectic.

NOTES ON CHAPTER 2

1 Text originally reproduced in the press notes distributed with *Daddy Nostalgie*, Little Bear, 1991.
2 Bertrand Tavernier, 'I Wake Up Dreaming: A Journal for 1992' in Boorman and Donohue (eds) *Projections* 2, London, 1993, p 327.
3 Jean Cosmos is the co-scriptwriter of *La Vie et Rien d'Autre* and *Capitaine Conan*.
4 Jean-Luc Douin, *Tavernier*, Paris, 1988, Edilig, p 76.

5   Volker Schlöndorff also went on to direct films. His work includes *A Degree of Murder* (1967), *The Lost Honour of Katherina Blum* (1975), *The Tin Drum* (1979), *Swann in Love* (1984), *The Handmaid's Tale* (1990), *Palmetto* (1998). Schlöndorff was assistant director on Tavernier's first short film, *Le Baiser de Judas*.
6   Daniele Bion, *Bertrand Tavernier: Cinéaste de l'Emotion*, Renens, 1984, p 6.
7   Jean-Luc Douin, *Tavernier*, Paris, 1997, Ramsay, p 110.
8   Sketch from *Les Baisers*, a portmanteau of short films produced by Georges de Beauregard. The other films in the set were directed by Claude Berri and Charles L. Bitsch.
9   Sketch from *La Chance et l'Amour*, another portmanteau set produced by Georges de Beauregard. Again, the other films in the set were directed by Berri and Bitsch.
10 Tavernier cast Powell as Law in *Que La Fête Commence...* (1975), but the role did not make the film's final cut. Although Tavernier's *Death Watch* (1979) is formally dedicated to Jacques Tourneur in the end credits, he has also acknowledged it as a homage to Michael Powell's *Peeping Tom* (1960). He dedicated *Daddy Nostalgie* (1991) to Powell.
11 Tavernier was referring to the most fruitful period of Powell's career, his collaboration with producer Emeric Pressburger. The Powell-Pressburger works include *The Thief of Bagdad* (1940), *49th Parallel* (1941), *The Life and Death of Colonel Blimp* (1943), *A Canterbury Tale* (1944), *I Know where I'm Going!* (1945), *A Matter of Life and Death* (1946), *Black Narcissus* (1947), *The Red Shoes* (1948) and *Tales of Hoffman* (1951).
12 Bertrand Tavernier, *Qu'est-ce qu'on attend?*, Paris, 1993, p 125 (French version of 'I Wake Up Dreaming: A Journal for 1992', originally part of an article written by Tavernier in *Le Monde*, 12 March 1992, to coincide with the French re-releases of *The Life and Death of Colonel Blimp* and *Peeping Tom*. This is a very small extract from Tavernier's very detailed, heartfelt piece. The full version, to be found in *Projections* 2 (see note 2), should provide fascinating reading to those interested in the work of Michael Powell.
13 Colo Tavernier, who went on to co-script several of Tavernier's films: *Une Semaine de Vacances*, *Un Dimanche à la Campagne*, *La Passion Béatrice*, *Daddy Nostalgie* and *L'Appât*.
14 The French collaborating militia were notably covered shortly afterwards by Louis Malle in his *Lacombe Lucien* (1974), and also represented in Malle's *Au Revoir Les Enfants* (1987).

CHAPTER 3

POLITICAL FILM-MAKER

Do you know what they call Bertrand? 'L'Homme en Colère' [the Angry Man]. Because every morning, when he comes in to the office of Little Bear with his newspaper, he is angry about something – about the way the Government is acting, or how someone is being treated.

Frédéric Bourboulon, Producer, on the location of Ça Commence Aujourd'hui

At the start of *L'Horloger de Saint-Paul,* Tavernier's first feature-film, the protagonist Michel Descombes is sitting with friends around a table in a café sharing an evening meal, involved in a conversation about the death penalty which descends into jocular suggestions about the desirability and practicalities of its being televised. The ensuing drama concerning a father's painful realisation of the distance between himself and his son, and his gradual acceptance of his son's point of view, is played out in front of a social backdrop that reflects French politics at the time. Politics are central to the story's study of the differing attitudes between the generations depicted. The film includes a mass of detail which both reflects and criticises the prevailing attitudes of the day, represented through the media coverage of the killing of a factory guard by Bernard Descombes and Liliane Torinni, and the reactions to them of secondary and peripheral characters. Most under attack are ill-educated, simplistic attitudes, expressed in reactionary, vague political labels used to damn individuals in television sound-bites: the evidence of people's failure to seek some detailed understanding of the complex truth that lies behind the superficiality of television news. *L'Horloger de Saint-Paul* perhaps reveals most about the director's intended course, in that it deals with the very question of politicisation itself. Michel Descombe's apolitical nature, an essential part of his character, increases his sense of confusion over how to respond to his son's actions, and the uncertainty over how the possibility of Bernard's crime being turned into *une affaire politique* might affect the eventual judicial outcome for the two fugitives. Michel's own best friend, who is politically involved, launches his most furious verbal attacks on two targets: society's tendency to always seek to maintain the status quo, and the superficiality of television. Throughout Tavernier's career, the place of political expression in his cinema has informed much of his creative thinking, shaping the narrative content of his works as well as influencing his construction of mise-en-scène, the result of his concern with the notion of 'integrity of viewpoint' within an art-form in which viewpoint is very open to manipulation.

On the basis of his first four features – *L'Horloger de Saint-Paul, Que La Fête Commence..., Le Juge et l'Assassin* and *Des Enfants Gâtés* – Tavernier was widely regarded as being primarily a director of political films. When asked 'Do you agree that *Le Juge et l'Assassin* is a political film?' his answer was simple: 'I hope so'.[1] Tavernier's desire to express political feelings in his films has been criticised for getting in the way of his drama, his handling of politics sometimes being questioned within article reviews otherwise full of praise. One example by film critic Michel Ciment suggested plainly that Tavernier's politics were 'interfering with his films', citing scenes from both *Que la Fête Commence...* and *Le Juge et l'Assassin* as examples of the more problematic polemics residing within his cinema.[2] Ciment's difficulty in accepting the political aspects of Tavernier's work seemed to stem particularly from his objection to Tavernier's choice of cinematic devices for the final sequences of *Que La Fête Commence...* and *Le Juge et l'Assassin*, both of which have endings that stand out in clear contrast to the narrative style of the rest of the film. In the former, the peasant girl whose brother has been killed by the regent's carriage looks directly into the camera to deliver her line, 'And you too my beauty!' to the audience as well as to the regent's prostitute mistress whom she insists must watch the regent's carriage burn. The rest of her apocalyptic speech to her dead brother prophesying the events of *La Terreur* is conveyed in the past tense by third-person narration over a freeze-frame of the peasant girl holding up her brother's corpse to 'watch'. In the latter film, after scenes of factory workers hurrying to join a demonstration, a socialist anthem sung by Rousseau's mistress Rose is taken up by the crowd. Tavernier then reverts to Jean-Roger Caussimon's voice-over singing and a final sequence of documentary photo-images of factory children, with superimposed text comparing the evil of Bouvier's twelve murders to that of the 2500 children 'assassinated' in the mines and factories. By employing this verbally polemical ending, Tavernier seems to grab and turn the audience's heads to face his argument in a way which mirrors the actions of his peasant girl. In both films Tavernier disengaged from the organic character-driven narrative in order to create a more detached moment of reflection for the audience, and to communicate his own sense of political anger. Their inclusion seems to be based essentially on the director's desire to make his point as directly and unambiguously as possible, and the objection is simply that, as narrative devices, they are heavy-handed. Ciment's objection was not unusual, and is interesting in respect of Tavernier's output, in that it does seem to question the validity of placing political expression at the dramatic centre of film, as well as playing down the notion that Tavernier's films are in fact primarily political dramas. Alongside their fascination with inner human struggle, the drama in both of these films is intrinsically political, and it is worth noting that – even counting just the dramas – of 17 feature-films, there are only two that could be described as apolitical (*Un Dimanche à la Campagne* and *La Passion Béatrice*), with another two that contain very little (*'Round Midnight* and *Daddy Nostalgie*).

Des Enfants Gâtés differs in that its polemical approach is more generally overt throughout, with Tavernier's concerns about the exploitation of city tenants and the urban ruination of Paris explicit from the outset and maintained as a constant theme. Here again, Ciment had difficulty in accepting Tavernier's political position: the film was 'at times too demonstrative in its criticism of injustice'.[3] The political message of *Des Enfants Gâtés* is conveyed in a very literal way, through dialogue expressing the thoughts and complaints of the film's many characters. Almost every role, central or peripheral, comes armed with at least one barbed line pointing out some example of the evil of the urban system. The central narrative thread concerns Rougière's affair with his neighbour Anne and their personal crises, and although the script is already very wordy, Tavernier had more feelings about urban disintegration than could reasonably be included within the dialogue of a drama, and third-person narration conveyed further expressions of his dismay concerning the worsening state of Paris: for example, over the images of waste grounds and concrete skyscrapers, the narrator informs us that Anne's father died in a construction accident and that she was 'rehoused in the suburbs by the property developers who depopulate Paris and build offices rather than green spaces and playgrounds'. Ciment's analysis of the polemical elements in Tavernier's earlier works was made in the context of an acknowledgement of Tavernier's developing maturity, around the time that he made *Un Dimanche à la Campagne*, associating this growth with his shift away from the intellectual and political to the emotional. However, political feeling maintains a crucial presence across Tavernier's subsequent work, in films including *La Vie et Rien d'Autre*, *L.627*, *L'Appât*, *Capitaine Conan* and *Ça Commence Aujourd'hui*. The style of *Des Enfants Gâtés* switches so markedly beween its scenes of human intimacy and those depicting the urban decay of Paris that it sometimes feels as if a political message is being made by regularly arresting the flow of a human drama to keep us up to date with a social documentary. *Des Enfants Gâtés* is the last of Tavernier's dramas in which political feeling seems to overtly shape his structural approach to form. The subsequent *Death Watch* and *Une Semaine de Vacances* were just as passionate in their anger towards society's chosen direction, but marked Tavernier's shift towards a cinema in which politics is confronted through the emotions, struggles and, above all, the working lives of his characters the dedication and doubts of a young teacher in the latter film being themes which were to recur.

La Vie et Rien d'Autre is just as vocal in its condemnation of the obscene ease with which human life was devalued and expended to fuel the First World War as it is tender in its central portrayal of a man who is helplessly and, to him, inexplicably consumed by passionate love for a woman who crosses the path of his military mission, but the film's style remains consistent throughout. There is no sense that these two aspects of the film's drama co-exist uneasily, and what can be seen through the progression of Tavernier's fiction films is simply that he has become increasingly effective at weaving political feeling into his dramas, subserving his presentation of political context to the primary evocation of individual human dilemmas, political feeling being expressed directly through character and emotion. Behind this balance seems to lie Tavernier's attention to script and character, more than any other elements of cinematic technique, with no evidence that his adoption of elements such as voice-over or narration should be specifically associated with his communication of either political or apolitical feeling. There is no clear pattern of practical inclination towards either verbal or non-verbal expression, for example. Tavernier earlier used voice-over narration, along with the piece-to-camera and titles, with the specific aim of expressing political comment directly, but narration is just as important in his later dramas and voice-overs have remained a powerful element in the conveying of emotion. Equally, music and visual lyricism have played as strong a role in Tavernier's most political works, as in his most apolitical. His most political films are not his least emotional. Whilst acknowledging the fact that political feeling is essential to Tavernier's work, it is obvious that concerns over the dramatic disturbance caused by his polemical views focus on a direct and sometimes detached form of expression which now and then add an uneasy preaching tone to his earlier films. The applause for Tavernier's 'maturation' seems prompted by his switch to more perceptive and complex political examination, and one formal development in Tavernier's work does aptly reflect the essential difference between the singular political feeling of his early films and the more open political exploration of the later ones: the increased complexity and mobility of his mise-en-scène.

Des Enfants Gâtés is Tavernier's most cut-and-dried comment on politics and society, and it is also his least interesting film visually. In this work more than any other Tavernier seems preoccupied with the task of communicating views on society and politics which he had already decided at script stage, in contrast with the feeling of journey and discovery which is integral to films such as *Une Semaine de Vacances* and *Coup de Torchon*. In *Des Enfants Gâtés* the images are clear but disappointingly straightforward in their simpler narrative statements, when compared with the exploratory camera and intricate mise-en-scène of later films. *Des Enfants Gâtés* gives very little of the sense of searching and surprise that has come to be one of the richest features of the recent works. The key to Tavernier's greater success in integrating his political fears and passions into his dramas lies firmly in the scripts themselves.

Even in a film loaded with on-screen political debate like *Une Semaine de Vacances*, political feeling does not feel tacked on, because it emanates from the personal traits of the characters themselves, exemplified by the exasperated lecture which Pierre delivers to Laurence and Anne, pointing out that he could never stand 'intellectuals who say "down with culture"'. After *Des Enfants Gâtés*, Tavernier generally avoided having characters directly lecturing the audience, or loading the authority of polemical statements with printed titles. He has remained attached to third-person voice-overs, but without using them to express a political viewpoint, choosing them instead for the poignancy generated by the sense of distance which they evoke. *La Vie et Rien d'Autre* expresses as much political anger as any of his films, but the script ensures that it reaches us directly through the passionate indignation of Major Dellaplane, whose life-long experience and personal involvement in the issues we can trust, written as they are into every expression on his face, through the way he moves, and in his voice.

The political content of Tavernier's dramas is shaped equally by the documentary element apparent in all of his works, a feature reinforced by his use of camera, favouring an 'uncomposed' style which prefers to follow characters closely, with wide shots appearing to be used in order to accommodate the movements of characters whose movements are not prejudged, as if what they will do next cannot be known. Tavernier's first major work of non-fiction was *Philippe Soupault et le Surréalisme* (1982), a lengthy documentary produced for video about the elderly surrealist painter, which he developed with Jean Aurenche, and he has continued to make documentaries at regular intervals, once describing his need to return to the form as a way of 'getting back to reality' and 'coming out of the dream' again, 'rediscovering how to open one's eyes and think quickly'.[4] Tavernier's co-producer at Little Bear, Frédéric Bourboulon, said, 'the word that always comes to mind when thinking about Bertrand is "cinéaste citoyen" – "citizen film-maker"'. Identifying his director's commitment to society as the most defining aspect of his cinema, Bourboulon stressed the dialogue between Tavernier's dramas and his documentaries, regarding them as inseparable. His attitude is not surprising, he having been already closely involved with Tavernier as producer around the time when the latter created two works of non-fiction that are hugely important in defining his attitude as a political film-maker: *La Guerre Sans Nom* (*The Undeclared War*, 1991) and *De l'Autre Côté du Périph'* (*The Other Side of The Tracks*, 1997).

Tavernier had been very interested in the Algerian war for a long time, having prepared himself to be sent to Algeria when he was drafted into the military service during 1960 and 1961, enrolling for the army's cinema service. He did not want to take part in the war, but passed the service exam, only to be given a subsequent dispensation from military service due to an eyesight problem. Following the creation of his own production company, Little Bear,[5] one of his first projects was to co-produce a film about torture in Algeria, with his former assistant director Laurent Heynemann, *La Question* (*The Question*, Laurent Heynemann, 1977). Tavernier wanted to cover the subject of Algeria himself, but could not find the way to deal with the conflict which he felt would do the subject justice, until he was contacted by writer and modern historian Patrick Rotman and producer Jean-Pierre Guérin. Rotman and Guérin's concept was to tell the story of the Algerian war purely from the point of view of the conscripts, rather than the professional soldiers. Tavernier's enthusiasm for their idea was instant, but he remained worried about the prospect of scouring France for the most colourful and interesting testimonies and turning the film into a documentary of extraordinary stories. Searching for a way of localising the testimony story to strengthen the sense of ordinariness, and therefore touch a chord with the widest audience, he decided to take testimonies from a single town. He came up with the idea of using one of the locations where the biggest demonstrations against the Algerian war had taken place, and research finally brought the choice down to either Caen or Grenoble. The pull of Lyon and its environs already made Tavernier lean towards Grenoble, where a demonstration against the sending of army reservists to Algeria took place on 18 May 1956. He also came to his decision to begin from there as a homage to Marcel Ophuls, in reference to the region's link with *La Chagrin et La Pitié* (*The Sorrow and the Pity*, Marcel Ophuls, 1971), regarding Ophuls as 'cinema's number one documentary historian'.[6]

As with his works of fiction, Tavernier sought a single principle around which to build *La Guerre Sans Nom*, with the intention of ensuring both its originality in relation to other documentaries about the French conflict in Algeria and its integrity in representing its subjects – conscripts who had remained silent about their experiences for over 30 years, never having been given the chance to tell their own story. The principle which shaped *La Guerre Sans Nom* was simple: to remain committed exclusively to the personal testimonies of the conscripts and a few people directly involved with them. Tavernier stuck rigidly to his refusal of all testimony, information, documents, archive photos or film from official sources, excluding in this way the opinions of army and state, which had already had their say. All of the explanatory and illustrative material in the film – letters, documents and photographs – belonged to the interviewees. The result is a four-hour documentary dedicated almost totally (excluding a very brief introduction and conclusion) to presenting the memories and feelings of 28 veterans from all walks of life, most from the Grenoble area and all still living there. Tavernier's challenge was to take the time to listen to each witness, with minimal direction or manipulation of their testimony, then structure and shape their experiences in a way which would bring the audience close enough to listen to these stories, which he felt deserved very much to be heard. The most deeply affecting aspect of the many painful and moving stories that come out in *La Guerre Sans Nom* is their almost universal understatement. The spectrum of individuals from different backgrounds, interviewed in contrasting visual styles that stress their relationship with their current environment – either their workplace, home or a social setting – heighten the audience's awareness of the many thousands of other veterans all over France.

The film pursues a basic chronology, covering involvement in the demonstrations, conscription, service and demobilisation, but is structured thematically, the conscripts covering those subjects which affected them all: attitudes and reactions to being drafted; the fear and experience of death; the impact of the conflict on their families; personal experience of torture; the effect of thinking or talking about the war afterwards. Some of the witnesses bring humour to *La Guerre Sans Nom*, but as the film returns again and again to each of the conscripts, who add a little more each time, the overall impression it conveys of feelings long buried is very painful, evoking as it does the opening up of wounds and a need to release harrowing memories and emotions. Whilst the interviews are handled sensitively, the strength that many of the witnesses have to summon when recalling events which affected them so personally makes some of the interviews humbling to watch, the most heart-breaking testimony coming from those accusing themselves of lacking courage, in failing to desert or to speak out against some brutality. In taking its time to listen to the gradual opening-up of the conscripts, and accepting all the contrasts in the individual views expressed, *La Guerre Sans Nom* best represents Tavernier's politics in his stubborn refusal to compromise. When selling the film to television, Tavernier defended its lengthy running time vigorously as being essential to the integrity of the work.[7] His adherence to it, as well as his rejection of a historical theory-evidence-proof structure, places demands which require commitment on the part of his audience, although Tavernier prefers to talk of placing 'trust' in people.[8]

The film's open structure creates an identical sense of an undetermined journey to that which exists in dramas such as *Life and Nothing But* and *L.627*, and the narrative structure of *La Guerre Sans Nom* concludes with a reflection that touches directly on a later work, also about the effects of war on ordinary soldiers. In Tavernier's concluding voice-over for the film, he outlines the extent to which France has neglected the huge numbers of veterans scarred by their enforced service in Algeria, closing with images from a gathering of veteran psychiatric patients arranged by an association for veterans of the conflict. 'Look carefully at these faces', he asks, a plea almost identical to the words voiced later by a man broken by his experience of war: *Capitaine Conan*.

In complete contrast with *La Guerre Sans Nom*, the origins of *De 'Autre Côté du Périph'* have no direct connection with Tavernier's personal history, and the project arrived out of the blue during the period which followed the making of *Capitaine Conan*. Tavernier's previous film had been an almost overwhelming experience, conducted in a permanent state of tension, as daily failures in Romanian production support maintained a constant fear of shut-down. When shooting was completed, Tavernier and his crew felt that they had achieved something exceptional, but his early worries about managing to touch his audience with the film were to be confirmed: the exhausting journey ended with *Capitaine Conan* being released to wide critical acclaim but a lack of interest at the box office. Tavernier was still recovering his bearings when he became involved in a political protest, which began with a televised public statement and ended up being the premise of his next film. On 11 February 1997, 66 film-makers signed a statement of protest, initiated by two French directors, Pascale Ferran and d'Arnaud Desplechin, calling for civil disobedience against the new Debré Immigration Act, Article 1 in particular, which required mandatory reporting of suspected illegal immigrants. The following day each of the protesters received a letter from Eric Raoult, Minister for Urban Development and Integration, accusing them of an ignorance of reality. Inviting them to spend a month experiencing real problems first-hand, Raoult singled out the Grands-Pêchers area of Montreuil, a deprived area on the outskirts of Paris, as if it were the epitome of urban trouble. A few days later Tavernier was contacted by some residents of Grands-Pêchers, asking him to visit their area. He attended a meeting at which he was faced with 250 residents, hurt and offended at having a finger pointed at them – branded and stigmatised by officialdom. Tavernier stayed in Grands-Pêchers for three months, to make *De l'Autre Côté du Périph'* with his son Nils. Like Nils's documentary on his father's experience of *Capitaine Conan*, the film was shot on videotape for television.[9]

As with *La Guerre Sans Nom*, its stated remit was to give its subjects a voice, and the film is an extraordinarily frank picture of the district constructed mainly through the feelings of scores of characters from every walk of life: residents of all ages, both employed and unemployed, shop and café owners, teachers, social workers, youth workers and police. While providing an outlet for the residents' hurt, Tavernier and his son included sequences that showed conflict and crime and racism, but seemingly without the fear that they might risk supporting Raoult's argument, confident that the negative images would be forced into their proper context by the adjoining wealth of evidence. *De l'Autre Côté du Périph'* is one of Tavernier's most life-affirming works, ultimately a celebration of people's resilience and their own faith in humanity. Its kaleidoscopic array of first-hand views and reactions is built around a simple narrative line that plots Tavernier's systematic comparison of the minister's allegations with reality. Each stage seemed to dismantle further the validity of Raoult's statements, their brevity and dismissiveness contrasted mercilessly with the variety, depth and detail provided by each new contribution from the people of Grands-Pêchers. While exposing Raoult's distance from reality, Tavernier occasionally revealed a cutting delight in his retaliation for a remark of Raoult's, that 'integration isn't cinema'. 'Eric Raoult is no longer a deputy or a minster. I am still a film-maker. The other sixty-five signatories as well.' At the film's end, Tavernier confessed his adherence to 'the same errors of script and casting' which Raoult had accused him of, pointing out that his time spent in Montreuil had only confirmed his original feelings. Tavernier's defence of the maligned residents had gained strength from his determination to make Raoult pay for the personal insult of having suggested that he lived outside reality. As if to affirm his own convictions about the dialogue between his documentary and his fictional work, he tinted the emotion of *De l'Autre Côté du Périph'* with the most emotional sections of Philippe Sarde's score for *L.627*, and compared one shaken young police officer in the film with the lost and frightened Erlane from *Capitaine Conan*.

Tavernier's output of political documentary work has grown during the latter part of his career. Campaigning works which he directed personally, such as the episodes from *Contre l'Oubli* (*Against Oblivion*, 1992)[10] and *Lumières Sur un Massacre* (*Spotlights on a Massacre*, 1998)[11] stand alongside his commitment to producing the work of others through Little Bear, including Bernard Favre (*La Trace*, 1983), Laurent Heynemann (*Les Mois d'Avril Sont Meutriers*, 1987) and Jean-Paul Salomé (*Restons Groupés*, 1998). His increasing disillusion and concern over the state of France comes with a later tendency to lean towards younger characters, and his willingness to confront the political powers of the day is matched by a fusion of ideals across his documentaries and dramas that brings them closer all the time, never more apparently than with *De l'Autre Côté du Périph'* and *Ça Commence Aujourd'hui*. Throughout 'I Wake Up, Dreaming' – the diary which he kept for John Boorman, begun at the start of shooting on *L.627* – Tavernier adds to his wealth of historical film knowledge with continual reference to contemporary political battles of every kind, both connected and unconnected with the world of film and television. In line with his early championing of films which he felt were neglected or under-rated, Tavernier has always been involved in the political battles of film authorship, production and distribution. His creation of Little Bear for the production of *Des Enfants Gâtés* was a response to his dissatisfaction with the level of artistic control which he had as a director alone. For many years he has been an active member, then president, of the SACD, the Sociéte des Auteurs et Compositeurs Dramatiques, which campaigns for the creative and intellectual rights and interests of directors, writers and composers in film, television and theatre. At the society's regular meetings he met Louis Ducreux, casting him as M Ladmiral in *Un Dimanche à la Campagne*, and Jean Cosmos, whom he persuaded to write *La Vie et Rien d'Autre*. He also belongs to the SRF, the Sociéte des

Réalisateurs de Films, and the ARP, the Association des Réalisateurs Producteurs, and has been a representative of the production support foundation Film Europe (France). Increasingly, he has become involved in lobbying for fair access to theatrical and televisual distribution circuits for French and European films, and during the 1993 GATT negotiations he campaigned vigorously for the defence of European cinema's interests as part of an ongoing response to the growing American domination of the European audio-visual market. Tavernier's activities in support of cinema also take the form of an energetic commitment to the general promotion of the medium as an art-form. He is President of the Institut Lumière in Lyon, currently under the directorship of Thierry Frémaux, and regularly introduces special screenings and retrospective events there, as well as being involved in equivalent organisations and festivals in other European countries. His extremely detailed knowledge of world cinema and its history is regularly called on for television interview in programmes about cinema and at retrospectives of directors and particular schools of film-making. He is co-author of the major French history book on American film, *50 Ans de Cinéma Américain*.

In the short 'making of' section at the end of *Lumières Sur Un Massacre*, Tavernier points out that he is not a politician. 'I'm just a film-maker' is a phrase which he has used often, almost apologetically, implying that he would not have to get involved if those with real power would only do their job. In reality, it is unimaginable that Tavernier's own political engagement will dull in his future works. On the contrary, dialogue between the anxieties of his fictional characters and the problems of the society in which he lives has intensified as his career has developed, resulting in films whose direct attacks on the official status quo have provoked the fury of the establishment, such as the Ministry of Interior's attempt to discredit *L.627*'s portrait of a drugs squad left to flounder and nearing breaking point. In contrast, the film was defended widely by grass-roots police workers, despite its sometimes extremely unflattering image of their attitudes and performance. His parallel story of the work, struggle and exhaustion of one man within the education system, *Ça Commence Aujourd'hui*, produced an almost identical pattern of responses, although its devastating portrait was even harder for the establishment to talk down, faced as it was with the testimony of the real residents of the deprived ex-mining town of Anzin, some of whom acted in the film. For the director, politics and emotion do not simply go together; they are part of the same thing. Tavernier's political cinema is certainly angry, but increasingly its emotion comes charged with feelings of incredulity – gazing in utter disbelief at the state's inability to recognise the wealth that lives within its citizens.

NOTES ON CHAPTER 3

1. Bertrand Tavernier, *Cinéma Français* no 1, May 1976, p 46.
2. Michel Ciment, 'Sunday in the Country with Bertrand', *American Film*, October 1984, p 35.
3. Ibid., p 36.
4. Bertrand Tavernier, quote from the press release for *La Passion Béatrice*, Little Bear, 1988.
5. Tavernier called his production company Little Bear in reference to the Silver Bear awarded to *L'Horloger de Saint-Paul* (1973) at the Berlin Film Festival in 1974. The silver teddy-bear logo adorning the company letterhead was changed to a gold bear when *L'Appât* (1995) won the Golden Bear at Berlin in 1995.
6. Bertrand Tavernier, interview for Neuf de Coeur and l'Association des Professeurs d'Histoire-Geographie, December 1991.
7. Bertrand Tavernier, 'I Wake Up Dreaming: A Journal for 1992' in Boorman and Donohue (eds) *Projections* 2, London, 1993, p 257.
8. Bertrand Tavernier, Interview for Neuf de Coeur, December 1991.
9. *De l'Autre Côté du Périph'* was screened in two parts as *Le Coeur de la Cité* (*The Heart of the City*) and *Le Meilleur de l'Âme* (*The Best of the Soul*).
10. *Contre l'Oubli* (1992), produced by Béatrice Soulé for Amnesty International, is a film made up of 30 segments by different directors, each defending a different political prisoner. Tavernier's film pleaded the case of the Burmese prisoner Aung San Suu Kyi, and took the form of a formal request to the Burmese leader and message to Aung San Suu Kyi, written and read by the actress Anouk Grinberg.
11. *Lumières Sur Un Massacre* (1997), co-produced by Tavernier and Frédéric Bourboulon through Little Bear for Handicap International, was a series of short films by ten directors against the deployment of anti-personnel mines. In Tavernier's film, Sandrine Bonnaire made a plea direct to camera in response to a letter which she read out, written by a worker involved in dealing with landmine victims.

CHAPTER 4

HUMANIST FILM-MAKER

> I believe that every one of our works is just a part of this big work which is our whole life. After all, our whole life also belongs to the whole world.
>
> Jean Renoir

Since the release of his very first feature, analysis of the political content of Tavernier's cinema has been offered alongside evaluation which tends to single out for comment the humanistic nature of the drama. An early review which typifies this emphasis directed its praise at the perceptive humanism of *L'Horloger de Saint-Paul*, citing the fact that the film showed characters who were 'breathing human beings, with ties to a place and a time, who are as real in our memory as people we once knew'.[1] The humanist side of Tavernier's films has been the single most consistent aspect of his famously eclectic body of work, an aspect whose importance is increased by an apparent difficulty in defining his work in other terms. One programme review for an early retrospective of his work defined Tavernier's cinema by stating that it 'lacks both the literary qualities of Truffaut and the theatricality of Chabrol', without going on to explain any defining quality it does possess, and might share with them, or indeed any other film-maker,[2] not unusually finding it easier to define the director's work in terms of what it is not than what it actually is. Problems of definition can be attributed to that side of Tavernier's films which has often been developed from a reaction against certain things which disturb him, whether they be cinematic conventions (the anti-genre visualisation and casting of *L.627*), over-reverence for period décor (the detached acceptance of the physical world in *Que la Fête Commence...*), filmic reference to painting (the avoidance of static composition and impressionism in *Un Dimanche à la Campagne*), or general perceptions of his own nature as a director (the nihilism in *Coup de Torchon*). Tavernier admitted that the pessimism of *Coup de Torchon* was partly a reaction against what he perceived to be the particular value that had been attached to the warmth of his earlier work, culminating in the tenderness that creates the optimism of *Une Semaine de Vacances*. 'I made the film because I wanted to break the image of my nobility; because I was being labelled as a humanist director.'[3]

In principle, Tavernier was irritated more by obsessive pigeon-holing than by his being equated with humanist values, and would later reaffirm his personal distrust of the crude categorisation of artists: '... I reject all labels and categories. To lump so many directors as the *tradition de la qualité* or the *nouvelle vague* and now *la nouvelle qualité française* is the best way to ignore the individuality of each film-maker. I'd say that the definition of *tradition de la qualité* applies when academism stands in the way of expressing emotions... in the attempt to reinvent *la nouvelle qualité francaise*, I was lumped together with Claude Miller, Alain Corneau and a dozen others. We're not at all alike.'[4] Tavernier's dislike of the analytical defeatism that lies behind conveniently vague labels is a deep-rooted conviction that fits with his acute sense of human complexity, but is also very easy to accept in the light of the spurious categorisation that had been applied to his own cinema, essentially on the basis of his decision to work with Jean Aurenche and Pierre Bost. Tavernier's collaboration with the writers has been interpreted as both a fundamental alignment with the post-war 'quality' cinema of other directors such as Claude Autant-Lara, Yves Allégret and Julien Duvivier and a conscious stance against the New Wave. These assumptions, at best an exaggeration and still persisting to an extent, take no account of the practical situation facing Tavernier at the time as a budding first-time feature director who had experienced great difficulty finding a producer for his first film due to his lack of track record, and often play down contradictory evidence of his clear approval of much that the New Wave had brought to the cinema:

> I thought that 'If I am going to do a first film and I go to well-known screenwriters they will turn me down, or take me among other projects', and I was seeing that well-known screenwriters were always doing two or three films at once and even the directors I was working with as press agent were complaining they could not have any re-writes, that the writers were onto another film, immediately after the second and third draft, so I thought to myself 'Maybe I should take people who are not in demand. They will be more with me. They will really have something to prove

again.' Part of the theme of *L'Horloger de Saint-Paul* was dealing with the question of generation, so I thought 'Let's take people older than me' because it's part of the subject. I decided to watch a lot of films of the past again, to listen to the dialogue, to the words, and I picked up the name of Maurice Auberger who was the screenwriter of a film by Jacques Becker, *Falbalas* [1952], and of a wonderful, totally under-rated film directed by Henri de Coin called *La Verité sur Bébé Donge* [1952], and other than that, there was Aurenche and Bost. When I was watching the films, I was always surprised by the extraordinary quality of the dialogue, which was not made of *mode auteur* as they say, I mean the dialogue was alive, was fresh, was perceptive, was original. Their subjects were always original, and when the film was heavy-handed, or sometimes wrong, most of the time I thought that was due to the director – a scene, a line done in a close-up when they should do a long shot, things like that. I thought 'It's not them who are old-fashioned. It's not the writing which is dated.' I remember seeing a film by Jean Delannoy called *Dieu a Besoin des Hommes* [1950], and I came out and I said, 'If I was doing exactly the same screenplay, people would not recognise the film. It was full of composed, artificial shots and I thought the screenplay was full of life, of energy, of violence. It should have been dirty. It should have been full of mud instead of those composed images. The direction was taking out all the life out of the project, and the screenplay was incredibly original, and I thought that the film was attacked by Truffaut on completely the wrong basis. I thought, 'He is attacking Aurenche and Bost, but it is Delannoy who is totally mad'. If you gave the same screenplay to any number of directors – to Louis Malle or to someone like that – you would not recognise the film. So I decided to go to them... Pierre-William Glenn was a kind of new cameraman – he had done a few films – I knew that he would use hand-held camera and I wanted that a lot. I knew that I would shoot the film with direct sound, and there were a lot of things from the *nouvelle vague* which I wanted to adapt. It was very, very important for me not to have an old-fashioned cameraman, and to have somebody who was ready to experiment, who knew the American cinema.

Awareness of Tavernier's stronger affinity with *Positif* – Truffaut was linked to the more vociferous yet less politicised *Cahiers du Cinéma* – may have been responsible for inflating the perception of Tavernier's reaction against Truffaut. In reality he was a great admirer of much of Truffaut's work – never making any secret of it – but simply had a number of very specific disagreements with some of his strongest attacks on directors as well as writers, which he regarded as unfair and clearly the product of Truffaut's over-enthusiasm in defending his own heroes, especially Hitchcock. In the case of Truffaut's famous attack on Aurenche and Bost,[5] Tavernier eventually discovered that Truffaut himself regretted the article, and had been insincere from the start, at least in relation to Bost.[6] Tavernier was on very friendly terms with

Truffaut, whom he admired for *La Chambre Verte* (1978) especially, while the New Wave's own humanist had admired Tavernier's fresh approach to directing historical drama in *Que la Fête Commence...*, as well as writing to him in praise of *Une Semaine de Vacances*, *Coup de Torchon* and *Un Dimanche à la Campagne*. Their mutual admiration was communicated through Daniel Bion,[7] and an occasional exchange of letters until Truffaut's death in 1984.

The nearest thing to a clash of principle between Tavernier and the New Wave falls somewhat short of being an opposing cinematic credo: a comment dealing mainly with practical working methods is interesting in that it touches on the approach to film-making which is at the very heart of everything that Tavernier is praised for: 'I also think we trust actors more [than the New Wave] and we work with them in depth'.[8] His emphasis on working with actors provides the key which positions Tavernier along a continuum of film-directing methods which has, at one extreme, a pure storyboard approach, where an almost cartoon approach to directing would slot actors into precisely pre-conceived visualisations; at the opposite extreme is a mise-en-scène which remains undetermined before the director, camera, sound and actors arrive on location or set, where drama is shaped during rehearsals. Tavernier's preference for an approach to directing that is close to the latter scenario, centred on human communicaton, matches the definition of his work by Volker Schlöndorff, who said of his former classmate, 'He won't seek originality, nor (human) perfection, nor fashion, nor ideology. His cinema will be without system, without rules, heterogeneous, organic...'[9] Tavernier finds it impossible – and increasingly so – to pin down a small number of film directors who represent the essential influences on his own cinema. There are simply too many – short lists of names which change constantly, as the emphasis of his interests shifts; but as regards his directing style during location shooting there is one director with whom Tavernier was compared early on, and whose name keeps coming up: Jean Renoir.

The first time that Tavernier recalls his directing style being compared with Renoir's was while shooting *Que la Fête Commence...* Tavernier's philosophical affinity with the master director is apparent from his own natural avoidance of the type of approach which he knew was taken by directors whose films he often admired, but whose way of handling people appalled him, such as Claude Autant-Lara, Marcel Carné, Julien Duvivier and Jean-Pierre Melville. The tyranny of the last of these he had experienced at first-hand, as his assistant director. Tavernier still regards the comparison with Renoir as one of the greatest compliments he has received, revealing a man for whom the very act of film-making itself is as important as the film itself.

Twenty-three years later, with references to the atmosphere which he manages to achieve in production now well-documented, it is still an astonishing experience to enter Tavernier's set for the first time. Arriving in the infant school in Anzin, the main location for *Ça Commence Aujourd'hui*, watching Tavernier through a corridor window as he directs a tracking shot[10] of teachers and assistants and children, before being introduced to him, there is something unusual about the atmosphere, hard to define at first, but in the end simple – obvious even: the entire atmosphere is lit up by an enthusiasm which gives the impression of watching a director making his first film, and which infects the entire production. There seem to be none of the barriers between director, key crew, actors and assistants which are often invisible but powerfully tangible on film sets, and Jürgen Vollmer, the film's veteran photo-publicist of around 40 features from France and Hollywood, from Alain Resnais to Francis Ford Coppola, is more amazed than anyone. After shooting finishes early for the day, and everyone has had the chance to get freshened up, there is an air of celebration in the Grand Hotel, Valenciennes, where the cast and crew live together during the entire shoot. In his element, Tavernier hands out all the drinks to his entourage as they are placed on the bar, then everyone strolls into the hotel's function suite to view the rushes which have just arrived from Paris. There is much teasing and hilarity in the air, the surprisingly child-like laugh that belongs to the big man as apparent as anyone else's, save perhaps that of Michel 'Tonton' Desrois, who began recording sound for Tavernier on *L'Horloger de Saint-Paul*, and whose dedicated work has apparently entitled him to rib his director mercilessly in banter that is part of a long-standing game. Tavernier is clearly used to it all, but is treated to an extra surprise this time. The last reel ends with a shot that he doesn't remember directing. With the aid of one large pole and an ocean recreated by out-of-vision crew waving a huge, blue tarpaulin frantically, one male and one female member of Tavernier's cinematic 'family' re-enact the emblematic 'flying' scene from *Titanic* (James Cameron, 1997). During the general collapse into hilarity it is hard to decide who enjoys the prank more, the practical jokers or the outspoken scourge of cultural imperialism himself.

Although the apparent openness of Tavernier's 'little world' was heightened during *Ça Commence Aujourd'hui* because of his decision to involve and integrate the local population with the film, it is a quality which many of his collaborators regard as fundamental to his work. The atmosphere in which Tavernier's crew feel both valued and free to share ideas which may or may not be accepted is something which he has consciously nurtured, as well as making sure that he leaves a door open to 'outsiders':

> Maybe people like to work with me because I never demand something very difficult then change my mind totally, doing the opposite and making their work unusable in the film. Ninety per cent of the time, what I have specifically demanded is on the screen. *Capitaine Conan* was a tremendously difficult film – maybe the most tiring film I have ever done – but everything that we fought for is in the film. I have seen so many crews absolutely dead, without any energy, any impulse, because the director was asking a lot then never using what they gave – like asking for two streets to be lit then doing a close-up against a wall. That is something which can destroy the spirit, which destroys the spirit of the film. I never keep people away from each other. When I read the Powell book[11] I felt that I was working very much like him, when he had that constant group and they had discussions. I always try to work with new people. I always try to combine a kind of family of actors, composers, even people who write songs like Jean-Roger Caussimon, with new faces. Instead of having the group totally closed, I always try to leave it open so that people could get in, like Gerard Lanvin, Eddy Mitchell. If you look at my films, you see that I discovered many actors that way, from Christine Pascal to Philippe Torreton.

As well as aiming for a working relationship with his cast and crew based on the creative trust which he both offers and requires, Tavernier also attaches enormous importance to relationships between the rest of the cast and crew, especially that between the camera operator and actor, and talked about Pierre-William Glenn, his first director of photography/camera operator, being 'in sync' with Philippe Noiret and the other actors – not only sensitive to their way of communicating but tuned in to their physical expression, to the extent of literally anticipating their exact movements. Pierre-William Glenn and Alain Choquart, who have covered most of Tavernier's work as camera operators, both understand the priority which Tavernier places on the operator-actor relationship as well as the actor-camera dynamic. Naturally disposed to empathy with their subjects, they are both equally aware of the fact that actors are far better able to push performance to the limits of their emotional expression when they know that a state of complete respect and trust exists between themselves and the camera operator, who is at times working in extremely close physical proximity to them. If Tavernier's cinema can be defined essentially as humanist, that definition can rest on the simple basis that there is nothing more important to him than achieving what he regards as emotional truth in his films, and this has a major impact in shaping his work. Once Tavernier begins shooting, whatever visual ideas he has, or are offered to him, his mise-en-scène is always shaped around the actors' performance to a very great extent. In this respect, his working method is exactly like Renoir's – something of which he is very well aware. While using camera movement as a form of emotional expression, he always avoids tight camera moves which constrain the movements of his actors, seeking to keep them as free as possible, every camera movement being related directly to the emotions within each scene that stem from the characters, whether they are in the frame or not.

Always in search of the hidden side to characters and of what is 'unspecified in the script', it has become second nature for Tavernier to direct an atmosphere that actively encourages people to bring him ideas, something which he regards as yielding huge benefits of quality, and indeed quantity, of material which he is offered at every stage of production. The notion of keeping a door open to new faces is crucial for what Tavernier refers to as his need 'to be astonished'. The humanist centre of Tavernier's cinema is characterised always by a sense of wonderment of every kind, sometimes joyous but more often appalled, even heartbroken. Those who are closest to Tavernier while he is working often refer to a child-like or vulnerable side to his nature, as well as the deep doubts to which he admits himself. Regardless of the subject or circumstances of his productions, his working world tends to be full of laughter and warmth, as if to provide some kind of protection against the deep sadness that is most often evoked in his films.

Frédéric Bourboulon, Producer:

> Bertrand is always anxious, frightened. He is someone who carries his anxiety. When he gets up in the morning, he has a stone in his stomach. 'Am I doing the right thing? Is this the right sequence? The right way to do it? It is unbelievable for a director of such stature to always be so anxious. He needs to have people near him who are very loyal; in whom he has complete confidence, so that he can unload his anxiety. He needs to discharge himself of his anxiety. He can kill his anguish with the help of someone else, and he can only do that with somebody close, a friend who is complementary. I know that I serve that function sometimes. It's a big part of our relationship. He needs me to take his problems so that he can feel lighter and go and shoot. Maybe it's a bit like a couple – one is obliged to share one's anguish with someone so that one can feel lighter, and I sense that very strongly in him. Betrand is a kind of sun at the centre of a galaxy around which all his satellites gravitate, and his family of satellites is very large. He has always succeeded in integrating everyone. Everybody knows each other, and knows that it is important for Bertrand that there is a cohesion, a coherence. He is afraid, Bertrand. He is afraid of birth, of death, of powerlessness, of not having inspiration – that is what makes him a being who is full of doubts, who is very anguished. Everyone knows that we have to be there to reassure him. When he has everybody around him,

he is the Sun King – everyone is just there, the women, the men, the friends, and it's a very familial circle. He needs to have that.'

Alain Choquart, Director of Photography/Camera Operator:

In a way, Bertrand likes, and doesn't like, to change crew. He likes always having something new, but also, every film he directs is so different that he needs to have a different mentality on every film. I think the reason why we have done a few films together now is that he felt that I could change my way of thinking from one film to another. The reason he never acts like a dictator is because he knows very well that everyone will surprise him and give him even more than he was expecting. He is a spectator of his own film while he listens to the actors. Quite often, he doesn't even look at the video-assist and he likes to watch the crew around. Like the cameraman in *Death Watch*, he would like to have a camera in his eye and be able to film everything that he sees. He is also a real spectator of his own way of shooting and he enjoys it a lot. The laughing on set comes half from the scene we are shooting and half from the way we are shooting, and we always play with words a lot while making the film. Laughing is part of the concentration anyway. On *Ça Commence Aujourd'hui*, we were a bit like children ourselves – we were playing at making cinema.

Tiffany Tavernier, Co-writer:

Sometimes Dominique and I wrote sequences[12] which had a very definite beginning and precise ending, and my father said, 'No, we're going to remove the beginning; remove the end. What I like in a story is to feel that I am arriving in the middle of something.' So if two people are shouting, he doesn't care about the beginning or the end of the argument. What he likes is to be a kind of invisible man, a kind of mouse, who arrives suddenly in a crisis, and disappears in the middle of the crisis – this is typical of him. He likes to integrate the comic and the dramatic. It's his way of seeing the world. It's a kind of kid's vision of the world – a kid is just moving in the crowd and with his eyes he's picking up things, like the beauty of a woman's dress, then somebody else's anger, then the red shoes that belong to someone else. He doesn't like to have just anger in a sequence. He is spraying emotion. The dramatic and the comic and all the elements of life are dispersed around. I think he is horrified by something that exists in human nature. Each film is a fight against the horror of human nature and in each film I can hear a kind of voice saying, 'No, it's not true. I don't want to admit it'. He took maybe two months to accept the suicide in *Ça Commence Aujourd'hui*. Then another two months to go up to the point of shooting it. All his life is like this – there is a fight with the writing, and then there is this fantastic period during the shooting, because this moment is a kind of victory. I think he is winning against the darkness around him. The time he is shooting is when he is most enthusiastic – he will say, 'When I'm shooting, I'm alive'. In *Capitaine Conan*, sometimes he had to wait two days just for some element of the production to arrive, so for two days he was stuck, and that is the worst thing for him: to be stuck in the mud with his head full of ideas.

Tavernier's 'child-gaze' is most obviously apparent, and certainly most sustained on screen, in his second major documentary work, the film of his visit to the Deep South of America which is like a personal pilgrimage for him. The project was released in two versions, the first being a series of four hour-long programmes for television called *Pays d'Octobre* (1983), the second, better known version, being a 90-minute feature called *Mississippi Blues* which was released on video. Tavernier co-directed the project with Robert Parrish, the American director who was also John Ford's editor for many years, Mississippi having been where Parrish spent his childhood. *Mississippi Blues* is the film in which Tavernier's sense of discovery is clearest, the film being largely based on his own active discovery of the place which existed in his dreams through books and films. With *Mississippi Blues*, Tavernier allows himself to marvel in fascination with the physical world itself, in a way that he avoids with his dramas, and the impression of innocent wonderment at the 'big country' is as striking as that in the fictional films of Wim Wenders,[13] another European 'outsider', albeit with a far more conscious feeling of exploration and a search for answers that is rooted in the film's concern with people, their history and culture. *Mississippi Blues* is a search for the hidden South, its neglect being the factor which draws Tavernier in as much as its authenticity. His discovery of the real, uncommercialised blues in the documentary is not very different from what he so often does in his dramas. While his fiction so often seems to be made to serve as a window into the distant past or contemporary history which France would prefer to forget or ignore, *Mississippi Blues* is a loving document of a part of America which has been totally removed from the corporate presentation of a nation by the political establishment and Hollywood. Even in its drastically cut form, the film impresses in the time it takes to listen, allowing the singers, ministers and activists to fix the meaning of their stories with a context, a history. One of the most important aims of the film is to document the expression of a collective history as well as a collective contemporary emotion through music, and the rich variety of music caught in churches, homes, shops and bars is left intact. Tavernier would no more cut his subjects' performance than he would expect viewers to leave one of his films before the final credits and music had finished.

As Parrish takes Tavernier inside the reality of the romantic land that holds his young memories, we also see a film being made. The journey is stitched together by scenes of the crew setting up, on the road, playing in between shooting the interviews and the music; but as well as Parrish and Tavernier we also see the members of the crew just sitting and listening to the stories and the songs. *Mississippi Blues* was

Tavernier's chance to merge totally the pleasure of the crew in the act of filming with the audience's enjoyment of their subject. We see Pierre-William Glenn (Lighting/Camera), Michel Desrois (Sound), Albert Bonomi (Key Grip) and a very boyish Alain Choquart (Camera Assistant), soaking up what seems like a huge reward for fidelity, growing up in Tavernier's film, like his daughter Tiffany, whom we have seen change from a little girl to a woman through most of his films, even if we did not realise it. Seeing the faces of Tavernier's crew in the film we know that *Mississippi Blues* is not about work – it is about learning. One way or another, Tavernier's films are all about education, and *Mississippi Blues* conveys more openly than any other of his films the sheer pleasure of learning and his confident knowledge that wisdom is best acquired with patience and respect. Dealing with two men whose attachment to the South is very different, and listening to subjects who have remained in Mississippi all their lives, through all the emotional upheaval of the civil rights years, the film also traces the roots of education and growing up. It contrasts Tavernier's feeling for the South with Parrish's, Tavernier's affection having grown at a distance and been created largely through film. Alongside its primary interest in the connections between history, religion, politics and the path of education in its widest sense, *Mississippi Blues* is partly a reflection on the notion that emotional roots are at least as important as physical ones: Paris failed to pull Tavernier away from Lyon, after he moved away so early in his life.

While taking in the new, Tavernier and Parrish keep returning to the old, their conversation turning to film as the young director seeks the views of an old hand. Memories of real life and of cinema collide and blur in a sequence in which the film drifts seamlessly through documentary and fiction, colour and monochrome, while Parrish reminisces with Tavernier about being made to cross onto the other side of the road before passing the Catholic church. Again, Renoir's name turns up. The best film about the South? *The Southerner* (Jean Renoir, 1945), Parrish tells Tavernier, going on to relate a conversation he once had with Renoir, having asked Renoir how he, a Frenchman, could know so much about the South. Renoir's reply was that he knew nothing about the South, but did know about peasants. The side of *Mississippi Blues* that is shown through Tavernier's lens deliberately avoids the pretence of instinctive prior knowledge, its gaze alternating between the quietly attentive and the wide-eyed. Before setting out with a small crew to bridge the half-imagined dreams of his youth with the real towns, characters, voices and music of the present, Tavernier may have known little about the land of the authentic blues, beyond what literature and cinema shaped in his mind, but he does know about learning. *Mississippi Blues* is the clearest vision of Tavernier's insatiable curiosity for knowledge, the essential element of his work that steers his humanist vision.

The other defining element which informs his pensive cinema is an almost paradoxical blend of definite convictions regarding injustice and its perpetrators, and a frequent feeling of mystification about the individuals who populate his films. Tavernier's characters are often seen thinking, as if disappearing into their own past, searching for answers, but very often he feels no need to tell us what their thoughts are. In truth, he doesn't know what his characters are thinking any more than any of us can be totally sure of what our past means. For Tavernier a certain amount of obscurity is far more truthful and personally identifiable than neat explanations, which goes some way towards explaining his strong desire to get away from the chronological pattern of plot. Tavernier's cinema has always displayed a particular sensitivity towards the side of human nature in which the meaning of past events seems almost tangible, but impossible to verbalise, exact understanding just beyond our reach. This aspect of his humanism is diametrically opposed to the conditioned fixation which constrains Hollywood and almost all television drama in Europe as well as America: stories primarily driven by the logical connection of events which hold plot-intrigue together. In relation to *Une Semaine de Vacances*, Tavernier talked of critics who found a lack of construction and plot in the film, defending his drama by saying that if they 'talk about not finding a plot there, they do not see what the film is about'.[14] Tavernier is well aware that his own doubt reflects something which is an essential side of the human condition, and the ambiguity which has been resident in his work from the start suggests a belief on his part that to pretend full understanding of Laurence Cuers or any of his characters would mean the betrayal of truth.

NOTE ON CHAPTER 4

1 Ruth M. Goldstein, 'The Clockmaker', *Film News* no 5, 1973 (review of *L'Horloger de Saint-Paul*).
2 Tavernier retrospective programme, National Film Theatre, London, August 1980.
3 Joseph Hurley, 'Tavernier et Noiret Encore', *Films in Review* vol. 34 no 4, April 1983, p 232.
4 Dan Yakir, 'Painting Pictures', *Film Comment* vol. 20, Sep./Oct. 1984, pp 19–20.

5   Truffaut's article was entitled 'Une tendence certaine du cinéma française', and appeared in *Cahiers du Cinéma* in 1954.
6   Bertrand Tavernier, 'I Wake Up Dreaming: A Journal for 1992' in Boorman and Donohue (eds), *Projections* 2, London, 1993, p 287
7   Ibid., p 288. (Daniele Bion has written extensively on the work of François Truffaut, and is the author of *Bertrand Tavernier: Cinéaste de l'Emotion*, Renens, 1984)
8   Michel Ciment, 'Sunday in the Country with Bertrand', *American Film*, October 1984, p 33.
9   From Volker Schlöndorff's preface to Bion, *Bertrand Tavernier*, op. cit.
10 A 'tracking shot' is one where the camera is moved along tracks which have been laid down during a take. It is the method of camera motion which provides the smoothest and (usually) most unobtrusive movement. Walking with a hand-held camera is sometimes described as 'tracking'.
11 Michael Powell's autobiography, *My Life in Film*.
12 Dominque Sampiero co-wrote *Ça Commence Aujourd'hui* with Tiffany and Bertrand Tavernier.
13 One moment in the film seems to make a cheeky reference to Wim Wender's *Paris Texas* in one of Tavernier's rare close-ups: a sign saying 'Paris Postal Service – Paris, Miss.[issippi]'.
14 Lynda K. Bundtzen, interview with Bertrand Tavernier on *'Round Midnight, Film Quarterly* vol. 40 no. 3, Spring 1987, p 10.

> If everything was clear to me, if I knew exactly where I was going, I would not make the film.
>
> Bertrand Tavernier

THE DRAMAS

CHAPTER 5

L'HORLOGER DE SAINT-PAUL (1973)

Black screen. The sound of a train approaching fast. Rapid fade up. Night. A passenger train rushes across the screen, revealing a sign when it finally passes: LYON 15km. Cut to train interior. Slowly track along a couchette wagon corridor towards a little girl leaning against the window, staring out absently. Cut to the girl's point of view. The train passes a car blazing fiercely. Cut back to the child who seems unperturbed by the scene as she turns and goes back slowly into her compartment, pulling the door closed behind her, shutting out the camera. The train's rhythmic sound is gradually replaced by a growing, pulsating drumbeat. Cut to exterior. The camera pans and tracks past a typical level-crossing and guard's house until it finds the gutted car still ablaze, lighting up the night. The drumbeat sweeps into an ominous theme, which seems to promise a *policier* thriller, as glaring red opening credits slam in to fill the screen, then scroll rapidly onto the screen in quick succession: Raymond Danon présente… Philippe Noiret…

Nine years after completing the two shorts *Le Baiser de Judas* and *Une Chance Explosive*, neither of which he felt was very good, and following his period spent working mainly as a press agent and film writer/critic which he used to develop his ideas and direction as a film-maker, Bertrand Tavernier chose for his first full-length feature for cinema to direct an adaptation of Georges Simenon's novel *L'Horloger d'Everton*. What became *L'Horloger de Saint-Paul* (*The Watchmaker of Saint-Paul*) proved to be an assured and deeply personal debut feature-film whose successful release brought to light a film rich with many of the elements and themes to which Tavernier has returned again and again in his subsequent 16 feature-films for cinema, not to mention his documentaries for television. The opening sequence alone is laden with suggestions of several of Tavernier's main concerns and preferences: the train as a nostalgic emblem of the emotional past and symbol of the human wandering in search of meaning; the burning car as first embodiment of the film-maker's detestation of materialistic status within French society; a love of the potency of words and their interplay with the non-verbal, given first illumination in the form of the 'LYON 15km' sign, underscoring his conscious decision to root *L'Horloger de Saint-Paul* firmly within his own past and experience, as well being prophetic of his professional advocacy of a diverse, regional French cinema. The train's hurtling towards his home town prefigures the emotional return to roots that would be made by so many of his characters in later films, as well as his own reflective and healing journey to the city for his poignant documentary *Lyon: le Regard Interieur*.

His use of a novel – though radically transposed in both epoque and milieu – as the basis for the screenplay was a handling of form which the literature-loving director would repeat in *Coup de Torchon*. The deceptive title style was early evidence of his desire to turn cliché around, and his determination to subvert any formulaic expectations of genre. The film's primary engagement with the paternal-filial relationship between Michel and Bernard Descombes would recur repeatedly, although in profoundly contrasting forms, from the bitter-sweet loves experienced by M Ladmiral and son Gonzague in *Un Dimanche à la Campagne* and by 'Daddy' and daughter Caroline in *Daddy Nostalgie*, to the false, pseudo-parental nurture offered by Judge Rousseau to Sergeant Bouvier in *Le Juge et l'Assassin* and François de Cortemart's appalling ruination of his daughter's idealised adoration in *La Passion Béatrice*. Following his acclaimed portrayal of the watchmaker whose world was turned upside down, Philippe Noiret went on perform another four lead roles and two smaller parts for Tavernier – a fidelity mirrored in the creative dedication of several other recurring collaborators, and which became an essential aspect of the director's production environment. The tracking camera leads straight to the heart of Tavernier's *oeuvre*, setting out his most profound concern by anchoring a moment of emotional reflection to a child-image, expressed through a lyrical camera move. It is significant that the first human being we meet in Tavernier's first feature-film is a young child, and even more so that the little girl in the train corridor is in fact his own daughter Tiffany. As the first of many instances where Tavernier put close family members into his films – acting, being interviewed, writing, crewing and co-directing – Tiffany's opening of *L'Horloger de Saint-Paul* is consistent with the huge emphasis

'Your son has killed a man.' Inspecteur Guiboud gives Michel Descombes the news, going on to court and gain his friendship, though it is to be short-lived.

placed on family by Tavernier, an importance which exists for him as much in terms of his creative production needs as in the content of his films, which display his endless fascination with the painful love that characterises the inter-personal politics of family relationships.

When Tavernier wrote his treatment for *L'Horloger de Saint-Paul*, Simenon had already been adapted over 40 times in French cinema, and he admired several classic versions such as *Maigret Tend un Piège* (Jean Delannoy, 1957) and *En Cas de Malheur* (Claude Autant-Lara, 1958). All the same, and despite being immensely struck by Jean Aurenche's screenplay for the latter, for his own film he wanted to remove all that was for him superficially Simenon, feeling that the famous atmosphere for which Simenon was always praised – the fog, the wet pavements, the feeling of oppression – had become clichéd. The 30-page treatment which he gave to Aurenche and Bost was already very close to the final structure, identifying most of the scenes and new characters, including the police inspector, placing the action in the 1970s and setting the story in Lyon at the height of summer. Recognising such radical changes, Tavernier does point out that Lyon was still for him 'a very Simenonian city,' and his adapted version of the title kept intact the essence of a sense of place, but by far the most important reason for shooting his first feature-film in the city was his desire to root the film in a reality stemming from his own experience:

> I wanted to charge it with memories of my youth. The film was shot in many places where I loved to walk, to go when I was ten. The Parc de la Tête d'Or was my favourite park in the world. As soon as I could walk I went there. I put a lot of places in L'Horloger which were related to my discovery of the world.

Tavernier's desire to make this Lyon of his own experience a real part of the main characters' lives explains the notable absence of classic images of the city, such as the striking Fourvières basilica or the Place Bellecour in the film. Tavernier consistently avoids using familiar establishing shots, which are for him a kind of *cinema touristique*, but the way he wove Lyon into *L'Horloger de Saint-Paul* represented far more than his almost obsessive desire to avoid cliché; it established, at the outset of his film-making career, his fascination with the complex metaphysical relationship between character, environment and event. The film is saturated with the suggestion of meaningful connections between the distant and recent past: conversations about an old family home due to be demolished; stories about objects old and new in Bernard's room; Michel Descombes's seemingly trivial tale about the encounter with the child which marked him deeply. Tavernier is certain of the significant nature of memory, but not of its precise meaning. We see Michel being transformed from a state of total disorientation to one of absolute conviction of his chosen stance, but Noiret's watchmaker is striking, more than anything else, for his detailed portrayal of a man consumed by deep personal uncertainty. When Michel tells Bernard the old tale about his rebellious attack on a superior officer, he admits to being unsure why he is telling the story, and the doubting side of his nature is the one which he shares most with Tavernier himself. Like the enigmatic images of Lyon, Tavernier includes Michel's memories to show the all-pervading connections which shape the watchmaker's existence within the physical world, but in doing so he draws relationships which defy absolute verbal definition and, typically, he portrays a world literally beyond understanding.

One key visual characteristic of the film is the ease with which scenes are introduced with characters off-screen, showing an aspect of the décor or location which is not concerned with the plot. The opening restaurant scene which immediately follows the title sequence introduces the group of diners via an image of the café they inhabit: a close-up of photos of anonymous characters on the café walls, presumably regular clients, friends or family. When Michel and Antoine walk out of shot during their conversational stroll home, the convention of cutting as soon as characters leave the frame is substituted with a focus-pull,[1] in order to show clearly the constant rush of the huge stone fountains they have just passed. The cumulative effect of these and the many other images of the town is to heighten the feeling of the city's complicity in the story. While Michel's relationships with Antoine, Commissaire Guiboud and Bernard develop and are fractured or renewed, the city projects an air of strength and constancy which is somehow both comforting and hurtful. When the first journalist intrudes on Michel, waking him up to pester him for 'background', Tavernier links tranquil images of the city with one of several variations of the film's music score and uses them in a reflective montage to form a frame for Michel's loneliness, following the conversation about his marital status:

> Journalist: You are a widower, aren't you?
> (Camera tracks in quickly to hold Michel in close-up.)
> Michel: No, I'm not a widower. My wife died, but we were already separated. Still, I'm a widower all the same. I was as unhappy as a real widower.

Earlier in the film, while suggesting the metaphysical element of the drama, Tavernier creates a mise-en-scène drawing expressively on a relatively unconventional camera move, which has perhaps become his most singular trademark of visual style. Shortly after Guiboud has told Michel that Bernard had killed Razon, the factory security guard, we see him drop Michel off in Lyon, to make his own way home. Next the camera pans to pick up Michel as he walks to the tram stop, then tracks on, leaving him to take in a view of the city, closing in on the distant cityscape, with people standing around and walking casually past in the foreground. What the camera does is to separate Michel from his surroundings in our eyes, and this seems to reflect his mental detachment from the world around him. The view is a picturesque one of Lyon with its River Rhône on a beautiful sunny day, and its idyllic impression clashes with Michel's emotional state. Several seconds before we cut away from the view, we hear the tram's bell. Michel has already gone, oblivious of any views around him, and the final image serves to create a strong impression of Michel's deepening loneliness by excluding him from the frame. Although Tavernier was far more concerned with script than visual style during pre-production, the nature of this type of scene was already deeply embedded by his plans:

> I wanted to do that kind of shot. For me it was clear. Willy[2] made fun of me because I was always asking for shots of the landscape without characters. I wanted to root not only the characters but the film with the city. I wanted them to be part of that city, because for me Lyon was a very Simenonian city and I wanted to get away from the characters a few times in the film and go with landscape shots. Very often directors use that kind of shot to introduce a new set, to explain a kind of topography. Those kind of shots in this film and my other films are always, for me, emotional. They are

half-musical. They are like a kind of moment of pause. It's a moment where you give a little space to the character, a little time, and it is a way to root the character and the story in the place. I was very much influenced at that time by a lot of directors, and in people like Losey[3] who was working very much on the relationship between the décor and the characters, not only as a social element but as a kind of metaphysical element. I used to, and I still do, like the Westerns of Delmer Daves,[4] where very often you have a crane shot, in *The Hanging Tree* [1957] for instance, which is like a moment of music and it suddenly reintroduces the country, the places which are around the characters. I liked that in some of the films of Pierre Granier-Deferre, who did that in two adaptations of Simenon – *Le Chat* [1971] and *La Veuve Couderc* [1971], moments where you were taken out of the story – of the central plot – to have a moment of grace and of pause. It's a way of widening the angle, the story.

Tavernier also widened the scope of Simenon's novel most noticeably by introducing the film's rich political backdrop, setting the events around 1971 when French politics and media were audibly riddled with the paranoid obsession over 'gauchistes'[5] in post-'68 French society. Television and radio broadcasts speculating on the political dimension of Razon's killing punctuate the film, and Tavernier uses them to stress Michel's apolitical nature, but they also reflect Tavernier's horror of a generalised naivety, through which a nation is taken in and carried along by media analysis which amounts to little more than shallow comment disguised with a superficial air of authority. Michel is apolitical, and his witty suggestions that the death penalty be televised tell us more about his opinion of the degree of depth offered by television than his true feelings on capital punishment. Television is Tavernier's main target of attack, for its culpability as the main message-bearer for materialism and defence of the official status quo. Bernard burns Razon's car – an act which appals one commentator more than the guard's death – and in doing so destroys the main symbol of 1970s French consumerism. Michel and Antoine both make direct attacks on television, never more disparagingly than in Antoine's furious instruction to the photographers outside court to go back to their televisions following Bernard's conviction and harsh sentence. Antoine's anger is generally directed at groups or the masses, and this is consistent with Tavernier's reluctance to judge individuals.

Tavernier's distrust of easy answers, as well as his avoidance of cliché, partly explains the characterisation of Inspector Guiboud, who was not in Simenon's novel. Far from being a symbol of the state and the right wing, Guiboud is often vocally sceptical of the official line, and is more outspokenly scathing of simplistic explanations for Bernard's actions than anyone else in the story. He is ultimately incapable of

Distance between the generations – Michel listens to his son Bernard's confession on tape.

understanding Michel's unconditional support of his son's stance, causing Michel to break off their friendship before the trial is over, but he is genuinely concerned for Bernard's welfare, as well as to avoid injustice. Tavernier's main reason for including Guiboud, with his tales about his own son, was to reinforce the film's concern with middle-age and the loss of communication between generations. The ex-housekeeper Madeleine Fourmet is a generation older than Michel but has an easier and relaxed relationship with Bernard, emphasising the acute difficulties existing between the more immediate generations. These painful divides form the emotional heart of the film that Tavernier sought to convey, a reminder also that the age difference between himself and Aurenche and Bost was one of the reasons why he decided to collaborate with them.

L'Horloger de Saint-Paul indicated Tavernier's leanings as a political and a humanist director, but it also introduced the essentially lyrical nature of his cinema, and the political and humanist themes are drawn together hauntingly, below the layer of dramatic dialogue, through the interplay of key images and the film's developing music score. The driving, ominous theme which opens the film over images of Razon's burning car does not appear unconventional for the superficial *policier* premise of Simenon's novel, but the music returns several times throughout the film in a variety of guises to form a complex expressive element. We never discover the exact circumstances surrounding Bernard's killing of Razon, but the warlike drumbeats which set the theme off reflect the confrontational aspects of the contemporary political situation into which Bernard's crime is dragged. The musical theme recurs throughout the film. Several times we hear versions in which the violent tempo is reduced to create a more constant, melancholic air linked with languid montage sequences of views of Lyon, and the more aggressive version returns with a scene of Razon's burnt-out car, forming a counterpoint to the clean-cut tourists posing for photographs with the car. It is only towards the end of the film we find that the theme's source is hidden within Lyon itself: the emotional score is finally heard as a simple melody of clock bells in Saint Jean Cathedral, where Michel has gone to sit in peace and to decide what he must do. All along, the music has been associated with pictures of Lyon, and its connection with Bernard's crime comes from Antoine when he addresses the injustice of the sentence, serving as an indictment of the 'satisfied comfort' of those 'respectable people' of Lyon whose peace must be preserved at all costs, people whose tradition Michel has symbolically served all his life through his work on all the old clocks in Lyon. The scene perfectly encapsulates Tavernier's passionate concern with the complex plight of the individual in the face of society's state-driven, uncaring, selfish tendencies, and it is this crucial viewpoint which has consistently underpinned the humanist expression within all of his subsequent films, both drama and documentary.

Tavernier combined *L'Horloger de Saint-Paul*'s lyrical qualities with a rich impression of realism, using perceptive observation of the superficially ordinary daily routines of Michel and Guiboud to accentuate the watchmaker's lonely anxiety. Right from the outset, Tavernier committed himself to a performance-centred cinema. In addition to Noiret's quietly simmering emotional performance, Tavernier's desire to achieve something which seemed far more authentic was served by his choice of production methods, especially his desire to combine cinematographer Pierre-William Glenn's experience in highly portable location shooting with sound recordist Michel Desrois's skill in recording realistic direct sound. *L'Horloger de Saint-Paul*'s marked avoidance of formulaic convention was certainly at least as important as its announcement of Tavernier's political and humanist concerns. Crucially, in addition to the key collaborations with Pierre-William Glenn and Philippe Noiret, the film forged several of the close relationships which would give the director the confidence to discard convention and adopt an open approach to script and narrative construction. The film's success ensured that Tavernier would be quickly offered the chance to make another, allowing him also to work again with writer Jean Aurenche, editor Armand Psenny, actor Jean Rochefort and the actress

Christine Pascal, to whom Tavernier had given her first break in cinema as Bernard's quiet, enigmatic girlfriend Liliane Torrini. Sound recordist Michel Desrois could be found 25 years later still gathering direct sound for *Ça Commence Aujourd'hui* (1999) on the streets of Valenciennes, having worked on virtually all of Tavernier's full-length feature-films. Tavernier wanted to retain elements of the loyal production 'family' he had formed for his second film, but this consistency was not to be mirrored by any repetition of genre, and the shift in his attention from *L'Horloger de Saint-Paul* to his next project established another striking pattern in his output: that each film would be in stark contrast to the previous one, even a reaction against it.

NOTES ON CHAPTER 5

1 When the camera operator (or focus-puller) has to adjust the focus of the lens to deal with subjects which are at varying distances from the camera.
2 Cinematographer Pierre-William Glenn.
3 Joseph Losey, the blacklisted director on whose films Tavernier worked as press agent. Losey's films include *The Servant* (1963), *King and Country* (1964), *Accident* (1967), *The Go-Between* (1971) and *Don Giovanni* (1979).
4 Delmer Daves was a prolific director, mostly of Westerns, thrillers and war films, throughout the 1940s, 1950s and early 1960s. His *3:10 to Yuma* (1957) is another film which Tavernier cites as influential. Daves's other works include *Destination Tokyo* (1943), *Dark Passage* (1947), *A Kiss in the Dark* (1949), *Broken Arrow* (1950), *Return of the Texan* (1952), *The Last Wagon* (1956), *The Badlanders* (1958) and *Youngblood Hawke* (1964).
5 Literally 'leftists'.

CHAPTER 6

QUE LA FÊTE COMMENCE... (1975)

> But all this love which I shall give, where shall I get it from?
> Jacques Audiberti

Que la Fête Commence... (*Let the Party Begin...*) marked a complete switch in genre from Tavernier's first feature, but although the director's preference to work with a completely new subject for subsequent films would be established as a consistent pattern, the film was less of a reaction to the previous one than happened in later years. Tavernier already had the project in mind when he resisted several predictable offers of books by Simenon from which to create his second feature. The film stemmed from one of the ideas which Tavernier and Aurenche were considering for their first project together, namely a screenplay adaptation of *La Fille du Régent* by Alexandre Dumas. It was in the process of re-adapting that screenplay for their second film together that Tavernier and Aurenche decided to throw away Dumas's novel and write an original screenplay which became *Que la Fête Commence...* The story is set in 1719, four years after the death of Louis XIV, when the film's protagonist Philippe d'Orléans was regent. Tavernier's interest was both in dealing with the period's restless change, which would eventually lead to the upheaval of *La Terreur*, and with the dramatic contrast between the reformist regent and the other two main characters, the Breton rebel Marquis de Pontcallec and the scheming, ambitious Abbé Dubois:

> I have always been fascinated by the transition period. After the end of the reign of Louis XIV which was totally puritan, stupid, closed, and which

had left France totally destroyed and famished under oppression because the last mistress of Louis XIV had become totally bigoted, it was like breaking or opening a window there. The film was a possibility to describe a world at the start of a new age where people were starting to think, and were beginning all the refutation of the church – all the roots were there. I was fascinated by the opposition between the three characters: the mad idealist Pontcallec and the practical politician l'Abbé Dubois – ruthless, a liar and a scoundrel but in a way pragmatic and with a result, because those were the only years when France was at peace – it was the first time in 60 years that the country was not destroyed by war. Then the Regent – the man who wanted to reform the world around him. He was very educated. He had all the vision and saw everything beautifully. He started a lot of things and a few are indicated in the film: he started building the roads, taxing the Church, started free education for everybody – he created a lot of high schools which are still here now, and it was the Regent who introduced the soldiers' barracks in France, which was something totally revolutionary, because before that soldiers were living in the houses of the peasants and they were stealing everything, raping girls. So in a way it was to protect the civilians that he did it and this was an incredible move – something which Jean and myself were never able to write properly without seeming to do a lecture. In a lot of historical films you have scenes where people are explaining something to the audience, and something which I insisted on with Jean in the film was that we should never have one character who is explaining something to another character that he should already know.

Despite Tavernier's fascination with the period, and its many characters' political motivations and manoeuvring, the drama in *Que la Fête Commence...* is as emotionally centred around the plight of Philippe d'Orléans as the previous work was around Michel Descombes. The focus of Dumas's title suggests that his story perhaps did not centre enough on the regent's own situation for the film director's purpose. The lines of text from Jacques Audiberti shown before the opening sequence provide the key to the film, reflecting the anguish and intractability of the regent's trapped circumstances – the aspect of the story which forms the heart of the film and which affected Tavernier most of all:

> The Regent saw exactly what he could do. He had a goal, an aim but he had neither the strength nor the possibility to do it because of the selfishness and stupidity of the aristocrats and the Church, who wanted to keep what they had. My concept was that he was someone who did not want the power that he had, and in a world, especially in the modern world, where you see so many people who are ready to do anything to get power, I was moved by that. My interpretation – which was something new at the time – was that he went to those orgies to forget and maybe to die, that it was a way out for him; it was absolutely suicidal. That was the concept that we

'Let the party begin…!' – orgies as Philippe's only means of escape from failure.

had of the character and I felt that all of those shades and ideas were very moving.

The context in which the regent exists is symbolised in the opening sequence, which encapsulates all the stupidities of the established powers of the time, and of the Church in particular: a priest standing on a cliff top with a small congregation, announcing gravely that unless the verminous field mice leave the area within three days, they will be declared 'damned and excommunicated'. In complete contrast to *L'Horloger de Saint-Paul*, *Que la Fête Commence…* is full of humorous moments, but the humour tends to be bitter, frequently with an air of dark incredulity at the idiotic and corrupt attitudes and actions of the aristocracy and the Church. Any possibility of the priest's condemnation of the field mice producing laughter is diminished by the ominous sound of an incessantly tolling bell in the nearby village, whose insistence finally leads us into a relentless tracking shot along the cliffs, following a man who is about to be caught and killed for trying to kidnap children for deportation to Louisiana. Most of the humour is bleak and sarcastic, and only the poor, outraged Marquis de Pontcallec is at times genuinely comic. The most savage humour comes regularly from Philippe d'Orléans himself, who is forever ready to display sarcasm and his utter contempt for the aristocracy who form his entourage. After he has ordered the execution of his murderous cousin, the Comte de Horn, and another cousin asks him, 'Is it a habit of yours, killing your family?' the contemptuous regent replies, 'No, it's an overwhelming desire I get when I look at you'.

Tavernier portrays the regent as someone far more intelligent and better educated than most of those around him, and who has a genuine understanding of the wider world, in contrast to the surrounding ignorance and narrow bigotry. He achieves some release from his frustration with them by rubbing their faces in their own lack of understanding, never missing an opportunity to point out to the insincere, self-interested nobles and clergy around him that he despises their stupidity and hypocrisy, and sees through their transparent ambition. The first words he speaks in the film are to suggest to Chirac the surgeon, who has just completed an autopsy on his daughter Jouflotte, that her death was more likely to be a result of his phoney medicine than from the 'gluttony' which Chirac had himself diagnosed. When a cleric suggests to Philippe that priests are 'not interested in politics', he replies, 'Jesuits giving arms to one tribe to kill another – I call that politics,' and goes on to express his disgust at the 'butchery' of the Spanish Inquisition. In reply to Maréchal Villeroy's defence of such action against 'the enemies of religion', the regent calls him 'an imbecile, a pitiful general and a third-rate Christian' to his face, then tells him to remember that 'I am as patient as you are stupid', after letting him know that he is fully aware of Villeroy's ill-concealed mistrust and disloyalty.

He is equally blunt with the ambitious Abbé Dubois, constantly making cutting remarks about his greed and his self-interest. When Dubois interrupts Philippe in the evening while he is entertaining his whores, to discuss an '*extremely* serious affair', the regent replies 'There is nothing serious after 7 o'clock except the supper menu,' sneering at Dubois's self-importance before sending him packing. Throughout the drama, marked by his unfolding discovery of Dubois's deepening treachery, he becomes increasingly outspoken towards the Abbé in his contempt for him, to the point where he openly expresses hate, telling the Abbé how much he likes to see him suffer. Tavernier had already criticised the established order in *L'Horloger de Saint-Paul*, but *Que la Fête Commence...* was the first film in which he targeted the shortcomings of the Catholic Church. Dubois might seem the obvious embodiment of the corrupt Church, having no real interest in the vocation of archbishop beyond the power and wealth it affords. He schemes to ensure the execution of the pathetic Pontcallec and his insignificant band of rebels, purely to placate the English king whose support for his bid for the mitre he desires. His obsession with ensuring Pontcallec's death, purely as a means to further his political ambition, is a cynicism which would be mirrored later in that of the judge Rousseau in *Le Juge et l'Assassin*. Dubois is at least open in his admission that his only motive for wanting to become Archevêque de Cambrai is his craving for riches and power; he describes himself as 'naturally pagan,' and jokes about becoming a cardinal, maybe even Pope. It is the worst hypocrisy, evil practised cynically in the name of God, which offends Tavernier most: we see Brunet the magistrate genuflecting in front of a crucifix before performing a travesty of a trial which consists solely of judging Pontcallec. When the Marquis refuses to kneel at first, saying, 'I kneel only before God', Brunet replies, 'God is here', indicating the crucifix behind him before condemning him to death.

The Marquis may have been Philippe d'Orléans's sworn enemy, but in *Que la Fête Commence...* he is seen suffering at the hands of the very same people who also torment the regent. In the film, it is Pontcallec himself who seems to set out Philippe's predicament in the lines which precede his first appearance, referring to regency banknotes, which he accepts with some distaste to fund his rebellion: 'When the wine is drawn, one has to drink it...' Music overlaps the two scenes linking them, enveloping the first images of the pensive, restless regent, whose apparent preoccupation is reinforced by a melody which is superficially light and restful, but marked with an air of sad anxiety.

The entire film score, which was re-transcribed and adapted by Antoine Duhamel, came from original manuscripts composed by Philippe d'Orléans himself, and the elaboration of his opera based on Euripides struck Tavernier, who felt that they represented an important side of the man which had never really been analysed. The director's use of the regent's own music was exactly in line with his interpretation of the orgies which Philippe attended, a way for the regent to escape his own torment. His compositions are certainly emotional, their quietly wounded tones matching Philippe Noiret's portrayal of a man hiding behind sarcastic anger, but who keeps letting his guard down and slipping into the demeanour of an utterly lost child, seeking some explanation for the events which have broken his heart. The final Dies Irae-sounding chorus, which carries the film's dénouement, leads us into the final descent of a man who has now slipped into madness, driven by self-loathing, first referring to himself as 'an old corpse', then hallucinating that his own hand literally stinks with deathly putrefaction. Tavernier used the regent's own music not because of any formal or classical purism but for the emotional integrity which he felt it could bring, a fact borne out by the style in which the film was shot:

It was a totally new challenge. In the *L'Horloger de Saint-Paul* we had rather a free style and I wanted to be even freer. I wanted to do all the film as if the camera was invented in 1715, exactly as if we were witnessing the film – it started at the writing stage, and went on during the film-making. In the case of a historical film it was something new, although a little bit had been done by Tony Richardson in *Tom Jones*. But normally, people were always shooting period films as if they were looking at the set and the furniture from a modern point of view; we feel that they are looking at, say, the furniture and thinking 'Oh my God it's beautiful, it's beautiful, it's really a work of art.' I wanted to do the film without ever thinking that. The characters were not – for them it was something which was contemporary, and I wanted them to treat the furniture and the palaces with a lack of care. Myself, in the framing, in the lighting, I never wanted to be in admiration of what I was filming.

The earthy colour and lighting gives the impression that Tavernier hoped to invalidate any simplistic label of 'costume drama,' and *Que la Fête Commence...* does look unconventional, to the extent that even the term 'period piece' seems thinner than usual. It contains no beautiful images of large rooms with smoke-enhanced light streaming through large windows, the camera never lingers on images of furniture or rooms or gardens, and there are very few wide establishing shots at all. Compared to most of Tavernier's other films, *Que la Fête Commence...* is shot unusually close in many of the conversation scenes. In fact much of the film is shot like reportage. Action sequences are shot as hand-held 'actuality,' and at times the camera follows people around from outdoors to indoor and through rooms, as though unsure where they are going, what they are doing, whom they will encounter. There is a sense of time running out for the characters' precarious lives, created by all the rapid camera work, right from the opening tracking shot, and this feeling pervades the whole atmosphere of the film, furthered by the brisk, frequently aggressive and contradictory dialogue. The film's documentary lack of formality also displays Tavernier's early preference for the removal of the formal predictability of shooting dialogue sequences in a series of matching reverses,[1] where medium shot is cut with medium shot, then medium close-up with medium close-up.[2] The dialogue scenes often adopt shot sizes which are less interested in a seamless, balanced aesthetic, more geared towards suggesting introspection and dependence, or subtly implying the current state of psychological power relationships. When the regent converses with Dubois about his clerical ambitions, Rochefort is often framed closer (larger) than Noiret, although the variation in shot sizes is not so dramatically different as to draw attention to itself. Closer framings often seem to reflect the viewpoint of the listener (the regent), most

An anguished regent's confidante – Émilie the prostitute and Philippe d'Orléans.

apparent in the scenes where the prostitute Émilie and the regent offer each other concern and support.

Noiret's frequent appearance in central roles for Tavernier has led to him being considered the embodiment of autobiographical elements in the director's works, and his school-friend Volker Schlöndorff referred to Noiret as the director's 'alter ego',[3] but in *Que la Fête Commence...* it is Christine Pascal's portrait of the regent's prostitute companion Émilie who often functions as the film's moral voice. She is the one who tries to counter the regent's dark despair when he is weary of trying to achieve what he knows should be done. When his courtiers amuse themselves with a fancy-dress ball in which they dress up as the poor, she reproaches Philippe: 'I don't like people making fun of the poor. It would be better to invite real poor people.' In subsequent films, it is often secondary or minor characters who reveal the essential truths hidden beneath the surface drama, such as the teacher Laurence Cuers' reproachful boyfriend Pierre in *Une Semaine de Vacances*, or the young detective who tries to make Nathalie understand the enormity of her crimes at the end of *L'Appât*. As with Émilie, the moral force also regularly comes from women, both in central roles (*Death Watch*; *La Passion Béatrice*; *Daddy Nostalgie*) and minor characters (Rose, Rousseau's girlfriend in *Le Juge et l'Assassin*; Anne, the teacher in *Coup de Torchon*; Kathy, Lulu's wife in *L.627*).

Michel Descombes in *L'Horloger de Saint-Paul* is a man shaken with uncertainty and indecision when his world is turned upside-down, but ultimately his darkest period passes and he comes out into the light of total certainty regarding his role as a father, whereas the regent in *Que la Fête Commence...* is eaten away by terrible, deep-rooted doubt that continues growing until he is on the point of literal self-destruction. Doubt is frequently identified as a recurring theme in Tavernier's films, something he readily acknowledges, but his portrayal of Philippe d'Orléans was the first of three profoundly religious works dealing crucially with the central characters' increasingly despairing questioning of the meaning of the human condition and the very existence of God: the other two were *Coup de Torchon* and *La Passion Béatrice*. *Que la Fête Commence...* is not quite as dark, however, and its clearer sense of hope is again provided by Émilie the prostitute. When the regent asks Émilie if, given the life she leads, she really believes in a God and a Heaven and a Hell, she replies, 'I trust that God will take pity on me'. Her suggestion that a shaved head, the pox and death in a hospice will be her penance is very similar to the view taken by Charlie in *Mean Streets* (Martin Scorsese, 1973): 'You don't pay for your sins in church, you do it in the streets...' The opening titles of *Que la Fête Commence...* read 'Brittany, Palm Sunday', the day on which the Passion and Crucifixion are played out.[4] The theme is expanded further at the very end of the film when the peasant girl whose brother has been killed by Philippe's carriage grabs Émilie's head and forces her to watch the royal carriages burning after the peasants have set it ablaze to avenge the dead boy. Her final words are quoted in a third-person voice-over, its tone reminiscent of Revelations, seeing the inferno as a penitential precursor to the events that would occur during the impending revolution:

> ...and the peasant girl lifted up the dead boy's head and said to him, 'Look, little brother, look. Look how well it burns.' And she added, 'We'll burn many others, little brother, many others'.

NOTES ON CHAPTER 6

1   A conventional approach to shooting dialogue sequences which is based on a symmetrical approach to cutting together shots of people who are facing each other in conversation, symmetrical both in terms of angle and shot-size (the relative size of subject to frame).
2   Shot sizes are most often defined in terms of their framing of the human body. The medium shot is roughly half-length, from the waist up. The

medium close-up is from just below shoulders up. The close-up is basically a 'head-shot', framed to the shoulders. A big close-up is a close facial image, cropping at least some of the forehead and chin.
3 From Volker Schlöndorff's preface to Daniele Bion, *Bertrand Tavernier: Cinéaste de l'émotion*, Renens, 1984.
4 The Passion and Crucifixion, starting with Jesus's celebrated arrival in Jerusalem on a donkey, are traditionally commemorated firstly on Palm Sunday, during which palm leaves are distributed near the start of mass. The same events are read or played out again on Good Friday, which marks Jesus's crucifixion and death.

CHAPTER 7

LE JUGE ET L'ASSASSIN (1976)

Bertrand Tavernier's next feature-length drama film was his last venture linked strongly with both Jean Aurenche and Pierre Bost, although he would work again with Aurenche, on the documentary produced for video *Philippe Soupault et le Surréalisme* (1982) and *Coup de Torchon* (1981), as well as using Pierre Bost's novel *Monsieur Ladmiral Va Bientôt Mourir* as the basis for *Un Dimanche à la Campagne* (1984). Philippe Noiret's formidable presence again in a central role, as Judge Rousseau, is the other key link which reinforces the sense of this film being the completion of a trilogy. Tavernier's interest in this piece of unfinished business dated back to the shooting of *L'Horloger de Saint-Paul*, during which he asked Pierre Bost if he had any other screenplays which had never been made. Bost gave him a 60-page treatment[1] for *Le Juge et l'Assassin (The Judge and the Assassin)* which he had done in 1948 for David O. Selznick, the producer of *Le Diable au Corps*[2] (Claude Autant-Lara, 1947), but which had not been developed further. The alterations which Tavernier made to the original concept gave a clear indication of the direction in which his cinema was heading:

> I immediately thought there were wonderful things in it and I started to develop it with Jean Aurenche. We changed the treatment, which was entirely focused on the relationship between the Judge and the Assassin in the jail. I introduced all of the first third of the film and a lot of later scenes which described the place, the period, the time. Although at least eight or ten scenes from the first draft are still there, it was a new screenplay – the idea of the film is totally different. The difference between the two is very interesting, because it is the contrast between two ways of making films.

> The first draft screenplay was very intelligent, very precise and full of very, very interesting scenes, but in a way narrower – it had been done as a kind of psychological study. I think the screenplay I did with Aurenche is freer, wider, is more musical. There is much more scope in it. It's less theatrical, more lyrical.

Tavernier also widened the scope of the story by developing further the character of Judge Rousseau's colleague Villedieu (Jean-Claude Brialy), the prosecutor, who existed in the original concept. He also introduced a completely new character, Rousseau's mistress, Rose (Isabelle Huppert). Both roles allowed the film's politics to be expanded explicitly, through dialogue sequences, but they also serve the purpose of adding depth and complexity to the story, especially in terms of the character of Rousseau. Like the earlier films, *Le Juge et l'Assassin* pursues the theme of justice, dealing with the judicial process to an even greater extent. However, whereas in *L'Horloger de Saint-Paul* political feeling was more directed towards a distant, untouchable enemy – state structure and the attitudes fed by its media messenger – *Le Juge et l'Assassin* seems to provide the audience with a much clearer political battle and establishment target: the cynical manipulation of a clearly insane killer by the politically motivated Rousseau. In fact, the lines are not so clearly drawn, and the dramatic conflict between Rousseau and Sergeant Bouvier was the strongest example so far of Tavernier's repudiation of simplistic notions of good and evil. In particular, Rousseau exemplifies Tavernier's rejection of the portrayal of Dionysian characters as totally bad. Despite Rousseau's distasteful and at times evil behaviour, Tavernier takes the trouble to show both the judge's human side and his point of view. Rousseau is truly appalled at Bouvier's crimes; whilst deviously ensuring that his convenient denial of Bouvier's insanity prevails, he sincerely finds it impossible to accept that Bouvier has no sense of culpability. His heartfelt plea to Bouvier that he face up to the reality of his actions is reminiscent of the sense of outrage voiced by the young detective who tries to force Nathalie to face up to the shocking consequences of her activities near the end of *L'Appât* (1995).

The director's affirmed belief in the combined influence of both personality and society on an individual's actions[3] explains his partly sympathetic portrayal of Rousseau, and is equally at work when we see characters performing selfish or evil actions throughout all of his later works, such as Roddy in *Death Watch*, François de Cortemart in *La Passion Béatrice*, Dodo in *L.627* and Conan in *Capitaine Conan*. Just as Bouvier pleads his own case by citing those events outside his control which led to his crimes, the inclusion of the judge's personal life in the film amounts to Rousseau's plea of mitigation, supported by the

'He doesn't listen to me!' – Bouvier comes
across Christ in the wilderness.

repressive quality of those tools employed by the society in which he had lived. The stifling influences of the army, the Church, the prisons, the asylums and the hospitals are all exposed in the film, and Tavernier's own ultimate refusal to judge either Bouvier or Rousseau is characteristically answered by his indictment of a more collective culpability.

Le Juge et l'Assassin is driven primarily by feelings of injustice, and these ideas are rendered more complex by the film's intertwined themes concerning insanity. The dramatic conflict of the plot revolves around Bouvier's sanity, but at every turn the film also shows an époque riddled with madness and violence; reactionary, intolerant, paranoid. In pushing Bost's original concept towards something far more reflective of the contemporary state of France, Tavernier was acutely aware of the inherent madness of the period's domestic conflicts and violent history. He has alluded to the fact that Bouvier's actions occurred between the death of Van Gogh and the arrival of Freud, and when asked what he wanted to say about madness with the film he made two crucial points: firstly, that he shared Foucault's view that a society can be judged on its treatment of the mentally ill; secondly, by citing an old popular belief that the insane are less insane than we believe – that they speak the truth – this leading to the question of whether it was really by chance that one of the first measures directed by Goebbels was against the mentally ill.[4] These two points inform everything that we learn in the film, about Bouvier himself and the dreadful world he inhabits. Bouvier cites, at every opportunity, the appalling treatment he has received at the hands of those who were supposed to treat him and care for him. There is never any hint that he is anything other than genuinely insane, but his most grandiose and crazed rantings are mixed equally (and at times uncomfortably closely) with the most cutting and perceptive observations about his immediate situation and surroundings, as well as analyses which display his acute sense of the wider injustices of the social order within which he exists.

Tavernier's reading of the prevailing madness of the time is offered through the reactionary outbursts of the army and the Church. The pulpit ranting of a priest who, in the process of denouncing secular schools, vilifies the ideas of Émile Zola and Victor Hugo seems remarkably similar to Bouvier's most feverish outpouring. Rousseau's own mother reflects the state and Church obsession with destroying Dreyfus, doing 'good works' on behalf of the Church by serving soup to the destitute, but only to those who will sign a petition against him in return, and refusing two men who claimed that they could not write. The film's representation of the Church provoked some very negative reviews including – unsurprisingly – from the Catholic journal *La Croix*, which was allocated two appearances in the film in the form of a poster reading 'La Croix – France's most anti-Semitic journal'. The poster, shown at one point behind the judge and his mother, seems to provide further ammunition for those who find Tavernier's polemical style too blunt, although there seemed to be a certain amount of mischief in showing it in the film – the director actually acknowledging his heavy-handed approach – as well as an element of joyful aggression.[5] This slightly anarchic quality recalls the character of Bouvier himself, and Michel Galabru's simultaneously comic and deeply tragic portrayal of the killer is hugely instrumental in setting out the tone of the film, as he swings from his gleefully contemptuous attack on human arrogance and pomposity to the darkest despair of someone who sees no way to avoid the abyss. The strength of Noiret's previous appearances actually serves to accentuate the ambiguous qualities in the film, and of the repressed, measured Rousseau himself, the sheer contrast with Galabru's explosive performance intensifying the profoundly tormented image of Bouvier, the demented yet eloquent voice of the film's deepest outrage.

The highly political content of the film continued the tendency already established by both of Tavernier's earlier features, embedding firmly his reputation as a political film-maker. *Le Juge et l'Assassin* is fundamentally more polemical than either of his previous films. However, his cinema had already been praised for its lyrical qualities, and *Le Juge et l'Assassin* also took this aspect of his work much further. The film combines highly scripted intellectual argument with intensely lyrical sequences, the latter created by the intricate weaving of performance, camera, music and words. In terms of performance, Tavernier's recollection of the work done by Noiret and Galabru demonstrates the huge importance he attaches to working style, also revealing a little about his own essentially co-operative approach:

> It's such a pleasure to have those superb actors who don't behave as if they are showing to everybody how difficult it is to act. With Noiret, it was part of his pride to give the impression to everybody that it was easy, and that there was no work involved, and even when he was working, he never wanted to show it, doing it when nobody was watching. Noiret does most of his work when he is choosing the costumes or the props. It's a wonderful way of examining the characters, without talking about them – to examine every part of the character without ever psycho-analysing. It was very easy working with Michel because he was easy to work with, funny – a little bit like Philippe, and they liked each other very much. He has a wonderful sense of humour, is one of the great raconteurs of all time and Galabru and I wanted to use that in the film. The only thing I was frightened of was the fact that he had done many low-grade comedies, sometimes without any script or dialogue, with directors simply indicating, 'So, OK, be funny... Action!' but from the very first day it was immediately clear that he had never been contaminated by those films. It was as if we were doing his first film. He was totally fresh, ready to experiment, to try anything and never relying on technique, on his knowledge. Michel would be telling funny stories and I would say, 'Michel, we are ready to shoot,' he would stop the story and go in front of the camera, I would say, 'Action,' and he would immediately be totally tragic, then when you said, 'Cut', he would go back, saying, 'I have to tell the end of the story' – and Philippe Noiret was like that.

Isabelle Huppert was the director's immediate choice for the part of Rose, and her casting represented the arrival of the classic Tavernier heroine:

> I had seen her in one or two films – she had small parts at that time and I wanted her because for me she looked like a model for Auguste Renoir. I thought that she had an incredible strength. There was something in the way she behaved; she had a mixture of softness, a lyrical quality, while you could sense that she was like a rock inside. I like that mixture and I think she is absolutely stunning in the film.

Even Christine Pascal's silent Liliane Torrini, Bernard Descombes's girlfriend-accomplice in *L'Horloger de Saint-Paul*, exudes pure commitment

'... Judas!' – Judge now accused by assassin, Rousseau tries to block Bouvier's words of sympathy to Rose.

and determination; and the striking combination of vulnerability and strength which Huppert shows in *Le Juge et l'Assassin* is an essential feature displayed by all of Tavernier's later heroines. Katherine Mortenhoe (Romy Schneider) in *Death Watch*, Laurence Cuers (Nathalie Baye) in *Une Semaine de Vacances*, Béatrice de Cortemart (Julie Delpy) in *La Passion Béatrice*, Irène de Courtil (Sabine Azéma) in *La Vie et Rien d'Autre* and Caroline (Jane Birkin) in *Daddy Nostalgie* all display Tavernier's image of gentle femininity and powerful inner strength expressed in a variety of forms, both positive and negative: persistence, stubbornness, bravery, defiance, reproach.

Lyrical expression sets off the film, with its feeling centred around Bouvier, his love letters to Louise and his anguished searching for peace and meaning as we see him wandering through the Ardèche. The film opens with Rousseau's voice heard over a black screen, solemnly explaining his own situation in relation to Bouvier's violent crimes, suddenly switching to images of Bouvier on the snow-covered mountains around Lourdes, supported by Philippe Sarde's original music. The sharp contrasts in this introduction instantly start to create the constantly changing rhythms which reflect Bouvier's alternately hopeful and demented state of mind. The lengthy opening title sequence consisting of images of Bouvier and the landscapes plays like poetry and music, with Bouvier's words of devotion to both Louise and the Virgin Mary forming a strange, dream-like turmoil with Sarde's eternally restless music, whose phrases and melodies hang in the air as an echo of Bouvier's emotions, only to suddenly drop down and swell ominously, ruining Bouvier's poetry of love with dark hints of the other side of his nature and the atrocities which he will commit.

Violent contrast continually dominates the film's lyrical themes, underlining the ambiguous connections between the main characters. Immediately after his arrest, Bouvier plays and recites the same Communard song which Rose sings to rouse the strikers and soldiers at the factory uprising. When Rose sings the anthem and her voice is ignored by the soldiers, its effect is to provoke anger at injustice. When Bouvier sings, the song's literal emotion is destroyed through Bouvier's own perverted morality, its words falling on the deaf ears of captors who ignore the pleas of a child-killer. Bouvier's flat delivery is in any case depressingly bleak and impotent through its association with his earlier recitations to Louise – gentle words of love, rendered empty through his attempt to kill her. The sadness in Rose's version is very far from Bouvier's, hers representing the pain of a justifiable plea ignored, instead of the tragic shame of soiled truth. But the reality is that Bouvier is on Rose's side: he is one of the few who speak out at the oppression which constrains her life through inescapable poverty. Natural sound is employed for similarly expressive effect. When Rousseau orders Rose to submit, then rapes her, the sound of sheeps' neck-bells is heard accusingly in the distance, faint echoes from the earlier scenes depicting Bouvier's crimes which draw the connection between Rousseau's appalling treatment of Rose and Bouvier's unspeakable acts. The solitary bleating from the darkness in the early scene where Bouvier bemoans pitifully his loneliness to Louise's mother further deepens the meaning of the symbol.

Natural sounds are also deliberately presented less naturally, isolated as a way of underlining emotion. The sequence of the factory workers running to join the demonstration consists of shots taken from several different perspectives, with the soundtrack almost exclusively emphasising the sounds of the army horses' hooves and the workers' running footsteps on cobblestones; the nervous apprehension of the workers gathering quickly to face the arriving soldiers is created almost entirely by the rhythmic, nervous intensity of their footsteps rising, falling and increasing in pace. The saturated feeling of conflict in *Le Juge et l'Assassin* is equally served by the pictorial approach which Tavernier and his cinematographer adopt. In sheer contrast with the later section, when Bouvier is held within Rousseau's domain, the expansive images of the Ardèche serve to create the feeling of an enormous distance between Bouvier's needs and the imperatives which pervade the world represented by Rousseau. The director's desire to 'open up the story' was fulfilled by his decision with Pierre-William Glenn to shoot the film in Panavision 1:2.35 wide screen aspect ratio,[6] which provided a frame that would reinforce the sense of visual conflict:

> I wanted the opening section of the film to be set free, wide. Then, for the relationship between the killer and the judge, I wanted the style to be different – to be closer, sharper; to be less lyrical... At the same time, I wanted to give maximum freedom to the actors within those frames, never to block them. This is something I insisted on from my first film – never to have any marks. I chose to work with a cinematographer who operated the camera himself, in order to get that freedom. I didn't want composed shots, even in the scenes with two characters and I'm still critical of one or two moments in the film now when I see it again. If I was re-doing the film now, there would be two or three scenes where I would take out the close-ups and do them in longer takes.

As well as offering Noiret and Galabru the freedom which could facilitate spontaneity in performance, the wider frame specifically assisted the projection of their uneasy relationship. As the scheming judge manipulates the unsure Bouvier into a position of trust, the wider possibilities of composition allow the visual impact of their spatial relationships to be fully projected, with Rousseau carefully stalking his prey, deliberately maintaining his distance until his flattery and deliberate sowing of doubt begins to break down Bouvier's guard. As well as accentuating Bouvier's loneliness, the frame's width helps to visualise the wariness which his unpredictability causes in those around him.

Bouvier and Rousseau were based on real characters who did live during the period that the film recreates, and the film's impression of historical 'truth' in social attitudes and forces operating at the time was Tavernier's central goal, far more important than the authentic surface recreation of 'period' which typically gains Césars for Art Direction, important as that may be. Tavernier studied the book written by the real judge of the case, and all of the interrogation files and letters of the real life Bouvier. He wanted to inform his presentation of both men with their own ideas of reality, but just as important to him was the sense that any 'truth' achieved was still relevant and meaningful. *Le Juge et l'Assassin* did succeed in picking up awards, but Tavernier's attitude to his work seems best summed up by his obvious satisfaction in relating one famous *juge d'instruction*'s admission that he identified with the character played by Noiret while watching the film, and the fact that another expressed amazement at hearing phrases which he was convinced had come from the dossier of Bontemps and Buffet.[7]

Le Juge et l'Assassin closes with troops raising their rifles towards Rose and the striking factory workers, ignoring her call to them for solidarity, then freeze-frame images of ragged children and a red flag, finally ending with the still image of a child looking into the camera over which titles fade in, setting Bouvier's murder of 12 children in the context of a society which allowed 2500 children to die in the mines and silk factories. The accusatory tone is comparable with the ending of *Que la Fête Commence...*, but far more direct in its delivery of a polemical viewpoint, and this seemed to indicate a definite direction for Tavernier.

NOTES ON CHAPTER 7

1 A treatment is basically an outline for a film project which gives an idea of how the subject will be handled ('treated'). The length of a treatment can vary enormously, sometimes including very detailed proposals for specific scenes covering visuals, sound and dialogue. It is usually far from being like a 'shooting script', which is more of a set of clear instructions for how a narrative is to be filmed.
2 Pierre Bost wrote *Le Diable Au Corps (Devil in the Flesh)* with Jean Aurenche, which was directed by Claude Autant-Lara.
3 Bertrand Tavernier, *Blending the Personal with the Political,* Cinéaste, vol. 8, no 4, 1976 – interview with Leonard Quart and Lenny Rubenstein.
4 Interview in: Jean-Luc Douin, *Tavernier,* p 94, Paris 1988.
5 Interview in: Dan Yakir, 'Painting Pictures', *Film Comment,* vol. 20, p 20, Sep–Oct 1984.
6 Aspect ratio refers to the shape of the screen: comparing the ratio of the screen's horizontal plane with it's vertical plane. The shape varies greatly. The very wide 1:2.35 ratio which Tavernier used for *Le Juge et l'Assassin* is often wrongly referred to generically as "'scope" – short for *Cinemascope* although the format exists in other versions, such as the *Panavision* ultilised by Pierre-William Glenn. The format does tend to be associated with more spectacular types of drama, its introduction owing a certain debt to cinema's need to compete with the arrival of television. The original standard 'Academy Ratio' is 1:1.33, much squarer, but still affected slightly by television cut-off. (Television cut-off is less serious with the incoming wide-screen television, which has an aspect ratio of around 1:1.78). The majority of films are shot for the cinema at 1:1.85. Another standard is 1:1.66.
7 Bontemps and Buffet were the last people to be guillotined under the state death penalty in France. They were executed for murder in 1972.

CHAPTER 8

DES ENFANTS GÂTÉS (1977)

Tavernier's fourth feature-length drama was the first to present a completely contemporary image of French society, differing even from *L'Horloger de Saint-Paul*, which had been set in a defined recent past contextualised clearly by the specific politics of the day conveyed by the radio and television broadcasts shown in the film. *Des Enfants Gâtés (Spoilt Children)* does share a tangible autobiographical aspect with *L'Horloger de Saint-Paul*, although that of the earlier film exists obliquely through its sense of place, deriving essentially from childhood memories. In *Des Enfants Gâtés* it is directly suggested by the main character Bernard Rougerie, played by Michel Piccoli. Rougerie is a film director who decides to rent an apartment, away from his family, in order to get peace and quiet to write a film-script he is working on, but soon becomes deeply involved in his new surroundings, having a love affair with a young unemployed woman, Anne (Christine Pascal), who lives in the same building, and being dragged into becoming an active member of the apartment block's tenant's defence committee. Tavernier insists that only part of the premise of *Des Enfants Gâtés* was autobiographical, although it is clear that Tavernier's identification with Rougerie informed much of the character detail in this portrayal of a director whom we see frequently in a quandary about which paths to take, within his film project as well as in his life and work. We are specifically informed that Rougerie is forty-six years old, the exact age which Tavernier reached in 1977 when the film was released, and there are, both in aspects of Rougerie and incidents which happen to him, obvious reflections of Tavernier himself:

The idea of the screenplay came from a personal experience – not the relationship with the girl but about the tenants' strike. All those things took place when I was living in my real apartment and I became the president of the tenants' movement. I was much more involved in the social elements than the character played by Michel Piccoli, but it was more interesting to have a character who wants to get away from his home in order to be completely free and to have no problems, but suddenly gets involved... For me, it was like the starting point for a comedy and although the film was not exactly a comedy, it has many comic moments. His was not my way of working. I didn't rent a flat in order to work, but I had seen many directors do that, such as Claude Sautet and Jean-Pierre Melville, who used to live in a hotel when he was preparing a film, and I can understand him having to cut himself off in order to be alone to write, and not to see anyone, not to have the phone, or the problems of daily life. When I did *'Round Midnight* and *Sunday in the Country*, I took a hotel room. It's a little bit selfish, but you have to be selfish when you are making a film. You have to have those moments of isolation when you do a film on location, in a city, far away from Paris. Yes, I share many of his doubts – those *were* my doubts.

The central thread concerning Rougerie's experiences in the apartment block is inter-cut with others which include scenes relating the effects of urban building programmes, or showing Rougerie's new-found girlfriend Anne's personal situation, or his wife Catherine's work treating children with communication problems. The doubts to which Tavernier refers are expressed mainly through this last thread, juxtaposed with Rougerie's life while preparing his fictional film. At one point Rougerie tells Anne about Catherine's work, and how he wishes he did something similar – 'real' and 'concrete'. Here, Rougerie admits to a profound doubt far more serious than the root of his hesitancy when trying to map out the elements of his screenplay, questioning the very point of making films at all, and ultimately his entire role in society. Tavernier has frequently alluded to doubt forming a key element in his nature, and admits that he sometimes even shares this fundamental questioning of his own place in society as a film director, a feeling which probably never affected him more seriously than the experiences which occurred much later on, during the making of *Capitaine Conan* (1996). *Des Enfants Gâtés* was a very different experience from his previous films for Tavernier. It was his first step away from those closest working relationships which he had enjoyed during the first projects connected with Aurenche and Bost, and in particular he was working for the first time without either Philippe Noiret or Pierre-William Glenn, both of whom he had worked very closely with, had given him support and confidence through the difficulties of preparing and shooting his first film, and with whom he had established a way of working which he felt suited his temperament:

I am impatient – sometimes too impatient. This is a quality and a problem, but I like people who are fast, and Glenn is very fast – not only while he is shooting but when we were preparing scenes. I suffered on a few films with people who were slow, because when people are not coming up with the answer I want, or the response I want, or the energy I want, suddenly the fear, the doubts take over...

Regardless of the pace of shooting, *Des Enfants Gâtés* was a very difficult experience for Tavernier. Whilst he praises the work of Michel Piccoli, Christine Pascal (Pascal also co-wrote the film with him and Charlotte Dubreuil) and others such as Michel Aumont (Pierre, the script-writer) and Geneviève Mnich (Mme Bonfils, one of the tenants) with whom he worked again in *Un Dimanche à la Campagne*, he admits that he did not like the film when it was finished, relating this partly to the problems he experienced during production. Tavernier did not get on as well with the crew as he had during the previous three films; he occasionally found it difficult working with Christine Pascal, and was frequently having to shoot in small, cramped locations. Most importantly, *Des Enfants Gâtés* was his first experience of shooting a feature-film in Paris, something which he finds very difficult in itself. In the diary which he wrote for John Boorman, kept during and following his shooting of *L.627* in 1992, Tavernier mentions the difficulty of achieving the same working family atmosphere which he was used to having, when working in Paris, later suggesting that his great enthusiasm for *L'Appât*, which he was developing then with Colo Tavernier-O'Hagan, was spoiled only by the prospect of having to shoot a film in Paris again.[1]

Tavernier's other drama set mainly in Paris, *'Round Midnight*, was mostly shot in film studios. Like *L.627*, *L'Appât* presents in the capital city and its contents the metaphysical element in society which seems both to feed and reflect the destructive actions of its characters. Tavernier may have been apprehensive about shooting the film in Paris, but he knew that the drama had to be set there and nowhere else. Paris is often associated with suffering, or referred to negatively in his films: a telephone call from Paris is the source of Irène's distraught flight in *Un Dimanche à la Campagne*; Caroline is staying in Paris when she receives news of her father in *Daddy Nostalgie*; the city is the physical aspect of the existential prisons which hold Dale Turner for most of *'Round Midnight*. Even *Le Juge et l'Assassin* begins with the voice of Judge Rousseau saying, 'I was still in Paris, employed at the Ministry of Justice. I was bored...'

All the same, *Des Enfants Gâtés* does not strictly associate the destructive effects of the social and economic policies portrayed in it specifically with Paris, but attacks the city planning practices which prevailed in French society at the time, as the culprit responsible for the capitalism-driven depopulation of cities which causes destruction by building office blocks in place of playgrounds and parks. While engaging with these problems head on, Tavernier placed the element concerning a fiction film-maker's philosophical doubts about his own worth within a film which expressed his social and political concerns far more directly than ever before, framing its polemical nature with more forceful elements of documentary. The film's apparent message is presented immediately as its lengthy title sequence piles on image after image of dismal-looking tower blocks, building sites and waste ground, grim and increasingly claustrophobic, while the opening song 'Paris Jadis' rocks on and on drunkenly, laced with cutting irony and the black humour of collective human self-destruction. The song's ending is followed by a single shot of a little crowd of people walking to work in the rain through a city park, apparently huddled together under their umbrellas, with the quote 'every caress, every trust survives' superimposed. Through this image of a small group of people struggling against greater forces the film continues inwards to an intimate sequence of a woman trying to reach through to the creativity and imagination of a young girl who refuses to engage with her, creating the social juxtapositions which dominate the film's dramatic and visual style.

The scene between Rougerie's wife and the introverted child introduces non-communication as a central theme apparent at many levels in the story, and like *L'Horloger de Saint-Paul*, *Des Enfants Gâtés* deals in particular with the difficulty of communication between the generations. Rougerie's search for an apartment is a trail of encounters marked by misunderstandings and mutual distrust: he breaks off bluntly a discussion with Anne and M Bonfils when they first appear at his apartment asking him to attend their defence committee meeting, and it is the communication problems between him and Anne during their brief love affair which forms the film's other main narrative thread. Just after they have met, and they accompany each other to a launderette at night, it is an old man who sparks off their first moment of spontaneous warmth: they are both taken by his stubborn vitality of spirit as he enthuses about the aria from *La Traviata*, coming from the only channel working on the television which Anne agrees to let him watch. This image of the older generation managing to create a small bridge between two members of a younger one seems to echo Madeleine's more conscious, delicate efforts to help Michel Descombes understand his son's point of view in *L'Horloger de Saint-Paul*, and the rapport is warm between Anne and another elderly character, Mme Descombes (played by Andrée

Tension and uncertainty – Rougerie and his neighbour Anne edge towards an impossible love.

Tainsy who was also Madeleine Fourmet in *L'Horloger de Saint-Paul*), who defends her decision not to take a militant role in the fight against their exploitative landlord by saying, 'No, I'm too old,' adding, 'Besides, it's not women's business'. Through this, the theme of conflicting sexual politics between the generations is introduced and prefiguring ingrained attitudes within Bernard himself which would later reveal his difficulty in accepting Anne's political activities and her challenging, intransigent stance.

Throughout the film, people seem incapable of listening properly to each other, and both Anne and Bernard have to fight to get across their point of view and to be understood, both during encounters with other people, and with each other, with conflict seldom far away during their meetings and conversations. Bernard is clearly having a casual, short-term affair with Anne, but he is truly fond of her, despite the fact that she constantly irritates and provokes him, calling his standpoint into question directly, through her reproaches of his behaviour and his assumptions, and indirectly, through actions which make him feel guilty about himself. Their relationship is constantly inter-cut with the developing battle between the tenants (including themselves) and the landlord, Mouchot, but the sense of conflict is further deepened and complicated by the fact that Bernard and Anne are both struggling with their own personal battles concerning work, or the lack of it, and within themselves.

The dramatic structure of *Des Enfants Gâtés* is fairly simple, intercutting the strands concerning different aspects of Bernard's and Anne's life, the tenants' struggle, and Catherine Rougerie's work, but the multiple and interconnected conflicts which cross continually throughout the entire narrative made it Tavernier's most psychologically complex film so far. His approach to the narrative seems to have been informed partly by the experiments and decisions taken in his earlier works, partly out of a conscious desire to develop further and depart from what he had already done:

> 'I was afraid of routine. The first three films were more like chronicles than a real plot. I wanted to get even further away from the idea of a plot, to change that, and instead to have situations; to have stories, or one main story and lot of things around that. The film was a new experience for me.'

When he made *Des Enfants Gâtés*, Tavernier seemed to be striving to find the essential nature of his cinema. So far, he had seemed to be more primarily concerned with the issues concerning film narrative form, and although still engaged with questions about narrative and drama and convention he was apparently also wrestling with an inner debate about the purpose of his films. During an interview following the film's release, he identified the desire to achieve a very exact image of contemporary France as one of his essential aims in making the film, and affirmed his belief that films should project an identity based on national and social reality, stating as his worst fear for the art-form '...the development of a stateless cinema'. He also explained his desire to make a simultaneously intimate work, but acknowledged the film's less involving quality: 'It's necessary to be able to stand back a little – the film's kaleidoscopic structure allowed me to do that. In fact, the film is a kind of puzzle which obliges the viewer to do more or less the same work as the director, to be very conscious of what it is that he or she is watching.'[2]

The film seems less involving than the earlier works, especially *Le Juge et l'Assassin*, this quality arising mainly from conflicts between the different elements which Tavernier was dealing with. The character of Anne is integral to the political voice of the film, but at the same time the disturbing intensity of Christine Pascal's striking presence, both visually and in the wounded beauty of her writing, seems to conflict with the film's wider issues for our attention and concern. Pascal came to collaborate with Tavernier on *Des Enfants Gâtés* after an exchange of letters with him which drew his attention to her beautiful prose. He had introduced Pascal to the screen as an actress in *L'Horloger de Saint-Paul*, and he knew that she wanted to be more than an actress. Pascal's portrayal of Anne is subtle and complex, and she is totally convincing in conveying the young unemployed woman's relationships and anxieties,

'I'm just a film director' – Bernard Rougerie, the reluctant campaigner.

but her open pain, her direct intimacy, and her quiet desperation seem frustrated by the film's other distancing qualities. Whilst the film rarely puts aside its comment on urbanisation for very long, the lingering images are of Anne looking directly into the camera, demanding our attention. Pascal[3] committed suicide in Paris in 1996, and it is hard not to feel perturbed now, watching the scene in *Des Enfants Gâtés* in which, following a young woman's suicide in one of the apartments, Anne talks to Bernard, in graphic detail, about what it must be like to swallow 200 pills and watch oneself die in the mirror, giving a forensic description which almost suggests personal experience. The film closes with a poignant speech about suicide and self-pity, but ultimately the story ends optimistically, with Bernard and Anne apparently having learnt from each other, and able to move forward again. The development of their relationship is perfectly apparent, but its significance is weakened by the film's multitude of characters and concerns.

Des Enfants Gâtés was widely praised for its perceptiveness and the heart of its message, but it is not widely regarded as one of Tavernier's best works. The detail in its acute human observation is undeniable, and it is rich with perceptive humour and bitterness rooted in the social realities of its day, but its layers of meaning are obscured by the intricacy of its structure and the forceful grasp of its continuous verbal argument. The ambiguity in its title is best represented visually by a shot in the opening title sequence which shows monstrous concrete office blocks seen through the swings of a children's playground. All the same, in addition to some memorably inspired scenes – such as Bernard and Anne's embarrassed hesitancy when they both sense their mutual attraction – *Des Enfants Gâtés* is a fascinating work because of the insight it provides into the direction Tavernier was taking. When they first meet, Anne asks Bernard if he is the director of *La Mort en Direct*, the French title of *Death Watch*, which Tavernier had yet to make, and was developing as his next project. Bernard encourages Anne to explain her disagreement with the film's ending, indicating Tavernier's gradual movement towards an increasingly open approach to narrative, driven more by characters and places, less by dramatic plot. Through the character, Tavernier opens up about his anxieties as a director in a way that Bernard does not, providing many references to his own character, both serious and amusing. The impatience to which he refers is very apparent, including a dig at clueless television journalists who conduct interviews without doing proper research, when Bernard has to correct the reporter who wrongly attributes to him a film by Granier-Deferre.

It was for the making of *Des Enfants Gâtés* that Tavernier created his production company Little Bear, the name under which he has co-produced all of his films since in order to have more creative control over his work. The director's clear desire to engage directly with political problems within contemporary society would not be discarded or even weakened, ultimately going on to form the basis of some of his most successful works, fusing outspoken political concern and anger with fundamentally humanist narratives. Towards the end of *Des Enfants Gâtés* is a scene which serves as a wonderfully apt prediction of one of Tavernier's later projects, one which was to also to be one of his most important political works: Bernard is interviewed by a television journalist who points out that the political activity he is engaged in is not his job, and questions why he has to do it. Twenty years later, Tavernier would respond to government minister Eric Raoult's accusation of ignorant meddling by going into the poverty-stricken high-rise suburb of Grands-Pêchers in Montreuil for three months to make his most profoundly political documentary *De l'Autre Côté du Périph'* with his son Nils.

NOTES ON CHAPTER 8

1. Bertrand Tavernier, 'I Wake Up Dreaming: A Journal for 1992' in Boorman and Donohue (eds) *Projections* 2, London, 1993, p 343.
2. Bertrand Tavernier, interview: 'Spoiled Children', *Ecran*, 1977. Interviewed by Guy and Monique Hennebelle and Michel Euvrard, translated by Tony Rayns.
3. Christine Pascal was also from Lyon. She played Liliane Torrini, Bernard Descombes's girlfriend in *L'Horloger de Saint-Paul*, Émilie, the prostitute in *Que la Fête Commence...*, a cameo as one of the factory workers at the end of *Le Juge et l'Assassin*, and Sylvie, Francis's wife in *'Round Midnight*. Pascal also directed four films: *La Garce* (*The Wench*) (1984); *Zanzibar* (1988); *Le Petit Prince à Dit* (*And the Little Prince Said*) (1992); *Adultère: Mode d'Emploi* (*Adultery: A User's Guide*) (1995).

CHAPTER 9

DEATH WATCH (1979)

The next drama also dealt with the anxiety of a film-maker, but *Death Watch (La Mort en Direct)* is unique within Tavernier's oeuvre, being his only film to be set in the future. Established as a director who seemed to be primarily concerned with history, both past and contemporary, his treatment of David Compton's science fiction novel *The Unseeing Eye*[1] seemed almost out of character. However, the film is set in a very near future, and just as he believed in the contemporary relevance of the themes in his 'historical' films, so Tavernier hoped to connect the future with the present, pointing out that the seeds of the film's fictional television documentary existed already in contemporary television's ghoulish voyeurism.[2] Relating the film's 'fantastic' premise of a reporter with a video camera implanted in his eye to medical developments in electro-optical imaging to cure blindness, and citing an American television programme called *Lifeline*, which showed real operations which might result in the death of the patient, Tavernier pleaded the urgency of the film's subject in much the same way that Stanley Kubrick drew attention to the disturbing realities behind the fantasy of the Ludovico treatment portrayed in his *A Clockwork Orange* (1971) by talking about brainwashing experiments which had taken place within the American penal system.[3]

Death Watch was Tavernier's first English-language film. Intent on retaining the anglo-saxon qualities of the language, he chose to work with successful American scriptwriter David Rayfiel, whose previous collaborators included Sidney Pollack, and selected an international cast: Romy Schneider, Harvey Keitel, Harry Dean Stanton, Max von

Sydow. Tavernier's desire to set the film in Glasgow, brought him into conflict with the film's German co-producers and general advice, his insistence on shooting in the city being one of several creative decisions which typified his tendency to challenge previous convention, as well as reflecting his own admitted contrariness:

> I remember practically everybody in England saying that we were totally mad to shoot a film in Glasgow – that it was like going into the worst areas of the Bronx – and it was one of the happiest shoots I've ever had in my life; we never had any problems with people in the streets. I was going against most of the futuristic films of the time which always took place in very modern buildings, and which I felt were a kind of cliché. I think you can have a story taking place twenty years from now where people are still living in a nineteenth century house. Why should they be destroyed? Why, as soon as you are writing something in the near future does everything have to be changed? You already have all the change contained in the story – technological change, social and scientific change – but certain things are still stable and it's very interesting to oppose those two things. I love the look of Glasgow – I liked the look of the light in the streets. It's the same thing that attracted me to Lyon – that it's a mysterious city, that it has a certain look, and you have to go beneath the look and you discover many ideas.

His comparison of Glasgow with Lyon is also a reminder of his desire for a more diverse, regional cinema, eschewing London as a location just as he would refuse the 'natural' choice of Paris locations unless the city's character seemed to be genuinely integral to the script. Glasgow also allowed Tavernier to present a less familiar, more anonymous world, vaguely European, served by an apparently American-run television network NTV, whilst the film's images of its most depopulated urban areas also carried forward the visual warnings of *Des Enfants Gâtés*. The film's absence of the trappings of science fiction – gadgets, shiny surfaces and robots – can be compared with Tavernier's refusal to visually worship the Louis XIV furniture in *Que la Fête Commence…*, but it also reinforced the film's vision of a near future characterised more by urban decay and population displacement than meaningful progress, an antagonistic picture which is in this respect somewhat closer to Jean-Luc Godard's *Alphaville* (1965) than more conventional views of future society, driven by art direction which imagines sterile, modern fashion and technological wizardry.

Death Watch makes little specific reference to Scotland,[4] but the film constantly makes use of the visual opposition between the imaginary country's historical environment and the symbols of a new culture; enormous, centrally managed and state-approved, figuratively growing in the shape of street posters for *Death Watch*, which build their victim's image piece by piece. When Roddy, the human-eye cameraman is arrested after being caught in a street brawl, the police take an instant dislike to him because of his connection with the world 'down-town', with its all-powerful 'cultural centre', and Tavernier used his natural working environment to express the media's involvement in both the trivialisation of humanity and the cultural sterilisation of a society: over a stark image of decaying tenement blocks, an emergency siren screams out against a city atmosphere, trying to drown the sound of a horse and cart seen in the frame, a clinging vestige of Glasgow's past, representing cultural roots being actively stifled in the anaesthetised society of the film. Tied to the expansive and bleak city image, the normally casual symbol of the threat of urban crime seems to be directed at something much greater, some all-pervading cloud which engulfs a city or a people.

The same fear for the survival of people's true roots is also what splits the emotional feel of the Scottish lullaby sung at the church refuge where Roddy follows Katherine: it generates a pitying sense of his childish nature, and also evokes a feeling of quiet grief more like a nation's lament. During shooting, Tavernier decided to include the guitar-playing lullaby singer to create a moment of reflection, like the player in a western, a homage to form which happens to coincide with the fact that the accusations of *Death Watch* are directed more towards the increasingly cynical and exploitative television networks than American global culture in general, which would be dealt with more face-to-face later on, in *L'Appât*. *Death Watch* came before the invention of the miniature camcorder, and 20 years on, the proliferation of 'real life' television across every major western television network has rendered the film more chilling than ever. The film expresses its greatest horror at the prospect of a person forced to endure the stare of the masses, but without even daring to contemplate the now very near reality of entire cities covered by the CCTV. The urban settings in Tavernier's film are littered with images and sounds which confirm the complicity between television, state and commercial control, but he designed this apprehensive premonition to operate in the background while remaining focused on what he regarded as the heart of the film: a tragedy and a love story, undoubtedly his most romantic work to date.

Death Watch seems now like the crucial turning point in Tavernier's work, at which he consciously placed lyricism at the centre of his mise-en-scène, discovering the creative direction which would best represent his personal style and lead ultimately to his best work. Apart from Tavernier's real concerns about the film's general subject, his main interest in *Death Watch* was in the central characters, and whilst his earlier films had all shown the importance he attached to character, this was now taken further, in that he allowed the emotions of his central

A selfish child heads blindly towards tragedy – Roddy Farrar plays the caring companion, while secretly transmitting Katherine Mortenhoe's 'escape' direct to NTV.

characters to shape mise-en-scène and visual construction through camera movement more than any other element. These developments coincided with another notable change: Katherine Mortenhoe was Tavernier's first truly central female protagonist, a woman who not only carried the drama's moral outrage, but formed its emotional centre as well; she was to be followed by several others:

> The feminine characters were often the ones who expressed my moral point of view, but they were not the central character, although *Spoiled Children* was already a new departure. The character Anne played by Christine Pascal was very important to me; but Katherine was something else – the central figure of a tragic story. For me, she was like Antigone. She had everything that I could relate to. I needed to take a star – somebody very powerful, very lyrical; all those qualities which I found in Romy. She taught me not to cut too quickly, because she was always giving me moments at the end of the scenes which were so striking, so beautiful, so I let the camera roll. I think I opened up, working with her. I already had the feeling, with Noiret or Galabru or Christine, of working with somebody who is inspired, and with Romy you could really touch it – the sense of somebody who was inspired during a take, and was suddenly going beyond what has been written. I had a feeling of exploring unknown places with her.

The whole idea of entering the unknown was now becoming fundamental to Tavernier's approach. *Death Watch* and all the later films appear much less constructed in their writing than the earlier films, a contrast which is strongest between *Death Watch* and *Des Enfant's Gâtés*. Tavernier seemed to have gathered the confidence which allowed him to move towards a more instinctive and organic method of handling characters and narrative, which was now consistent with his belief in the fundamental ambiguities and paradoxes of the human condition:

> When I work, I try not to study, or to be totally conscious of what I am working on. I try not to psycho-analyse. I want to know the direction, the principle of what I am saying, but I also want to have a lot of obscurity. Sometimes there are scenes which, when I write them, I don't understand them totally – why they are there, and I like that. If everything was clear to me, if I knew exactly where I was going, I would not make the film. The things I have missed sometimes were when I knew too much in advance – either about the character or his evolution. For instance, I think I should have made the Judge in *The Judge and the Assassin* bring more ambiguity. I would go a little deeper and make him a little bit nicer, on two or three occasions, but in a puzzling way. When things are too clear, I lose my marks – there is something which makes me uncomfortable. I like the situation to be ambiguous, the characters to be ambiguous. Sometimes I like not to know the frontiers between what's good in them and what's bad in them. I know, more or less, where I want to go, but I do not know the way to get there.

The television producer Vincent Ferriman (Harry Dean Stanton) is the immediate instigator of the wicked exploitation of Katherine, but his character is even more ambiguous than Judge Rousseau in *Le Juge et l'Assassin*, alternating between the utter selfishness of a man whose instant response is to call for a camera crew when Katherine apparently collapses and the almost innocent warmth of the programme creator who can feel as genuinely touched by Katherine's on-screen personality as the masses he is exploiting. When he argues that bringing the dying 'back to the people' via *Death Watch* is much better than shutting them away in homes, out of the society which has banished death by disease, he is passionate and sincere in his conscious conviction, and even seems partly justified, within the social context he addresses. Alongside Katherine's battle to outwit NTV, the central drama of *Death Watch* concerns the internal struggle and painful education of Roddy (Harvey Keitel), the eager young cameraman who participates in Ferriman's experiment by having a camera implanted in his eye, transmitting everything he sees back to NTV to be taped and edited. Tavernier saw a vulnerable aspect in Keitel's screen persona which he felt had not been tapped, and drew some connection between himself and the naïve cameraman who is incapable of understanding anything unless he has filmed it:

The pain of truth – Katherine tells stories and Roddy's deception starts to falter.

I think a film-maker should stay like a child and have the same astonishment and admiration as a child. There is a lot of that in me, and I like to have that in many characters. Harvey had that – the smile, a childish guilt. I felt that he had something reminiscent of John Garfield, who is one of the actors I admired most in the American cinema. He had a proletarian quality, and a sense of guilt. Harvey has a wonderful, childish smile and it was never exploited at the time. I wanted him to play like a child, and was always saying to him, 'Don't play tense. Play – like Sinatra sings. Don't work.' I have a lot of affection for Harvey. He is demanding, which sometimes puts him in conflict with directors who do not understand him, but I saw that he was dedicated, and when he was demanding, it was never in order to have power, or to control the film. I've seen actors who try to do that, being demanding in a stupid, selfish way. With Harvey, it's never that – he wants to be very good but he also wants the film to be good, wants to make the film better. He was always working, filming blind people, then coming with all these tapes for me to look at, then watch him acting, and that was sometimes exhausting, but when you shoot he is tremendous – first take. Harvey was method-like, asking thousands of questions, refusing to rehearse, always wanting to shoot. That was one of the difficulties of the film. He worked in a totally different way from Romy, who didn't need to ask so many questions. They found each other great as actors, but did not like each other's working methods and that created two or three big moments of tension. She felt that he was not fair with her because he refused to rehearse, but I think that helped the relationship, provided tension in the scene – maybe they did it on purpose or maybe it was an unconscious way of working which helped the scenes, but every moment when they are together, they are alive, watching each other, circling around each other, like two wild animals – really working together.

Until the point where Katherine and Roddy's quite separate dramas merge into one, their relationship is laced with tension, and it is both Katherine's confused emotions and the sadness of Roddy's naïve moral blindness which drive Antoine Duhamel's tragic and violent original score. Tavernier talks about the need for him to have music in his head long before shooting, hoping ideally to be in a position to construct specific sequences and even the structure of a film in relation to the planned music. He often praises the quality of his actors' physical performance in musical terms, and his decription of Schneider following the release of *Death Watch* summed up perfectly his growing ideal of an inextricably linked marriage of performance and music. 'She's a musical creature, a sort of Mahlerian orchestra who explodes with a terrible violence as soon as she's found the note, the chord.'[5] Duhamel's music for the film is very reminiscent of Mahler, and his own earlier score for Jean-Luc Godard's *Pierrot le Fou* (1965) influenced Tavernier when working with Duhamel to create a similarly threatening and passionate soundtrack. The other vital element involved in creating the film's intensely tragic atmosphere is Tavernier's use of voice-over. He had used them in every film so far, usually in the third person, such as the bitterly ironic comment on the world outside Bernard's prison at the end of *L'Horloger de Saint-Paul*, but *Death Watch*, like *Le Juge et l'Assassin*, includes the first person narration of a main character, Roddy's estranged wife Tracey, a role which Tavernier badly wanted to be played by Julie Christie. Christie declined the role, but did agree to perform Tracey's voice-overs and dub Thérèse Liotard's on-screen voice.[6] Tavernier knows the debates about form concerning voice-overs, being used to discussing them when justifying them,[7] and he rejects totally any purist notion which favours the visual and the non-verbal as a cinematic ideal:

> To be anti-voice-over is to be like the people who were anti-sound, anti-colour, anti-steadicam. For me, it shows a lack of intelligence. One might as well say, 'Green is not a cinematic colour – you should make films without green.' Cinema is a combination of light, emotion and sound. Voice-over is like music, it's as important. Some of the most beautiful films in the history of the cinema have been done with voice-over – *The Diary of a Country Priest* [Robert Bresson, 1950], films from *Le Roman d'un Tricheur* [Sacha Guitry, 1936], to *Four Friends* [Arthur Penn, 1981; the film was called *Georgia* in Europe] thrillers, film noir. Voice-over can be musical, evocative; can be a way of creating a distance, of bringing the characters closer. Some of the most cinematic of films have a mixture of images and voice-over. The first line and voice-over of *The Go-Between* [Joseph Losey, 1971] is superb. The voice of Jean Cocteau in *Les Enfants Terribles* [The Strange Ones, 1950] is something only cinema could achieve. The relationship

between the images of Melville, the voice of Cocteau and the music of Vivaldi is something that you cannot have in any medium. What is cinematic? It's something which does not exist in theatre or books – where you cannot have that strange mixing of sound, images and music which is what creates an emotion that is totally special. You have films where it is used without imagination, without style, without poetic quality – many FBI investigation films and the *March of Time* films have the most exasperating voice-overs which you want to get rid of because the voice is bad, the writing is bad, it's over-explanatory. I like voice-overs, although I never use them to explain the things that you see. It's more a way of creating a distance – so voice-over is important.

Christie's voice as Tracey creates a unified effect with Duhamel's music, which generates the tone of regret, defining the sadness of *Death Watch*. The film's entire gaze feels like a combination of love and sadness, even towards Roddy and Ferriman in their treatment of Katherine – precisely the same impression created when Tracey is talking about Roddy. The things that Tracey says about Roddy do not give clear explanations about Roddy's motives, or even his exact personality – it is the tone of instinctive worry in her phrases which helps to form the picture of Roddy's essential nature. Tracey's words evoke a much deeper knowledge of Roddy than he has of himself, and their pain lies in their understanding of Roddy's true blindness. The impact of the song-poem which opens *Death Watch* has less to do with the literal message of the bold lyrics than the more abstract, disturbing contrasts which it conjures. Two lines of a childish rhyme form a disconcerting counterpoint to the underlying music's sense of dread, only to have their own banality demolished by the truly shocking third line:

> The wind, the wind, the wind blows high,
> The snow keeps falling from the sky.
> Katherine Mortenhoe… she will die…

Nothing is explicit beyond the film's title, but the presence of childhood, the combination of the grave and the trite, and the implicit contradictions touch on all of the main concerns that follow in the rest of Tavernier's films.

All of the film's contrasts and oppositions are enhanced by the 1:2.35 wide frame which Tavernier reverted to. He was working again with Pierre-William Glenn, who suggested using the Fuji film stock which is balanced more to handle green and blue,[8] allowing more complex rendering of all the available shades, tones and contrasts, especially the range of green tints to be found in Scotland. This allowed them to exploit the particular colour and light of the Scottish landscapes which interested them, especially by allowing the coldness of light around Roddy and Katherine's travels to be retained,[9] at the same time as ensuring that the depth of the colours remained. The cinematography also allowed them to maximise the contrasts in colour between the foliage and water of open landscapes, and the stony grimness of city images. The most striking aspect of the cinematography is its fluidity: compared even with the similarly open and expansive *Le Juge et l'Assassin*, Tavernier uses a moving frame far more than in earlier works. Camera movement in *Death Watch* seems more directly engaged with the emotion of the film, continually shifting, searching anxiously, whilst reinforcing the drama's unease over voyeurism, frequently rushing forward intrusively, but ultimately holding back slightly. The approach to camera that Tavernier took with the film was an exploration that has continued ever since, a search for the right way to frame the mysterious relationships between people and the world they inhabit.

NOTES ON CHAPTER 9

1 Compton's novel, published in 1974, has also been published as *The Continuous Katherine Mortenhoe*, *Death Watch* and in France as *L'Incurable*.
2 Bertrand Tavernier interview: '*Death Watch*', *Cinéma Français*, no 31, 1979.
3 Stanley Kubrick, interview in Michel Ciment, *Kubrick*, London, 1982, p 149, interview no 1 on *A Clockwork Orange*.
4 Except for a story which Gerald Mortenhoe tells Katherine near the end of the film, concerning a musician around the time of the Battle of Bannockburn – a tale about creativity and destruction.
5 Bertrand Tavernier interview in '*Death Watch*', *Cinéma Français*, no 27, 1979, on career to date, intervewer anonymous.
6 Julie Christie featured in an earlier futuristic film for another French director – *Farenheit 451* (1966), for François Truffaut.
7 Bertrand Tavernier interview in Jean-Luc Douin, *Tavernier*, Paris, 1988, p 110.
8 In the opinion of cinematographer Pierre-William Glenn, the Fuji stock, new at that time, appealed less to an American taste than the usual Kodak film which had enjoyed a near monopoly in 35mm stock for cinema.
9 Tavernier also adopted Pierre-William Glenn's idea that they exploit the use of *les faux tintes*, literally 'false tints', referring to the way the colour balance of colour film stock changes when the light source alters, such as when bright sunshine is suddenly covered by thick cloud, making the image more blue. Conventionally, such mis-matches would be evened out with the use of colour filters. Tavernier allowed Glenn deliberately to exploit Scotland's sudden light changes without correction, sometimes waiting especially for imminent light changes before going for a take.

CHAPTER 10

UNE SEMAINE DE VACANCES (1980)

Seven years after shooting his first feature-film during a hot summer in Lyon, Bertrand Tavernier returned to the city to make *Une Semaine de Vacances (A Week's Holiday)*, this time during winter. Working again with Pierre-William Glenn and many other members of his original crew, the film was like a reunion of the family that made *L'Horloger de Saint-Paul*, even allowing Tavernier to introduce the watchmaker Michel Descombes (Philippe Noiret) again, appearing as a character whom the film's protagonist, Laurence Cuers (Nathalie Baye), meets briefly during a week of rest imposed by her doctor following a nervous breakdown. This portrait of a young French teacher during a week when doubts about her work and her life have overwhelmed her is one of Tavernier's most modestly scaled works, its unassuming intimacy deceptively obscuring the important position which the film occupies in his creative journey. Following the clear indication of Tavernier's shift towards lyrical expression as the pivotal element of his cinema, seen in *Death Watch*, *Une Semaine de Vacances* confirmed his ideal of a cinematic form centred on emotion as a primary goal.

Tavernier quotes Jacques Prévert near the start of *Une Semaine de Vacances*: 'National Curriculum: everyone condemned to live will have their heads stuffed'. Whilst the film contains very strong political elements, including direct criticism of the impact on French youth of prevailing attitudes within the education system and society as a whole, its political feeling seems more integrated with his aim for a melodic, emotionally-driven mise-en-scène and approach to camera movement, always expressed directly through the emotional reactions of its characters throughout the film. Tavernier followed on from his previous film with another female central character, and Laurence Cuers as a persona is even more essential to the drama of *Une Semaine de Vacances* than Katherine Mortenhoe was to *Death Watch*, her presence in every scene in the film ensuring that, politics aside, the film communicates primarily as an intimately detailed portrait of human fragility. *Une Semaine de Vacances* is less concerned with dramatic concepts than *Death Watch*, more shaped by emotional feeling and atmosphere, which are simply far more character-centred.

Une Semaine de Vacances predated *Death Watch* as a planned project, and originated from Claude Duneton's experiences as a teacher, related in his book *Je Suis Une Truie Qui Doute*.[1] Tavernier decided to adapt elements of the book to create a drama involving a female character, and was encouraged to work on a screenplay with Marie-Françoise Hans by Duneton, who was reluctant to re-live his writing but provided Tavernier and Hans with memories and stories. Following research and interviews with teachers, Tavernier felt unhappy with the lack of cohesion in the material, the result of the diversity of the sources, and it was only on his return from shooting *Death Watch* that he returned to the project and completely reworked the screenplay with Colo Tavernier.[2] The intimate style of the film suited Colo's forte for characterisation and dialogue, which she would employ again later on in *Un Dimanche à la Campagne* (1984) and *Daddy Nostalgie* (1991). Bertrand had already been trying to persuade her to write for the screen for years, enthusiastic about her style, which favoured emotion over psychology and poetry over realism. Tavernier's own recollection of his decisions in making the project indicate the extent to which he felt that he had 'found' his style, and reveal the level of assurance with which he shaped the film.

> After *Death Watch* I really wanted to go on having female characters as very important in the story. I was not happy with the framing of *Des Enfants Gâtés* and certain things in it,[3] and I wanted to do things which I was not allowed to do in *Des Enfants Gâtés* because of the types of places where it took place, because of Paris, because of the flat. I wanted to combine the approach of *Des Enfants Gâtés* and the lyrical style of *Death Watch*, and have a kind of pensive, reflective mood at the same time. I wanted to pursue the things which I had done in *The Judge and the Assassin*, *Death Watch*, and to really have the places and the light as part of the emotion of the film. It's one of the films where I was freer and I have always been very happy with that film. I think within certain limits the film was successful in doing what it was intended to do, and I have always been very proud of that film. I had an impression of going beyond what was written, and a feeling that I was developing, that I was reaching places which I had not reached in the previous films. *Une Semaine de Vacances* was a departure because that was

> my first with a young couple and with new actors in lead roles. Gérard Lanvin had not done anything. Nathalie Baye had never done a real starring role – she had done *La Chambre Verte* [François Truffaut, 1978], and was very good, but the main character was François Truffaut. In my latest films I wanted to put energy in the frame and I wanted the film to have the same style, the same speed, the same rhythm as the main character. When it's Noiret, the film has a certain way of advancing, quiet, but they never stop. When you deal with characters like Nathalie, the film must be graceful and tight at the same time. I knew that I had a little story and that it was not a film which had to be over two hours. It had to be more compressed, and I wanted certain scenes to be fast, and to allow me certain ruptures, to have moments where it becomes more pensive, more reflexive. It's exactly like music – I mean that film was worked in the editing like a music piece.

Tavernier's desire for a rythmic relationship between character and camera, which informed his mise-en-scène for the film, is the crucial factor which he has retained as a central principle ever since, fully engaging with the notion during the film's making. His ideas concerning rhythmic expression seem to have been consistent with the timely casting of Baye, a former dancer, in the demanding central role, and his assessment of her contribution to the film reveals his fascination with character and performance through physical expression:

> Nathalie was in every scene, so that is very difficult – especially to play someone who does not do very much, who is sometimes in a depressive mood – it can be ungrateful for an actress, and she overcame all the problems. I think she is one of the most graceful actresses I have ever filmed. Whatever she did was always graceful – a way of moving, of sitting, of walking – they are a perpetual inspiration for a director, and on a film where very little was happening, most of the things had to depend on the charisma of the actress and on a relationship with some emotion. Nathalie had a real grace which allowed her to develop some very deep emotions and she is one of the most powerful and erotic actresses I have ever worked with – she knew how to be at the same time strong and delicate. I have very often worked with great actresses – Isabelle Huppert, Christine [Pascal], Romy [Schneider], Marie Gillain, Julie Delpy, Charlotte [Kady] and Sabine [Azéma], of course. I think there is a consistency in the choice – the different types. There are those who are lyrical and those who are full of fire and energy, very different. Isabelle has the two aspects – she is totally introspective and lyrical in *Le Juge et l'Assassin* and still full of fire and totally inventive and funny and wild in *Coup de Torchon*, and there was that wild side in Nathalie.

Tavernier's decision to cast relative unknowns Baye and Lanvin as the lead couple indicated the degree of confidence he had reached by this stage, and was repeated several times later, when he chose to cast faces

'Your life is finished' – superficial taunts find Laurence Cuers's Achilles heel: doubt.

unknown to the screen for major roles, such as Julie Delpy (*La Passion Béatrice*), Didier Bezace (*L.627*), Marie Gillain (*L'Appât*), Philippe Torreton (*Capitaine Conan*), often very consciously trying to avoid the associated images created by the previous track records of 'stars'. Tavernier tends to express enthusiasm for actors in terms of their existing qualities, and always talks in terms of harnessing what they have already; rarely in terms of 'getting' a performance out of people. Noiret was in his mind while creating his Michel Descombes for *L'Horloger de Saint-Paul*, just as he asked Jean Cosmos to think of the actor when writing *La Vie et Rien d'Autre*.

His organic approach to characterisation and casting was also expressed by his words about Michel Galabru's traits, which had struck him during the making of *Le Juge et l'Assassin*, and which he employed later in creating the father of Jean, Laurence's troublesome pupil, M Mancheron, the café owner, for *Une Semaine de Vacances*: 'It was in thinking of his talent as a storyteller that I invented this "bistrot" character... You should hear Michel Galabru relating his memories! I'd love to persuade him to let himself go in front of the camera.'[4] Tavernier utilised Galabru's talents as a raconteur as an essential part of the Mancheron character, using it to create a character whose entertaining stories are capable of being bitterly poignant as well as hilarious. Mancheron's exchange of stories with Michel generates real warmth when they are shared with Laurence, but also sadness in the way the men's *joie-de-vivre* cannot help but emphasise the darkness which is behind her silence. Mancheron makes Laurence laugh, helping to distract her momentarily from her troubles, but he also finds the need to confide in her his own deepest worries. Delving back into his childhood again as he reminisces, Mancheron shares his most intimate fears with Laurence, as if seeking reassurance from her feminine warmth, but in doing so he pulls her back into her usual nurturing role, which is now exhausting her dangerously. As a complete stranger to Laurence, it is Michel who seems the only person able to give her unconditional support, however small, letting her know that Mancheron has told him she is having some difficulties, whilst asking for nothing in return, and creating none of the pressure which comes at her from all sides, even from Pierre (Gérard Lanvin) and Anne (Flore Fitzgerald), however well-meaning.

Tavernier's inclusion of Michel in *Une Semaine de Vacances* reinforces its connection with *L'Horloger de Saint-Paul*, beyond his mere presence, enhancing the film's temporal context. When Michel tells Mancheron that Bernard now works as a librarian, he explains to Laurence that his son has been in prison in Saint-Paul for five years, the image of his son's detention adding to the film's bitter sense of an era having moved on, but only to reveal a society which has grown little beyond adopting convenient cynicism in order to justify its defeatism. Tavernier had already used songs on several occasions as devices to expose the underlying political attitudes in individuals or societies – such as the army officer's blood-thirsty party-piece or Jean-Roger Caussimon's denunciative song about Bouvier in *Le Juge et l'Assassin* – and in *Une Semaine de Vacances* his use of the songs performed by Eddy Mitchell seems to emphasise the hedonistic mentality dominating French society in 1980, implying the superficially contented attitude of a generation through the glaring contrast between the jaunty records and the impassioned anger of *L'Horloger de Saint-Paul's*, driving music score, underlining the political turn-around from one era to another. The songs are more akin to the radio and television messages selling materialist ideals in the earlier film, and *Une Semaine de Vacances* also uses radio news broadcasts, firstly over the introductory white-on-black titles, to introduce the political backdrop to the story, and later on as a direct illustration of the pedagogical clichés trotted out by the policy-makers, who wear Laurence and her colleagues down in the process of turning pupils into guinea pigs for their theoretical ideals. One scene sees Laurence switch off the radio she is listening to while ironing, enraged by the comments of an official predictably selling the Education Ministry line in vague terms, with no reference to the practical realities and problems facing

Laurence and all the other members of her profession.[5] As an ordinary 'footsoldier' crushed by the stupidity or cynicism of her superiors, Laurence's frustration was to be mirrored later by that of drugs-squad detectives Lulu and Antoine in *L.627*, who also react to their designated minister's pearls of wisdom by switching off the television.

The impression created by *Une Semaine de Vacances*, that radio and television programming is an undiscerning conduit for virtually any message sanctioned by the state, expanded on feelings which Tavernier had already introduced in *L'Horloger de Saint-Paul* and *Des Enfants Gâtés*. In the case of *Une Semaine de Vacances*, his clear distaste for the materialistic and conformist messages given credence by the French media co-exist alongside a stylistic response to the dismay he felt regarding trends which he perceived developing in form and aesthetics of television and film, the factor which he cited as being partly behind his decision to shoot the film in the wide 1:2.35 Panavision Large[6] format:

> The widescreen format and the new Panavision lenses[7] were a great help for the film. I think it changed totally the nature of close-ups. It provides space around the characters. It showed the city, the place and the period. I was starting to be obsessed to fight against TV, and to give a certain look to the films which made them different from the TV films. If I had done the film on TV there would be no work on the light or the quality of image – it is disappearing on TV. That does not mean that certain films on TV are not well shot. Some are, but there are so few which are shot with the work on the image which is, let's say, like that in the films of some of the people I admire, or some of the great directors, like Jacques Tourneur or John Ford or Michael Powell. Most of the image on TV is the negation of image. I was already starting to find a kind of identity for my films, to make them different – now you have many films in the cinema which you cannot distinguish from TV films – they are photographed, shot, cut exactly like TV movies. I wanted my films to be different from that. I want to feel what is the point of view in every scene – the important moment. It has also been a cliché that 'scope was only good for spectacular films. I'm not the inventor, because many directors have done very intimate films in 'scope – Robert Altman's *Three Women* and many of his most intimate films are in widescreen, and I could name other directors.

The film's compositional frame created a stronger sense of place than Tavernier achieved in *L'Horloger de Saint-Paul*, allowing Laurence's surroundings to become an expressive part of the drama of her life, with less self-conscious reference to them. The format ensured that Tavernier could avoid the visual severance of character and décor which increases with the squarer aspect ratios which are taken to their extreme in television close-ups, creating purely facial shots.[8] The most important contribution provided by the frame is in supporting the film's dramatic concern with Laurence's state of emotional isolation, a factor which

The repose of undemanding love, the fear of ageing – Laurence visits her sick father.

works equally in the scenes of Laurence standing amongst her seated class, waiting in a bar or strolling through a busy market, as with those which show her walking along the quiet riverside streets and the alleyways of old Lyon, or sitting alone in her flat as she marks piles of books. The presence of Laurence's surroundings in the scenes where she has difficulty working, and drifts into pessimism, increases the impression of Laurence being at a loss as she looks around her flat for anything which might distract her from work, which connects her to a future she cannot face anymore. Tavernier's presentation of Laurence within such a wide frame always emphasises the vulnerability of her relationship with the world, but visualises a state of mind which is constantly looking outwards, as if searching for a direction, an escape route to some existence far from her present one, or simply looking around for some answers or some assurance that her life is worthwhile. Laurence is able to identify specific aspects of her work which disturb her, including her sense of failure in the face of her pupils' indoctrination with shallow cynicism, but she is also made uncomfortable by deep feelings which she does not fully comprehend, and is therefore not equipped to fight off. Her doubts about the validity of her existence are compounded by her increasing concern with old age and its inevitability. Leaving her doctor's surgery, Laurence is perturbed by the sight of a frail old man too old even to bend down to pick up the stick he has dropped; she is obsessed with the unknown figure of an old lady who lives in the opposite apartment, and her preoccupation with ageing is deepened by her realisation of just how physically weak her infirm father has become.

Une Semaine de Vacances generates a powerful sense of the way fear and vulnerability tend to grow and take over at night. Laurence tells her friend Anne about an early childhood fear in one of her stories, and it is in the dead of the night, after a seemingly pleasant evening with her friend that Laurence breaks down in the bathroom after Anne finds her throwing up. Laurence confirms 'it was the chocolates' they ate earlier, lying for the first time in the story through desperation, as with the second time when she tells Pierre that she had made love with someone else, trying to provoke him to leave her in another half-baked cry for help. Tavernier and Glenn's lighting scheme leans towards the night, supporting a drama which starts in the early morning when Laurence cracks, and nearly always sees her at her weakest in the morning and at night, when depression is hardest to shake off. The images of Laurence wandering through Lyon, and those of the rolling hills of trimmed vines where she visits her parents partly to put some distance between herself and school, are mostly shot around dawn, or in the magic hour between daylight and twilight when light fades fastest. Laurence's apartment is almost always lit like an interior at night, even during the day, creating the sense that she cannot escape from her vulnerable situation, close to the darkness inside her that threatens to envelop her. The fades-to-black, which are used as a separation device to help individualise the days of the week off, are also used to reflect the film's concern with dark inner despair. The first fade follows Laurence's tearful breakdown when she cannot verbalise her feelings of anxiety about her work to her friend Anne, and most of the subsequent fades follow moments when the prospect of returning to work has been mentioned. The most enigmatic fade is that which falls on Anne's happy face while she looks up at the newly falling snow as she and Laurence part one evening. It seems a strange down-beat end to the image, until we find out at the end of the film that Laurence's crisis has provoked Anne's own gnawing doubts, leading her to be the one who ends up 'throwing in the towel'. This explains the slightly disquieting dramatic weight attached to the earlier fading image of Anne.

Time passing creates the emotional melody of *Une Semaine de Vacances* as much as ageing itself, with all of the main characters talking mostly about the past, seeking explanations about the losses which time has brought, like Mancheron's dismay that children no longer resemble their family, but their époque: 'Jean is not a Mancheron, he's a 1980'. The film marks Tavernier's deep fascination with the effects of time and the relationship between the past and the present, integral to *L'Horloger de Saint-Paul* and particularly central to many of the films which followed his portrait of Laurence. The effects of the past on Laurence create an emotional violence in the film, in which moments of relative repose are shattered by the memories which trouble her, like the shocking words of a teacher unable to control her class, jolting Laurence violently out of her dream on the bus and back to a cold reality dominated by the angry straining of a diesel engine pushed too hard. For all Laurence's despair, darkness fails to take over *Une Semaine de Vacances*, directly as a result of Laurence's relationship with the children, whose need ultimately convinces her of the value in her own existence, regardless of the pain which teaching them inevitably involves.

It was the scene introduced by Colo, in which an embarrassed and introverted young pupil, Lucie, comes to Laurence's flat to confide, 'I don't think I'm intelligent' which finally persuaded Tavernier to make the film, and it is Laurence's totally natural involvement with Lucie's needs, at a time when the teacher herself is at her lowest ebb, which creates the feeling of distant optimism which never quite disappears. The film was a revelation in its intimate contact with the thoughts of children, since children exist mainly in Tavernier's earlier films as distant, enigmatic figures, as if representing something lost in the adults around them, like Roddy and Katherine in *Death Watch*. Several times, voice-overs from Laurence's pupils recur in the film, expressing their innermost thoughts and fears through the exercises which she set, asking them to complete phrases like, 'I would like...', 'I dreamed...', 'Nothing is more...' When the voices return over the images of Laurence's bus travelling back to Lyon, their implications begin spreading outwards in all directions, strengthening the connection between the childrens' fears and her own, whilst creating an impression of her pupils drawing her back. Whilst the unspoken effects and influences of her own childhood hang in the air, the voices hint that the children are with her, and even raise the possiblity that they have some sense of her anxiety. Maybe Laurence is remembering the childrens' reading. The possibility that a loving phrase about an unnamed person might actually have been directed at her is present. Nothing is totally clear. In *Une Semaine de Vacances*, Tavernier cinematically softens and blurs the precision of words with sound and images, creating the kind of ambiguity which seems to suggest a conviction that understanding is not a prerequisite of love. The poetic possibilities of voice-over is an element which he has returned to often, including in the use of spoken poetry in *Ça Commence Aujourd'hui* (1999), a later work equally immersed in the problems of education.

NOTES ON CHAPTER 10

1 Literally translated as 'I am a doubting sow'.
2 Bertrand and Colo Tavernier were already separated by this time. Colo had not yet changed her professional name to Colo Tavernier-O'Hagan.
3 Tavernier also talked about having 'turned against the characters' in *Des Enfants Gâtés*, which would seem to have some bearing on the particularly warm view of his characters in *Death Watch* and *Une Semaine de Vacances*.
4 Bertrand Tavernier interview in *Cinema Francais*, no 27, 1979.
5 It was this kind of sympathetic observational detail which prompted film director Karel Reisz, himself a former secondary school teacher, to write to Tavernier in high praise of the film's portrayal of teachers' experience. Reisz's films include *Saturday Night and Sunday Morning* (1960), *Night Must Fall* (1964), *Who'll Stop the Rain* (1978), *The French Lieutenant's Woman* (1981) and *Everybody Wins* (1990).
6 A version of the widest 1:2.35 film format which is sometimes referred to generically as 'scope.
7 Basically, to obtain the wide frame on normal 35mm film stock anamorphic lenses are used for both filming and projection, compressing and decompressing the image respectively. The widest anamorphic film formats such as Panavision Large had been somewhat restricted by the properties of the special lenses necessary for shooting, namely a relatively narrow depth of focus. The newer lenses offered deeper focus than previously experienced.
8 It is worth noting that *Une Semaine de Vacances* suffers particularly badly from the practice of 'panning and scanning' wide-screen images to fit into a television screen without black bars at top and bottom. Much of the visual relationship between Laurence and her environment is removed. In selecting the 'most important' part of the image to be transmitted, panning and scanning reframes and effectively re-cuts the film in removing approximately 50 per cent of the image. Characters are frequently removed from the frame and two-shots showing two characters become sequences of single-shots. New movement of the frame, comparable with camera movement during shooting, is introduced when actual scanning of the image is transmitted on-screen.

CHAPTER 11

COUP DE TORCHON (1981)

Interviewer: Do you think of yourself in any sense as a religious film-maker?
Bertrand Tavernier: I think... I think that I believe in God.

From the quiet, introspective study of a young teacher's uncertainties in *Une Semaine de Vacances*, Tavernier went straight on to another work revolving around themes of loneliness and doubt. *Coup de Torchon* (*Clean Slate*) concentrates just as intimately on the internal struggle of a single character, but Lucien Cordier, the lazy, ineffectual, corrupt Police Chief of Bourkassa could hardly have been more different from the fragile, dedicated Laurence Cuers, seeming to have little connection with her beyond sharing the same initials. *Coup de Torchon* was Tavernier's third film to come directly from a novel, *Pop. 1280* by American crime writer Jim Thompson.

He chose to work on the adaptation with Jean Aurenche again, and it was the last drama they created together.[1] Like their earlier re-working of Simenon, Tavernier and Aurenche transposed the narrative to another place and time, but this time even more radically, substituting the American Deep South for French colonial West Africa. The setting allowed Tavernier to maintain the elements of endemic racism present in the novel, and to take another opportunity to confront French audiences with a chapter in their country's history that was open to serious moral questioning. Tavernier and Aurenche also moved the story forward from around 1917 to 1938,[2] just before the outbreak of World War II, showing once again the director's fascination with a world on the brink by choosing to expose his protagonist's anxieties and doubts against a backdrop of impending upheaval, just as he had done in *Que la Fête*

Commence.... The celebratedly eclectic nature of Tavernier's output could already be traced simply in the contrasting dramatic situations, settings and period that framed his fictional works, but the contrast between *Une Semaine de Vacances* and *Coup de Torchon* seemed to run much deeper, amounting to a shocking, totally opposite perspective on the human condition. The sheer nihilism of *Coup de Torchon* ran counter to the apparently life-affirming attitude which underpinned Tavernier's 'humanism', and its essentially reactive quality reflects Tavernier's conscious rebellion against his own image:

> I very often like to do a film against the previous film, maybe using the experience of the film I've just made but going against it, in order to set a new challenge, and so as not to become the prisoner of certain routines. I had just done a film which had been pensive, lyrical, quiet, and I tried to do the opposite – a film which was in a way lyrical, but devastating, wild, angry, funny. I tried to get on film what I was finding in the books of Jim Thompson – the metaphysics and the humour, the farce and the sexual provocation and the despair – things which had already attracted people like Stanley Kubrick, whom I learned afterwards had wanted to do *The Killer Inside Me*[3] and who also worked with Jim Thompson on two screenplays – *The Killing* [1956] and *Paths of Glory* [1958][4] – you can see what brought Thompson to those films. *Coup de Torchon* was also a way of fighting against my image as a humanist director. I wanted to be faithful to Thompson, because he doesn't leave any easy way out. It would have been very easy to include some character making a kind of liberal statement which would have helped us judge the other characters and the situation, but that would have been the worst betrayal of Thompson. I remember showing the film at the Sundance Festival and two people saying, 'My God, how can we accept the fact that Philippe Noiret killed the black guy. It's impossible.' They were absolutely outraged and felt that it was not liberal to do that, not politically correct, but Thompson is not politically correct. I think that's what makes him alive, and fascinating. He is very much on the left, but he is not a clean-up, liberal democrat. He does not allow you any easy way to cope with the situation. He forces you to stay there with your wounds, your doubts, your fear and you have to find a way to get out of that yourself. It is something which I loved in the book, and I tried to respect it, and it was very difficult.

Lucien, the fourth lead role to be played by Philippe Noiret, was an extreme contrast with the actor's previous incarnations, and Tavernier's least sympathetic protagonist to date. All the same, this anti-hero's complex nature shared many essential qualities with those earlier roles that seemed to fit much more easily into the image of Tavernier's humanism, and Lucien reinforces Tavernier's interest in loneliness as an essential aspect of the human condition. Michel Descombes and Philippe d'Orléans are also lonely characters, but they both enjoy contact with people who provide real concern and support, something that Lucien lacks almost totally. The view that *Coup de Torchon* provides of the police chief of Bourkassa is as intimate and detailed as the previous portrait of Laurence in *Une Semaine de Vacances*, and matches the previous film in its sense of isolation. Lucien seems less bound by physical isolation than Laurence, but he is in fact a more profoundly lonely character: he may be visibly surrounded by other characters, but these are mainly people who do not care about him at all, and even despise him openly for being ineffectual or weak. Lucien's loneliness can partly be defined by his lack of any proper family, something that he shares with many of Tavernier's protagonists: Michel Descombes (*L'Horloger de Saint-Paul*), Philippe d'Orléans (*Que la Fête Commence...*), Judge Rousseau, Sergeant Bouvier (*Le Juge et l'Assassin*), Bernard Rougerie (*Des Enfants Gâtés*), Katherine Mortenhoe (*Death Watch*) and Laurence Cuers (*Une Semaine de Vacances*) all suffer from an absence of close family support because of decimated relatives, illness or broken marriage. The difference between Lucien's loneliness and that of others such as Michel Descombes is that he is not just aware of his lonely state, he is conscious of his situation to the point of becoming totally obsessed by it, allowing festering thoughts about himself and his position in a terrible world to turn over and over in his head, sharing them with anyone who will listen.

Throughout *Coup de Torchon*, Lucien's obsession with the evil that surrounds him grows to the point that he cites it as justification for virtually anything that he does, notably a series of murders committed with visibly increasing ease, and we see him in a vicious circle of petty revenge in the face of a world saturated with evil at every turn, being pulled inexorably into madness. Insanity is the other major theme of the film, and while Lucien is seen losing his grip completely on his own existence he shares some of the troubled facets of both Philippe d'Orléans in *Que la Fête Commence...* and Sergeant Bouvier in *Le Juge et l'Assassin*. Like the regent, Lucien is acutely aware of the problems that surround him, but he is overwhelmed by their sheer scale, expressing similar feelings of resignation and impotence. Lucien, like Bouvier, seems to apply real logic and truth in the arguments that he uses to justify his murderous behaviour, making a compelling case that his isolated acts of violence amount to very little in the face of the systematic evil that surrounds him. Lucien too is highly perceptive, although he offers fewer ready answers, preferring to accept a view that the unknown explanations for all the troubles of the world are probably extremely complex, and this awareness alone establishes that he is far from completely insane.

Tavernier's previous films had all exploited characters' sense of humour, and included comic moments to offset or counterpoint the

Rose is led unwittingly into becoming part of Cordier's murderous scheming.

darker elements of the drama, but *Coup de Torchon* was his first real comedy. Lucien is constantly up to no good, using practical jokes as a way of getting his own back on those who spoil his quality of life with petty abuse and exploitation, and almost every speaking character in the film provides moments of comedy, from Vanderbrouck's descent through the vandalised floorboards of his own latrine, to Fête Nat's devastating dismissal of the friendly advance of Le Peron's 'ghost', to Lucien's mistress Rose's hilariously insincere shock at the news of her husband's death. As well as engaging in jokes and pranks, Le Peron, Chevasson, Nono, Rose and many of the white population of Bourkassa are seen to be actively revelling in their own comic activities, and the constantly erupting comedy is integral to the film's viewpoint on corruption and injustice. While everyone else seems content to protect their own status quo through self-indulgence, ignoring the darkening clouds around them, Lucien's ability to lose himself in satisfying his sensual appetites and shut out the horrors around him decreases. He becomes, like Bouvier, the reluctant visionary, at the mercy of terrible thoughts that he is unable to stop entering his head. Instead of respite from splitting headaches, all Lucien craves is to sleep and to find some rest from his increasingly tangled life and his own dark ideas, which he is unable to find. His sleep is constantly invaded, either by nocturnal visits bringing new troubles resulting from his latest murder or by nightmares about corpses or his own terrible childhood.

Lucien's confused uncertainty and the sense of impending chaos around him are the elements that shape *Coup de Torchon* stylistically. The film was the sixth and final collaboration on a drama between Tavernier and Pierre-William Glenn, and their work on the project resulted in a film that looked totally different from anything they had done before. In *Death Watch* they had already used the recently invented Steadicam[5] to follow Katherine in the flea-market chase sequence, and they decided to use the device very extensively throughout *Coup de Torchon*, harnessing its particular effect on movement in order to place Lucien's world within a peculiarly unsettling frame:

> I wanted to do a kind of experiment – to do practically an entire film on Steadicam. For me, the image of the Steadicam fitted in very well with the moral ambiguities of Thompson's world – giving the impression that you are never on stable ground and that nothing is ever quite solid in that. I wanted to use the Steadicam in the opposite way that Kubrick did in *The Shining* – not hide the way that I was using a Steadicam, but using it in order to gain the feeling from a certain kind of image that was the opposite of the typical image of all the old colonial French films. We watched a lot of those colonial French films before making *Coup de Torchon*, and the films taking place in North Africa were always very dark and pessimistic, but the darkness was announced, publicised, and done in a very obvious way right from the first frame, and the images were always very framed and stable, with a lot of importance devoted to the centre of image – the flag was always in the centre of image; the main character was always in the centre of image. In many of those films you knew that the people in them were condemned – I wanted to do the opposite in *Coup de Torchon*, to have nothing announced in advance. I wanted to create an image without any centre and without any diagonal composition, but having instead a sense that things are a little bit broken apart, that you never know where the central focus of the image is. *Coup de Torchon* was one of the films where the aesthetic principle was very clear long before starting the film.

Glenn's use of Steadicam exploited its inherently unstable quality, where its listing effect, especially during rapid movement, tends to create a disconcerting, slightly sickening effect. Following the opening sequence in which Lucien is first introduced as a malevolent figure by the heavy blows and swollen melodrama of Philippe Sarde's score, only to be seen lighting a fire to help the African children chilled by the sun's eclipse, we see him walking towards the town once daylight has returned. Lucien approaches hesitantly at first, as though he cannot face returning to the town, before gathering the strength to march in. As he does, the town's natural sounds of bustle are conveyed by a sweeping frame of Lucien's travelling point of view. The combination of Steadicam image and the stretched perspective of a wide-angle lens exaggerate the dizzying, chaotic impression of the milling crowds which cross the frame, and this sense of a sudden loss of control fixes the atmosphere of the film at once. The frequent use of Steadicam throughout the film also creates a frame that, like the protagonist, never seems to be quite at rest. Its effect is strangely supportive of the drama, in ways that are almost in opposition. The eerie fluidity enhances the sense of a dream-state, reflecting Lucien's sleeplessness and nightmares, yet at the same time it seems to assist Tavernier's typical desire for realism at some level, creating a frame that appears uncontrived, with the people of Bourkassa who form the story's background of poverty seeming to move in and out of the frame randomly, rather than being placed there.

Lucien's relationship with his environment is nervous, riddled with fear of the anxieties and threats that lurk all around him, and Tavernier employs a very reactive frame in *Coup de Torchon*, one which frequently moves rapidly in response to people's arrival, as if to suggest Lucien's increasing need to look nervously over his shoulder for yet something else to worry about, then deal with reluctantly. The sudden camera movements also serve as a mirror to the film's intrinsic violence, which is always just around the corner. The framing of the film is far more kinetic than anything that Tavernier had done so far, creating a visual restlessness that underlines the nature of Lucien's wandering – always searching for something, but never really knowing what it is that he is looking for. Tavernier's growing interest in using the camera to link people with their environment is more apparent than ever before, often linking Lucien and his world with a panning camera movement, but done in a specific manner in *Coup de Torchon*. Unlike most of the previous examples from the earlier films, the camera often takes us from an image of Bourkassa or one of its other inhabitants onto Lucien, but never in the other direction, in a system that conveys the idea that the community that exists in Bourkassa is exerting influence on him, but that he cannot hope to reverse the effect.

The visual style of *Coup de Torchon* is unlike anything that Tavernier had done, but Lucien has a very strong connection with two of Tavernier's earlier characters in particular: Philippe d'Orléans and Sergeant Bouvier, and the crucial element linking them is despair. He understands that none of the things that need to be done to create justice in the world will happen, just as the regent did, and his superficial laziness masks the true sense of failure eating away at the soul of a man who has given up completely on the possibility of being good, overwhelmed by his sense of impotence when confronted with the unnecessary suffering of the Africans around him. His despair leads him towards the embrace of violence and murder himself, diverting his remaining energy into the task of working out arguments that justify his actions. Like Bouvier, Lucien ends up referring to himself as Jesus

Christ, coping with his failure to find any apparent divine meaning or explanation by filling the void himself, using any method he chooses. Although Aurenche was anti-clerical by nature, and this was clear from some of his earlier work with Tavernier, this did not come across in *Coup de Torchon*. The priest, who replaced a different character in Thompson's novel, urges Lucien to show people that he can perform his duties properly and honourably. He unwittingly provides him with the motivation to commit another killing, but his words are intended to do good, and he is one of the few characters who does not seem to share the racism that contaminates most of Bourkassa's white population.

The only other truly benevolent character is Anne, the young teacher, who succeeds in provoking Lucien's small acts of generosity towards the African children, and who pricks his conscience painfully after seeing him avoid protecting an African who is being beaten by Marcaillou. At the time of its release, the film was, above all else, Tavernier's most religious work so far. Lucien's anxieties and fears do not relate to his concern with the aggravating obstacles that threaten his daily quest for a quiet and easy life; instead they are the consuming despair of a man who is finding it more and more difficult to shut out enormous evils that he can see and hear and touch. Lucien not only realises that he is utterly incapable of preventing the cruelty and injustice, but can actually sense it growing around him, as surely as the hints of the impending war that will engulf the world. He is aware of the small pieces of the jigsaw of his existence, such as his father's racial prejudices and the fact that he himself was the cause of his own mother's death in childbirth; he senses their importance in shaping his own life, but remains incapable of shaping them to help him cope. Having suffered constant blame and contempt at the hands of his bereaved father, both his childhood and the subsequent existence in Bourkassa that forces him to accept failure as a way of life have created a broken man whose destiny is mapped out by his desperate lack of self-worth. Lucien is the most child-like of Tavernier's adult protagonists, more poignant than Roddy in *Death Watch* because he is older and because he is all too aware of the fact that he has been unable to leave childhood at all, never mind unscathed. When he tries to convey his sense of self to the teacher Anne while they are walking alone together at night, she seems simply lost for words, as though resigned to the fact that any response is ultimately futile.

Following on from Philippe d'Orléans' soul-searching in *Que la Fête Commence...*, Lucien's confusion and despair render *Coup de Torchon* part of a trilogy of doubt, the second chapter of a terrible descent that would finally be completed in *La Passion Béatrice* (1987). In spite of the dreadful acts that Lucien commits and his claimed belief that his

Confident killer – Cordier now happy to threaten Nono openly with the worst.

increasingly spurious reasons for murder are justified, a small flame of human kindness still flickers in his soul, through his apparently natural tendency to at least try to assist the vulnerable and defenceless people who cross his path. His soul is not yet empty, and although Tavernier shows him clearly to be a man horribly contaminated by evils even greater than his own, there is little about him – including the worst of his actions, such as the merciless killing of Fête Nat – which could adequately prepare audiences for the terrifying chill and darkness to be discovered later in the soul of François de Cortemart in *La Passion Béatrice*. Philippe d'Orléans, Lucien and François de Cortemart express doubt over the intentions, presence and existence of God, but whereas *Coup de Torchon* shows us a man becoming worn out with the struggle for answers, *La Passion Béatrice* confronts us with someone who seems to have reached the end, having totally given up on God.

Coup de Torchon opens with titles, initially obscured as if by a shimmering heat-haze, which then rapidly clears to reveal the words, providing the impression of sudden revelations, similar to those which will hit the main characters as the drama develops. Lucien's twisted realisation of the path he must take is only one of several such moments. Anne is almost struck dumb when she finds out from Lucien's blackboard confession just how far he has gone, and this in turn seems to cause her to suddenly grasp the cynical nature of the situation in which she is mired, as she breaks off absently from her recital of 'La Marseillaise' with her class of African children. It is Rose who ends up with the task of trying to force Lucien to see the true nature of what he has done, her shocked efforts made all the more powerful because of their revelatory contrast with all the spoiled, childish naïvety she has displayed earlier. The film ends with Lucien seemingly having reached the inevitable point where his brutalised logic would take him: training a gun on some African children, murder having now been reduced to a casual event that finally requires no justification at all. The last thing we see is him lowering the gun, perhaps reaching another point of realisation, perhaps simply too exhausted to continue, having spent so much energy while constructing his rejection of God and explaining it to the world that he seems ultimately unable to let go completely. Ultimately, Cordier's doubts remain far more nihilistic than Tavernier expresses in real life, and it is Rose who seems to mirror the director's own words more aptly, in her exchange with the priest during the funeral of her husband, Mercaillou:

> Priest: Come on Rose – you believe in God…
> Rose: Well… yes.
> Priest: Yes what? Really!
> Rose: Well, I believe – but not really.

NOTES ON CHAPTER 11

1 Tavernier collaborated again with Aurenche on his documentary *Philippe Soupault et le Surréalisme* (1982), about the surrealist painter.
2 *Coup de Torchon* includes a scene which portrays the publics outdoor screening of *Alerte en Méditeranée* (Leo Joannon, 1938). Before the feature, we also see images of a publicity film directed by Jean Aurenche in the 30s, *Un Matin à Mexico*.
3 Jim Thompson's novel *The Killer Inside Me*, published in 1952, was eventually made into a film in 1976, directed by Burt Kennedy.
4 Kubrick's film *Paths of Glory* (1958), set in France during the First World War, has much in common with Tavernier's *Capitaine Conan* (1996) in terms of subject, themes and its viewpoint during combat sequences.
5 The Steadicam is a system designed around a series of very finely balanced counterweights attached to a body brace worn by the camera operator. It allows the operator to walk or even run over very rough terrain or even up and down stairs without the image shaking violently as with hand-held work. The main practical advantage is a very smooth, fluid movement without the need for tracks, although the 'look' is very different. Whilst absorbing jerky movement, the image does have less natural stability than tracks, and the precise quality of the frame's movement is still influenced considerably by manual handling and control of the operator.

CHAPTER 12

UN DIMANCHE À LA CAMPAGNE (1984)

Un Dimanche à la Campagne (Sunday in the Country) was completed three years after *Coup de Torchon*, the longest gap between feature-length dramas thus far, although Tavernier had completed other film projects in the meantime, including his final collaborations with Jean Aurenche and Pierre-William Glenn – respectively the documentary projects *Philippe Soupault et le Surréalisme* (1982) and *Mississippi Blues* (1983). Tavernier had acquired the rights to Pierre Bost's short novel *Monsieur Ladmiral va bientôt mourir*, his last work, and having a contractual obligation to make one more film with producer Alain Sarde he suggested an adaptation of the book, although at that time he felt that it would have to be for television. Sarde ultimately decided that they should make the film 'properly', for the cinema, the result being one of Tavernier's most successful films, both at the box office and with the critics, and *Un Dimanche à la Campagne* is probably still his best-known film. Ironically, this 'classic' Tavernier film is his least typical work in terms of its dramatic scope and formal structure; its confined, intimate portrait of one day in the life of an old painter, his housekeeper and family having no real precedent. For Tavernier to concentrate on the events of one day within a close family, in a restricted location, seemed to exclude any prospect of him exploring those relationships between characters and the influence of period, society and attitudes which interested him so much.

The film is totally different in structure and tone from the equally intimate *Une Semaine de Vacances*, but its most striking contrast with virtually all of Tavernier's films is the absence of concentration on any specific social and political context. The action is placed shortly before the First World War, but no specific reference is made to this in the way that the impending arrival of the Second World War was alluded to in *Coup de Torchon*. The era in *Un Dimanche à la Campagne* serves more as an atmosphere offering a sense of tranquillity which accentuates the inner ruptures created by small-scale yet profound pains. Visually, *Un Dimanche à la Campagne* shows meticulous period detail, yet its historical setting is less crucial dramatically than that in any of Tavernier's other films – instead the film reaches for an essentially timeless exposition of the love and tension and regret of close family relationships. It is not difficult to imagine Tavernier using the carefree image of the *belle époque* as a frame to expose hidden social injustices lurking beneath its surface just as at any other time, but in this case his focus is totally on the family. Depiction of an idyllic era approaching its end provided simply that feeling: the sadness of something drawing to a close, to be lost, like the life and the creative chances of M Ladmiral and his family, especially his son.

Tavernier had already demonstrated a special interest in the father, or father figures, in every other film, including central paternal figures such as Michel Descombes, Philippe d'Orléans and Judge Rousseau, as well as the importance attributed to more fleeting or distant relationships with a father, such as Lucien Cordier's dreams about the one who resented him deeply in *Coup de Torchon*, or Gerald Mortenhoe's calm and fatherly concern for Roddy in *Death Watch*. In *Un Dimanche à la Campagne*, the father and grandfather figure, M Ladmiral, is at the centre of a drama which pays close attention to all the interwoven relationships, but shows deepest interest in the individual relationships which Gonzague, Irène, Mercédès and Marie-Thérèse have with the old man. Once again, Tavernier includes voice-overs in his film, but on this occasion did the third-person narration himself, something which is consistent with the especially personal connection which he felt for the project.

Following the film's screening at the Prades film festival celebrating his work,[1] Tavernier noted how many people had interpreted the scenes in which the old painter questions the lack of ambition and passion in his work as a form of self-criticism, an idea reinforced by the fact that the director used his own voice. However, Tavernier insists that the assumption was completely misguided, explaining that the film's very clearly intended target was his own father, the writer René Tavernier. The gentle attack was on a father whom Tavernier felt had, like M Ladmiral, eventually discarded the risk and bravery and of his earlier formative creativity, settling instead for the easy security of playing safe, being content simply to turn out what seemed wanted. Tavernier did not hide the film's message from his father, and feels that his father responded in a way, redeploying some of his true talent in some of the last things that he wrote. In the film, it is not the son who questions his father's work – Gonzague is more concerned with his own failure to keep up with his painting – but the daughter, Irène, who criticises him directly, attacking the sterility of the paintings of dressed studio corners which command his creative attention.

Tavernier had dealt with the doubts of creation earlier, with the film director Bernard Rougerie's uncertainty in *Des Enfants Gâtés*, but the theme of *Un Dimanche à la Campagne* is more about the inevitable pain of creativity: regret over missed opportunities that always seem to overshadow small successes, and unending doubt about earlier decisions and directions taken long ago. Painting is Ladmiral's life, his conversation never going for long without some reminiscence of the excitement of a major exhibition of impressionists, or an amusing anecdote about a former teacher's clumsy handling of a fellow artist whom he felt suffered from sheer lack of talent. It is the old man's immersion in the art-form, and his well-practised display of contentment with painting the staged artefacts of his studio, that makes his confession to Irène about earlier creative doubts so poignant. In the outdoor café which they visit while out for a trip in her car, Irène criticises him again by saying that the young people dancing beside them are what he should have painted, and when Ladmiral tries to explain to her his attitude to his own work in the light of others he admired, he seems at the same time to be still struggling to make sense of what has happened, sometimes turning over his doubts as if still trying to convince himself that he really was right to choose the path he did.

Earlier on, while in the attic with her father rummaging for shawls to sell in her Paris shop, Irène finds a painting hidden in a trunk which he attributes to a nameless 'young man' from long ago. When Ladmiral approaches her to explain the painting, Irène takes hold of the hand on her shoulder but does not look at him, preferring to gaze on at the striking and emotional image which she senses is her father's. The reality of her father's creative expression deliberately buried is too hurtful, much worse than the hidden truth described by the voice-over at the beginning of the scene, that Ladmiral was sure that Irène had a lover, that they would never talk about it and that they were both right in that. It is only later on, in the café, when Irène's father tells her his dream about Moses's vision just before his death, that she fully absorbs the meaning of the discovery. Her request for him to dance with her has a desperate tone: a plea resulting from the fleeting sense that her chances

Bitterness momentarily swept aside – Marie-Thérèse, Gonzague and Monsieur Ladmiral delight in Irène's 'splendid' symbol of modernity and success.

to express love are running out. And so, Ladmiral and Irène get up and enjoy dancing together, communicating better without words, as ever.

It is understandable that the film, characterised by such strikingly modest dramatic action, has been referred to as a conversation piece,[2] but conversations do not carry the dramatic core of the film, serving rather as a relief against which the true drama comes out. Conversations frequently show a family not really talking, well-experienced in avoiding words that might create outward hurt, meanwhile ensuring the survival of inner pain through buried emotion. The day's conversations are filled with moments of misunderstanding, confusion and unspoken tension: Gonzague and his father completely lose the coherence of a story about work, success and failure; Irène was never meant to hear Gonzague's innuendo about how popular she is, and which made her angry; Ladmiral seems to want to patch up the quarrel but can only confront the issue obliquely, with a vaguely connected story about friction between him and their mother. He is incapable of tackling Irène for leaving him selfishly, instead taking out his displaced frustration on his two grandsons for misbehaving, having previously tolerated them with great indulgence. At various moments, other family members also seem to try and grasp little opportunities to really speak. When Gonzague rests on the couch with Marie-Thérèse in a darkened room after lunch, he opens up about his own regrets, perhaps finding it easier because she lies nearly asleep. Shortly afterwards, Ladmiral winces at Marie-Thérèse's banal suggestion that he put (another) cat in his latest painting, then the voice-over describes the formulation of his disdain for her; we see her take an opportunity when they are alone for a moment to express her reassurance about the validity of his repeated painting of the meadow in a most affectionate tone. At every turn we see family members who love each other but who experience the impossibility of matching such love with their own needs.

The impossibility of love and the impossibility of creation are utterly inseparable, and the ever-present aches of yearning are at the centre of *Un Dimanche à la Campagne*: Gonzague relates his decision to leave painting behind to the desire not to clash with his father's needs, and Ladmiral talks of the hurt his wife felt at seeing him constantly searching as part justification for his ultimate rejection of the journey towards stretching himself creatively. The intrinsic sadness of the familial condition seems summed up by Gonzague's situation. He is treated very unfairly by his father, taken for granted and exploited as attentive and reliable siblings can be, whilst his selfish and fickle sister Irène is held up to him as an example, even of the very qualities which are the source of her father's pain at her general absence. At the same time, Gonzague and his father are seen to be paying for the fact that they have not been a bit more concerned with self-fulfilment. The paradox of selfishness both as a source of conflict and as a personal and creative necessity is central to the drama, and Tavernier applies these characteristics to a quality which he attributes very much to himself and his work – 'You have to be selfish when you are making a film' – but he does not show any sense that Irène's selfishness brings her happiness. Irene's unsuccessful attempts to reach her lover in Paris by telephone only bring her anxiety, revealing that her display of effervescence hides a troubled character. When she finally receives a phone call from him, it brings her nothing but anger and upset, destroying her ability even to make a display of sensitivity to the needs of those around her again: she first ignores Gonzague's daughter Mireille's efforts to show her a drawing, then flees the scene completely, avoiding any discussion or further commitment to her father.

Irène's self-centredness does not bring her contentment, but it may well be essential to her survival – Tavernier does not make any judgement of her in the film, any more than he does with the other characters: 'All sorrows resemble each other,' coming as an allusion to the related sadness of the neglected father and the rejected son, seems the quintessential line from the voice-over.[3] Tavernier said that he used voice-overs from Pierre Bost's original text partly to pay tribute to the integrity of the author's original words, and the few moments of voice-over are balanced carefully to ensure that they serve to reveal equally the point of view of Ladmiral, Gonzague and Irène. Mercédès, Marie-Thérèse, Mireille, Émile and Lucien are all afforded time in the film so that we gain an impression of what the day is like for them. Mireille is the most enigmatic of these small portraits: she is sometimes seen just playing quietly in isolation as the camera lingers to watch her, and it is her loneliness which is important. Tavernier's voice-over only gives us Irène's romanticised image of Mireille, and we do not know what is going to become of her – just that Irène seems to identify with her vulnerability, and that whilst she is overly fussed over as the delicate one of the children, she remains short of the attention which she actually seeks, encouragement for her own budding creativity. It is little Mireille's situation which is used to carry one of the most evocative moments in drawing the film's atmosphere, as we see her in a darkened room for her afternoon rest, shut in away from the rest of the family's world, which can still be sensed in the form of muffled echoes and brilliant chinks of afternoon sunshine through the shutters.

Tavernier suggested that *Un Dimanche à la Campagne* fulfilled a long-standing aim to make a film which did not rely at all on intrigue or conventional plot, a film 'based entirely on feelings'.[4] *Une Semaine de Vacances* already showed signs of Tavernier's move away from the conventions of constructed intrigue, but *Un Dimanche à la Campagne* had no precedent in terms of its sheer sensuality. In place of plot, the film concentrates on emotion ladened with atmospheric detail, creating the almost tangible experience of the developing light and shade and heat of a long summer's day. As much as the sound of wasps and images of perspiration and heat and thirst quenched, the dream-like contrasts of interior sounds heard from outside and vice versa are used to conjure the undulating atmospheres of a large provincial shuttered house and its cool, placid interior on a blazing hot day. The immediacy of the film's sensory expression is in counterpoint with a style of cinematography that strengthens the film's impression of period at the same time as creating a feeling of distance that is poignant rather than cold: we may feel close to the characters, love them even, but we can never lose the sense that they are from another time, out of reach.

When Pierre-William Glenn was asked why he had not worked on *Un Dimanche à la Campagne* with Tavernier, he suggested that they had both agreed to seek new challenges apart because working together had become too easy, but also implied that Tavernier had been upset by unkind (unattributed) suggestions that the director relied unduly on Glenn in creating his films' visual style.[5] Glenn insists that people were attributing to him an importance which he never had, unequivocally stating his own position, that 'the cinematographer is an actor, not an author', but such hints could hardly have failed to affect the director. In any event, he consciously chose a cinematographer who had never shot a feature before, Bruno de Keyzer, for *Un Dimanche à la Campagne*. At the same time, he deliberately selected a young cinematographer who was known to be particularly knowledgeable about manipulation of the colour photo-chemical process, in order to help him create the film's photographic quality. Tavernier and de Keyzer conducted experiments with varying treatment of the film stock to mute or remove certain colours and tones (greens are pale and there is almost no blue in the film), and enhance others, favouring yellows and browns. Strong reds were avoided, since they were rendered as black, and this resulted in pale hues like the rose which Irène plucks from her father's bush. Blacks and whites were also enhanced by filtering and processing, producing an unusually monochromatic colour film. Tavernier specifically sought this particular effect in order to recreate the quality of the Louis Lumière autochromes of the period, rather than for some 'impressionist' effect stressed in many of the film's reviews, perhaps inevitably led by the (Auguste) Renoiresque images of the *belle époque* and the tavern where Irène and Ladmiral go dancing to read impressionism into the cinematography.

In reality, the film's images are in many ways almost opposite to impressionism, often with great depth of field (focus) and sharply resolved detail due to the slow pace of the camera movements. Tavernier did not study the work of Jean Renoir when preparing the film, but confirms inspiration from other approaches to camera movement, such as *Come Back To The Five and Dime, Jimmy Dean, Jimmy Dean* (Robert Altman, 1982) and *The Go-Between* (Joseph Losey, 1971). Camera motion is closely married to Fauré's music, which Tavernier sometimes played before shooting scenes in order to set the right pace,[6] and this bonding integrates the characters and environment in a way which contrasts greatly with the effect created by similar camera movement used in other works, such as *Une Semaine de Vacances* and *Coup de Torchon*. When the camera moves from a character to their surroundings (without the conventional 'motivation' of their own movement or look), it neither gives the impression that some message about cause and effect between the two is being drawn, nor tends to create a sense of detachment from the world they inhabit – quite the opposite. Every camera move serves to show the characters and environment as being in tune with each other. Whether the camera moves off Ladmiral to pick up some object around the room, or moves away from his conversation with his daughter to watch others dancing in the background, the connection between characters and surroundings is strengthened by the interaction of music and the moving frame.

Fauré's music assists the film's searching, contemplative frame towards an understated tone of gentle sadness, and the clearest impact is to

'... and if I didn't achieve more, at least I glimpsed what I could have done' – Monsieur Ladmiral opens up his sharpest critic, Irène: sharing a dream about Moses, and intimate doubts about his past choices.

forge an emotional link between people and their own domestic surroundings, tending to enhance the sense that the decor represents a physical reflection of the characters' individual humanity. Several fades to black used for scene transitions further support the film's generally languid pace, but without creating a downbeat effect – on the contrary, the series of fades used to punctuate the lunch table sequence provide an amusing episodic air to the long meal, adding a cheeky finality to the inconsequential 'pearls of wisdom' delivered at the end of each section.[7] The only deliberately powerful cuts used are those which introduce Irène en route to the country house in her car. She appears as a vision-figure in bright white, but dramatised into a darker shade by the fact that we do not see her face, further stressed by the jarring effect of her car engine's sudden intrusion on the idyllic peace experienced so far.

Faithful to Bost's original title, *Un Dimanche à la Campagne* is concerned deeply with death, as well as childhood and ageing. These themes exist in the film as fears and concerns which appear as if at random, like anxieties which seem to enter its characters' thoughts uninvited. Gonzague's thoughts are taken over suddenly by an image of his father just after death while they are walking through the meadow, haunted by the image of himself putting on his dead father's hat and 'becoming' him. There is no way of knowing whether we are seeing Gonzague's immediate vision, or a flash-forward to what will really happen, but it does not matter. Tavernier's handling of the scene is typical of his desire to get away from the constraints of chronology: what is important is the influence on the present of anxiety concerning the future, and this feeling is just as important as the voice-over near the start of the film which tells us how Ladmiral 'nurtured this false feeling of seeing himself abandoned – perhaps a final souvenir which stayed with him from his earlier relationships with women'. He is preoccupied by his impending death too, his half-jokes about possibly not being around in the near future revealed as prompted seemingly by a dream about death. When the old painter wonders out loud about the two little girls playing in his grounds, Gonzague patronisingly tells him not to worry, that they will be back, but despite his mild protest, Ladmiral is truly preoccupied with them. He does not know who they are, and finding out is one of many answers which he searches for, the most important being who he was himself when he was a young painter. The two girls in white, skipping and playing, might be real or imagined – again, their presence is ambiguous, but their importance is a haunting vision of childhood which can provoke feelings for any of the main characters and their relationship with their own past. When Ladmiral tells Irène about his dream, he seems to use it to convince himself that he made the right choices in life, and in doing so seems more childlike than at any other moment – not very unlike little Mireille, just seeking reassurance.

NOTES ON CHAPTER 12

1 Les Ciné-Rencontres – Tavernier, Prades, 18–24 July 1998.
2 Michel Ciment, *Sunday in the Country with Bertrand*, American Film, October 1984.
3 The line is not actually from Pierre Bost's novel but was written by Colo Tavernier.
4 Dan Yakir, 'Painting Pictures', *Film Comment* vol. 20, Sep–Oct, 1984.
5 Pierre-William Glenn interview in Daniele Bion, *Bertrand Tavernier: Cinéaste de l'Emotion*, Renens, 1984.
6 Interview in John Boorman and Walter Donohue (eds), *Projections* 9, London, 1999, p 86 (interviewed by Michel Ciment, Jean-Pierre Jeancolas, Isabelle Jordan and Louis-Paul Thiraud, Paris, 13 March 1984).
7 The fades also contribute to the style associated with early film-making. Instead of the now established practice of creating fades in the laboratory during the printing process, the fades were created during filming, by closing down the lens iris (aperture) at the end of the take. This pre-determined the exact timing and speed of the fade-to-black as it would be seen subsequently during theatrical presentation.

CHAPTER 13

'ROUND MIDNIGHT (1986)

In December 1986, during an interview at the Edinburgh Filmhouse, Martin Scorsese told a story about the time when he was in Paris with Irwin Winkler in 1983 on their first abortive attempt to set up *The Last Temptation of Christ* (1988), and Scorsese suggested that they call up Tavernier because he knew all the best restaurants. Tavernier's appreciation for fine cuisine is well known, but Winkler also learned about Tavernier's greatest artistic passion after film: jazz music. While exchanging ideas for personal film projects that they would love to do, Tavernier talked about a film on American jazz musicians in Paris clubs of the 1950s. A couple of days later, Winkler called him up and said he was interested in producing the film. Tavernier acknowledges a little assistance from Clint Eastwood, another jazz-lover, who went on to direct *Bird* (1988) about Charlie Parker, but was full of praise for Winkler, who pushed the project tirelessly, until Warner Brothers agreed to finance the film for $3.5 million, with any substantial overspend on the tiny budget to be set against the director's salary. Tavernier brought *'Round Midnight (Autour de Minuit)* in at $3 million. Scorsese ended up in the film, with Tavernier casting him as Dale Turner's New York agent Goodley, half-joking that a few lines from Scorsese would save him from any number of establishing shots of the city.

'Round Midnight is unusual for Tavernier in that it was shot mostly in the studio, including the street exteriors of the Blue Note, but it seemed predictable that Tavernier would one day tackle a subject involving jazz, and the connection between the film and his previous one, *Un Dimanche à la Campagne*, is very strong: *'Round Midnight* also

deals with an artist, and specifically with the relationship between emotional pain and creative expression. The film is loosely based on some reminiscences by French musician Francis Paudras about his relationship with Bud Powell. His memory of having no money and standing outside in the rain listening to Powell was the image which inspired Tavernier to take the script in the direction he did with David Rayfiel, their first collaboration since *Death Watch*. Jazz was already close to Tavernier's heart, but the film's central plot, concerning a young, struggling artist taking care of an ageing idol who is destroying himself, is rooted in some of Tavernier's own very personal memories which Paudras' story revived. Tavernier relates the relationship between Francis Borier and Dale Turner in the film to his own memories as a press agent, meeting his hero John Ford in Paris at a time when Ford was drinking a lot. Tavernier remembers having to stay in the same hotel room to make sure Ford was safe, and a scene in *'Round Midnight* where Dale brushes off Francis's open expression of admiration by asking for another drink is a replica of Tavernier's own description of John Ford's response to his high praise of the director's work.[1]

The film is dedicated to Bud Powell and Lester Young, and the Dale character is an amalgam of other jazz musicians too, not least Dexter Gordon. Francis's character was written clearly with direct reference to Tavernier's identification with him: Francis earns money as a film poster designer, and records his life with Dale on film, but Tavernier's primary concern is with Dale and the pain of his situation, seeking to catch some emotional truth which fittingly represents the jazz greats that he admires with no less awe than Francis does. The obvious joy that Tavernier finds in the music cannot be disentangled from the sadness that he recognises in the lives of the musicians – arising from their lack of rightful recognition – and in this he is reflecting Dale's own relationship with 'the music' that both lifts his soul and drains him of energy, never allowing him any rest. Dale's music is sublime, and is at the same time a drug whose presence is a permanent reminder of everything that is missing from his existence.

Unique as he is, Dale is a classic Tavernier central character in that he is an important father-figure to Francis, and yet their friendship is more complex. Francis looks up to Dale as a musical hero, yet Dale is both father and child in their relationship, having to be cared for and even protected by Francis. The ambiguity echoes comments made by Philippe Noiret in one interview in which he talked about the dual nature of his relationship with Tavernier, feeling fatherly towards the director, who is much younger than him, but also regarding him as the parent-figure because of the almost inevitable parent-child dynamics of

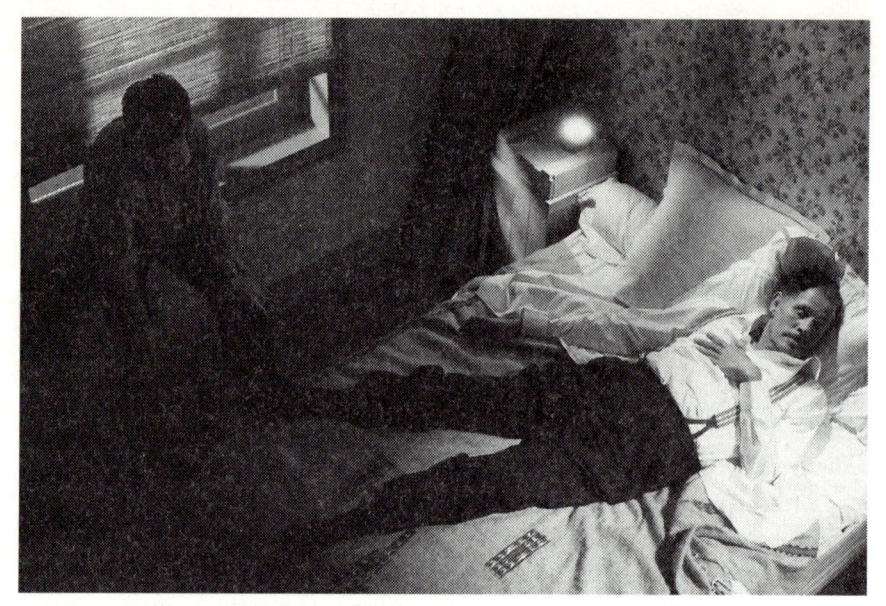

Francis watches over his alcoholic jazz hero in utter despair, fearful that he has no power to prevent Dale Turner from drinking himself to death.

the director-actor collaboration.² Gonzague Ladmiral's sensitivity towards, and respect for, his father's feelings in *Un Dimanche à la Campagne* does not alter the fact that their roles have in a way reversed: the son is now devoted to caring for his vulnerable, even childish, father. Dale's sometimes cutting dismissal of the adoring Francis is a vivid but minor detail within the film's themes of fatherhood, less important than Francis's own behaviour as a father. Totally absorbed in his obsession with music and his concern with Dale, Francis neglects his daughter Bérangère very selfishly (though not shamelessly), imposing on her the sacrifices that she must endure: being left alone for hours, living in cramped conditions, having to miss school, comforting her troubled father when he should be caring for her. For all the film's devoted sympathy with Dale, we know that those who love him have also had to make sacrifices as part of the deal. When Dale introduces a song for his daughter Chan's birthday, she has to correct him under her breath about her age, from 'fifteen' to 'fourteen'. Echoing Francis's demands on Bérangère, Dale has made Chan older than her years.

We know that there is pain attached to Dale's earlier affair with the younger Darcy Lee, and although their relationship is not detailed, their gentle communication suggests a real love rendered impossible. Francis's estranged wife Sylvie has also found herself unable to remain with him, but the rupture is far more destructive. Francis behaves with almost total selfishness towards her: he is exploitative and manipulative to the extent of using her guilt feelings about Bérangère as a weapon either in order to get his own way, or simply to retaliate in anger when she refuses to pander to his demands by taking Bérangère or giving him money. At least in terms of their passion for their art, and the inevitable neglect of their loved ones, Dale and Francis are two of a kind. The film focuses closely on Bérangère, recognising her lonely predicament as well as the small magic that Dale's attention brings to her world: she teaches him how to pronounce his French properly and mimics his gestures and phrases. The drama of Dale's impact on her perceptions is not played down: it is Bérangère who notices that Dale has withdrawn into himself at the table during her birthday celebration, the pan and zoom from her to a close-up of him creating the sense of her emotional rush to his side, as she shows her sensitivity to Dale's pain by responding with her own attempt at brightening up his existence, asking her father to light the candle on his slice of cake.

While Francis is shut outside the Blue Note in the rain, listening to Dale play, Bérangère is shut in the apartment in the evening, her containment adding to the themes of imprisonment, concerning mainly Dale, which dominate the visual style of *'Round Midnight*. When Dale talks to the doctor in hospital after his latest drinking collapse, he confides, 'My life is music. My love is music... and it's twenty-four hours a day,' making explicit the spiritual burden that is behind all the images of rooms, corridors, closed windows and doors. The opening line of the film has Francis's voice asking, 'Is this the room where Hershell died?' to which Dale replies, 'I don't know – they all look the same,' in an unconscious comparison with prison cells. The most haunting sequence in *'Round Midnight* is probably the one in which Dale tells the story about when he was in the army, 'part of an all-Negro unit, with all-pink officers', and was almost killed after hitting a white captain who had made 'one of those funny remarks' about his wife. The sequence's importance is conveyed by its stark isolation from the rest of the film's colour themes. Dale's first words, 'Yeah, I remember it rained pitifully that day,' are enigmatic, but offered without embellished drama, like everything he shares, and are followed by the visual shock of an unannounced point-of-view shot from a train window, depicting a journey with no time to consider the implications. The scene's bleached-out buildings and distorted foliage colours represent a disturbance of everything before and after, but create echoes which never leave the rest of the film. The stark, almost minimalist, quality of the words and images reverberate to attach their pain to everything that follows: the simple image of Francis on the train journey home is tinted with regret; rain is no longer just rain, but an invitation to contemplate the past. Every image of Dale sitting pensively with his head downward leaves us wondering about his past: how it has shaped the man he is and the music he makes. Dale's last observation, that Bebop was invented by those black men who succeeded in getting out of the army, confirms the music's status for many as the only alternative to death, either physical or in the form of a broken will.

The next scene brings the death of Hershell, announced by Francis, and the spectre of a death that threatens to bring oblivion instead of deserved recognition never quite leaves *'Round Midnight*. Hershell's death is first referred to in the opening scene, which then drifts seamlessly into the present, with a gentle camera pan and a slight warming of the lighting. Francis asks Dale about the past, transporting us back to listen to Hershell talking to Dale about the future. Dale is standing by the window in Hershell's room when we hear Francis's opening question, but when his question is repeated towards the end, Dale is lying down near the window; this deliberately weaves together Dale's encounters with Hershell and with Francis, fusing the past and present. This essentially cinematic dialogue between the past, present and future is an indispensable element in Tavernier's work, and *'Round Midnight* allowed him to express the emotional links between memories and both present and future more than ever before.

Tavernier's interest in jazz is second only to his love of film, and his decision to have Francis shooting film of Dale, the band and Bérangère with a home movie camera allowed him to use both elements together as a way of underlining the sense of communication across time and the influences of those long gone. Francis's images of Dale create many different effects: stressing the dark and light aspects of Dale's existence when inter-cut with him playing at the Blue Note; bringing the comfort of Bérangère's understanding and approval as she reminisces ('Aimez-vous basketball?'); signalling a warning reminder of Dale's mortality and time running out. Jazz music supports this dialogue through its very structures: when Dale breaks off from his tenor saxophone to give other players the space to grow, it also makes room for a visual dialogue between Francis's recordings of his life and the images of his sweat-covered face in between melodies, tired but never shutting off completely, still managing those looks that communicate with his band and audience, in spite of the secrets that seem to conspire to drag him back.

Of all the fears expressed in *'Round Midnight*, the fear of emptiness seems greatest. Several times, the camera tracks along empty corridors or streets with no sign of their end leading anywhere; these are lonely images that express the quiet terror of an isolation that is deeper than the physical. The worst fear of any artist about their art is that it

Brief respite from the pressures of Paris – Francis shares a few final idyllic moments in Lyon with Dale, just before the maestro expresses his need to return to New York City.

amounts to nothing. On several occasions, with a mischievous twinkle, Dale asks Francis, 'Was I good?' but the playful request for reassurance lives alongside real doubt. It takes the warmth of Darcy's presence to give him the courage to voice his deepest worry: 'I keep wondering if I still have something to give,' although Dale follows up with his usual humour, refusing to push the issue. For Tavernier, Dale's confession seems too serious, too poignant for the brutal intrusion of a cut to close-up, which only comes afterwards when Darcy tries to reassure him. The close-ups, panning between Dale and Darcy, draw them together, then most importantly reveal Darcy's understanding of Dale's fear by following her extending hand as it takes his in a move that connects the faces of two people who adore each other. Just after deliberately keeping at a slight distance from Dale's expression of his innermost worry, Tavernier uses one of the most insistent framings in the film. The purely visual gesture's strength seems to be validated later when Dale sits at another table with another person later on: 'Not everything has to have words to it,' Dale says to Chan after she asks if the music he composed for her birthday has any lyrics. The moments are fleeting, but are crucial to a film which expresses an utter conviction in the profound value of non-verbal communication, from the small acts of love that pass between its characters to the sorrows and raptures of the music itself.

Anxiety associated with the idea of emptiness also seems to be reflected in some scenes which are striking for their absence of music. Francis's deepening involvement with caring for Dale brings him increasing worry, until he too seems to reach an abyss, and it is the silencing of music which characterises these scenes. When Francis searches for Dale around the police station or the hospital, his nerves are exposed simply by the quietness of locations with almost nobody around. Neither is there any place for music in two of the most dramatic moments in the film which focus on Francis's fear for his hero: when Dale follows up his meeting with the doctor by arriving home dead drunk yet again, Francis's now total despair is shrouded in a suffocating silence, triggered by a disorientating overhead shot of him mopping Dale's brow, followed by shots of his face, at a complete loss; when they walk along the river in Lyon and Dale tells him that he thinks it is time for him to return home, Francis's inner panic is heightened by a rapid track round to his face, a move rendered more jarring by the near silence except for the faintest police siren. The sound seems to confirm Francis's fear that nothing can stop Dale, and sure enough its wail refuses to let up, carrying across a deceptively gentle cut to the river, then a smooth tilt up, which brings a shock: not Lyon, but New York City. Seemingly too fast for Francis, Dale is already back home.

'Round Midnight is also notable for its muted colour cinematography, but the scheme of colour tones and the effects they create are very different from those in *Un Dimanche à la Campagne.* Tavernier looked at some jazz films of the 1950s for inspiration, showing them to de Keyzer, and his original concept was to make the film in black-and-white, but Warner Brothers resisted the idea, arguing that shooting in black-and-white would harm the film's commercial potential. Tavernier's reaction was to set de Keyzer the task of shooting a highly monochromatic film, and lighting the film more like a film noir, similarly expressionistically. Cinematographer Bruno de Keyzer worked closely with art director Alexandre Trauner[3] and costume artist Jacqueline Moreau,[4] on the principle that the key to creating a monochromatic effect without actually draining out colours to a high degree, was to allow a single colour to dominate in any given scene. Set painting and dressing, as well as costumes and lighting are chosen to favour blacks, greys and browns in the film, as well as blue, which takes over the overall tone of many interior and exterior scenes to the extent of tinting all whites and pale tones. 'No cold eyes in Paris,' Dale tells Hershell, attracted by the prospect of at least some respite from the racism at every turn which he has lived with in America, but outside the warming cocoon of his music the world is cold and wet, and the blues of *'Round*

Midnight stress the feeling, as well as making people, whether black or white, warmer in contrast.

Tavernier and de Keyzer shot in studio mainly to have total control over the lighting, but the decision has other crucial effects on the drama. The studio-created Blue Note street exteriors create the impression of an unreal miniature world, accentuating the sense of Dale's imprisonment. The intensity of both Francis's and Dale's constrained lives is also greatly strengthened by sheer contrast between the studio designs of their cramped, blue-shadow environments and the few other real locations which are also used. This juxtaposition breathes air and life into scenes such as Dale's trip to a café, in which Francis is overjoyed to hear Dale order an *orange pressé* with his packet of Pall Malls, instead of his usual *vin rouge*; Dale, Francis and Bérangère's carefree trip to the beach; and Dale and Francis's stroll along the river quay in Lyon. We will never know exactly how different *'Round Midnight* would have been if Tavernier had shot in black-and-white, but the monochromatic impression of the colour version is solid, with blue leaving the strongest imprint. One interesting result of the use of colour is its contrast with Francis's own grainy black-and-white footage, rendering more poignant the relationship between the colours of the present and images from the past which will survive into the future. In any case, Tavernier was confident enough of de Keyzer's and Trauner's ability to keep the integrity of his central ideas intact that he was happy enough to put the Warner Brothers logo on the wall in the scene where the film distributors Redon and Terzian (cameos by Philippe Noiret and Alain Sarde) accept Francis's film poster design.

'Round Midnight showed Tavernier increasingly ready to frame the extremely natural human performances which his style always supported with more unnatural, expressionistic approaches to pictorial forms. The strong documentary basis of the film's content left him nevertheless unconcerned with realism, a fact matched by his approach to the film's music score, being perfectly happy for Herbie Hancock and Dexter Gordon to play with the harmonies and include some more modern sounds that were not necessarily authentic 1959.[5] *'Round Midnight* did come in for some criticism for 'fawning over these strange and wondrous Americans', with the added suggestion that if Tavernier avoided such an attitude, he 'could make a great American film yet'.[6] The simple problem with this analysis is that it rests on the implied assumption that Tavernier was trying to make an American film. The fact that *'Round Midnight* was shot in English does not change the fact that it is very French in its sensibilities. The film is reminiscent of his earlier *Pay's d'Octobre* (1983)[7] in its fascinated gaze on performance, but

more importantly, within its central portrayal of the French view of the American jazz players of the Paris clubs in the 1950s *'Round Midnight* engages directly with the very notion of passionate admiration. Tavernier was no more likely to make *'Round Midnight* as an American film than he was *Death Watch* (1979), for which he resisted the temptation to seek American backing which would have meant a loss of control over the subject's treatment. He remains hugely grateful towards Winkler, and forgave Warner Brothers' quibbles over production detail, knowing that ultimately they allowed him to make a French film, a Tavernier film as personal as any other he has made.

NOTES ON CHAPTER 13

1 Bertrand Tavernier interview on *'Round Midnight* in Lynda K. Bundtzen, *Film Quarterly*, vol. 40 no 3, Spring 1987, p 5.
2 Philippe Noiret interview in Daniele Bion, *Bertrand Tavernier: Cinéaste de l'Emotion*, Renens, 1984, p 85.
3 Veteran set designer Alexandre Trauner had previously worked with Tavernier on *Coup de Torchon*.
4 Jacqueline Moreau also worked as costume designer on *Que la Fête Commence...*, *Le Juge et l'Assassin* and *Coup de Torchon*.
5 Bertrand Tavernier interview in *Tavernier – 'Round Midnight*, Film (BFFS), vol. 3 no 1, January 1987, p 8.
6 William Hackman, 'A Parisian in America', *Film Comment*, vol. 2, Sep–Oct 1986, p 26.
7 Tavernier's television documentary search for the authentic blues music of the Deep South, better known in its shorter video version, released as *Mississippi Blues*.

CHAPTER 14

LA PASSION BÉATRICE (1987)

Béatrice de Cortemart: Where does this sadness come from, Father?
François de Cortemart: A dream. I was a ship with wind-filled sails, but God had emptied the sea of water.

Bertrand Tavernier had already looked into the darker corners of human nature in films such as *Que la Fête Commence…*, *Le Juge et l'Assassin*, *Death Watch* and *Coup de Torchon*, portraying characters steeped in doubt and cynicism, but the huge popularity of *Un Dimanche à la Campagne* and the success of other tender, observational works such as *Une Semaine de Vacances* and *'Round Midnight* led his name to become associated particularly with a cinema characterised above all by its warm view of humanity. For anyone who drew from Tavernier's signature the expectation that they might bask once more in the atmosphere of affection and gentle sadness that exists in such works, the terrible drama of *La Passion Béatrice* (*The Passion of Beatrice*) could only have come as a shock. Despite some high praise from critics in France and abroad, Tavernier was confronted with his first real box-office disaster, and *La Passion Béatrice* remains his least-known film, at the time of writing rarely seen and difficult to find, even in video form, outside France.

La Passion Béatrice cannot somehow be placed conveniently outside Tavernier's body of work as a way to explain its rejection. It is a project to which the director felt as personally attached as anything else he had done, and its historical roots, family relationships and religious doubt are themes which resonate throughout his other films. However, in confronting doubt about God and humanity through the damaged child François de Cortemart, and the impact on his daughter Béatrice of his dreadful brutality towards her and his son Arnaud,[1] Tavernier went further than he had ever done before towards contemplating the depths of the human soul. François's abuse of Béatrice especially was perhaps too uncomfortable for audiences to face, his character being even more disturbing because Tavernier portrayed him not simply as a monster but as a complex personality struggling against his own nature, even capable of feeling love for Béatrice despite the appalling crimes he commits against her.

La Passion Béatrice is unique in one sense, being the only one of Tavernier's dramas in which he has no writing credit, the screenplay having been written entirely by Colo Tavernier-O'Hagan.[2] Bertrand had tried to persuade her for a long time to write for the cinema, and included her poem *Le petit couteau* in voice-over at the end of *Des Enfants Gâtés*, although they only collaborated for the first time on a full screenplay for *Une Semaine de Vacances*. She went on to co-write *Un Dimanche à la Campagne*, and Bertrand also got her to write the French-language scenes between Francis, Bérangère and Sylvie in *'Round Midnight*, the rest of which was scripted by David Rayfiel and Bertrand. Colo had been interested in the idea of *La Passion Béatrice* for several years, and the project started as a few opening scenes intended to form the basis of a remake of *Beatrice Cenci* (Riccardo Freda, 1956). Despite Bertrand's lack of script credit for the film, his involvement in the project began during its conception, and when he first read the few scenes which Colo had written for Freda (who was originally to make the film, and to whom Tavernier dedicates the film), he asked her immediately to transpose the story from Italy during the Renaissance to France during the Hundred Years War, feeling that the period's violence would add to the drama of her story.

Like an antithesis to the previous family drama, *Un Dimanche à la Campagne*, the introduction of his own voice for voice-overs signalled his special attachment to the work: 'There are some stories that are like certain trees, of which it is necessary to know the roots in order to grasp the sickness that twists the branches, the rush of blood in the foliage, the poison in the sap'. Tavernier wanted the story's violent conflict to be set against the almost inevitable harshness of existence in that period, and in doing so he set out to shatter the conventionally romanticised Hollywood portrayal of the 'age of chivalry' with its mythical, over-lit images of shining knights, ladies, finery, castles and white horses. Cinematographer Bruno de Keyzer remembers with some amusement Tavernier's feeling that his first test shots with a double for Julie Delpy riding over the hills were 'too aesthetic', leaving him the task of taking images such as a beautiful young girl, wearing a flowing red cape, riding over hills on a white horse and somehow de-romanticise them. As with *Que la Fête Commence...*, Tavernier sought to avoid all conscious admiration of the film's décor, and the Cortemarts' world is hard and uncompromising. The human existence depicted in *La Passion Béatrice* is always harsh, creating the clear impression of life as a constant battle against the elements, with too little warmth, and not enough light, surrounded by exposed, wind-swept landscapes, rain-soaked mud which never dries, a lack of comfort and chronic difficulties in staying clean. The oppressive, heavy rain is matched by the stark qualities of the castle and its surrounding landscapes, with its rough terrain, covered in gorse and briar, and with grey rock everywhere.

The grim environment seems only to reflect the oppressive beliefs of the time: cruel mixtures of pagan superstition and Christianity, both of these twisted by the fundamental misogyny that coloured the period.[3] Prevailing attitudes have a hand in shaping François's supreme insult to his maltreated son, when he forces Arnaud to run into the wilderness wearing a woman's dress, to be hunted down on horseback as punishment for failing as a man in battle. The film depicts a world in which human cruelty seems a side-effect of the harsh nature of physical survival in the war-torn fourteenth century, and was shot entirely on location in the wild Haute Vallée de l'Aude at the end of winter, often in difficult, inaccessible places. Whilst the immersive nature of method acting is not part of Tavernier's background as a director, de Keyzer stressed the great importance which he attached to the prospect of involving every member of the cast and crew in the experience of living and working in the places which framed the events that they were recreating, generally rejecting the synthetic quality of studio-based work. The wild locations chosen, art director Guy-Claude François's imposing designs for the Cortemarts' chateau, and the wind and rain created an ideal backdrop for the uncompromising struggle between François and his adoring daughter Béatrice, but it is from the mouth of François himself that the explicit attacks on the illusions regarding the ideals of the age come, his persona riven with an anger that goes way beyond the cynicism of Lucien Cordier in *Coup de Torchon*. His bitterness and hatred drags him down into the abyss of complete despair: self-destruction, reaching that point only after validating his total self-loathing by setting out to ruin those who should enjoy the safe comfort of his unconditional love as a father.

Tavernier's interest in the savagery of the characters in *La Passion Béatrice* is typical of his concern with the way people are moulded both by their physical environment and their era. François's character might appear to be a departure for Tavernier, at least in terms of the extreme nature of his malevolence, but his portrayal can be related directly to a

Enlightened child – Béatrice shares with Our Lady her joy over François's impending return.

fascination which Tavernier had already established much earlier, in connection with *L'Horloger de Saint-Paul*, when he talked of the elements which interested him: 'I think that Simenon, who is one of the greatest novelists, has a way of getting inside the human soul, to find, according to his own expression, "l'homme nu" – man once you have taken out all the defence of civilisation, of education'.

Tavernier had already headed back far into the past to pursue his fascination with the shaping of character by environment and period, but the journey required to reach the world of the Cortemarts crossed a more demanding threshold, less marked by the sheer distance of time than by the necessary voyage of imagination to the characters' psyches, their behaviour driven by the intrinsic extremes of their values and beliefs. There seems little doubt that Tavernier recognised that the difficulty audiences might have in identifying with the characters posed a danger for this work, and there is a hint of worry about misinterpretation in the introductory titles, used to set out the film's tone:

> *La Passion Béatrice* is a film of emotion, rather than a psychological work. The people in it are guided solely by their internal impulses. Their universe is at the same time vast and fierce, haunted by the powers from up above, a universe where the Sacred brushes daily with the Barbaric.
>
> These are naked beings, possessed, too shaken by the Forces of Good and of Evil to perceive half-tints, shadows. These are savage children. They are what we still are at night, in our dreams. They are our unconscious.

La Passion Béatrice is a film of night, and all the connotations of darkness central to the beliefs of a time when the darkness into which the world was plunged every nightfall was never illuminated by more than the ever-changing moon or candles lit by those who could afford them. The desire to make audiences gasp in wonder at the minute detail in period reconstruction has never driven Tavernier's mise-en-scène,[4] but the conditions of lighting that the characters of *La Passion Béatrice* experienced were, for Tavernier, crucial to their state of mind, informing the central principle of de Keyzer's cinematography on the film. The film's primal qualities are illuminated by scenes which accentuate the natural light sources, usually single: sun, moon, fire, solitary window. Even the moon brings little comfort, if not diminishing daily, its cycle of growth leading inexorably towards the prospect of another full moon, bringing madness in many forms. 'Werewolf...' an onlooker explains when Béatrice's father screams out into the void, night having dragged him down into the worst anguish tearing at him, fear of nothingness: 'God and my love don't exist!' Arnaud also cries out into the night, tormented by nightmares born out of the terror he has experienced in facing the English in battle, and the fear of his father's hatred. François goes out of his way to ensure that his return to his chateau falls on the night of a full moon, deliberately aligning himself with the forces of evil, to which he has already consigned his own destiny. He has already decided on suicide, leaving only the task of ensuring the place in Hell that will confirm his own rejection of the God whom he hates for deserting him. Yet his most pessimistic thoughts do not even bring him the calm of confidence, his own deep doubt ultimately preventing him from letting go completely of either belief in, or love of, God.

Ten years old, François stabs his mother's lover to death with the blade which his father, before leaving for war, gave him to protect her. He seals himself in a wooden tower and maintains a lonely vigil for his father's return, enduring the pain of loneliness and the harsh elements for an entire winter on his endless lookout out across the hills and plains. Finally, a monk shouts up to him that he is released, because his father has been killed. François lies down beside a fire, holds his blade up to the heavens and, like a vow, says, 'My Lord God, I hate you'. During the depiction of François's childhood tragedy we hear Béatrice's voice describing the tale as she herself imagines it. The sequence blurs the sense of whether we are seeing the events as they happened, or in her mind, typifying the film's precarious balance between realism and dream. We cannot be sure of the scene's veracity, but have acquired crucial knowledge of how Béatrice views the father whom she is about to meet for the first time in four years: the image of 'this mad, noble child... so small, so wounded, so terribly alone'. Béatrice's tremendous sympathy for her imagined father includes hints that she is an enlightened child, unpersuaded by a seemingly superstitious prejudice against him, typified by her Grandmother's hatred of her son as a child because of his red hair. His long absence allows her image of him as a child to fuel her fierce sympathy for him, but the grown man whom Béatrice welcomes back to his home has been shaped further by experiences more recent and immediately affecting than the violent tragedy of decades earlier. Béatrice has to face the father who may have survived his early loss of childhood, but is now dealing with the disintegration of everything he has believed in, and his ability to cope has already been shattered.

The essential drama of *La Passion Béatrice* concerns the two intensely emotional characters whose relationship descends into a terrible conflict of love and hatred, and the film's single close-ups and medium close-ups always favour the intensity of the communication between Béatrice and François, François and God, Béatrice and the Virgin Mary. More than in any other of his films, Tavernier's sparing use of close-ups ensures that the images that echo longest after the film are human faces drawn by anguish: Béatrice's tear-stained face as she aches for her father to return, and regretting the plunder of his wealth which she struggled, but inevitably failed, to protect; François staring up into the night sky like a lost child looking for a missing parent, as he tells Béatrice, 'All I hear is Him bursting out laughing'. Their faces alone speak the drama of their first contact in years: Béatrice walks towards her father, barely capable of getting out the words, 'Father... Father...' as she is overcome with the emotion that follows her agonising wait; François's silent response comes from his pained expression as he tries but fails to contemplate the countenance of his own daughter's love. The very tone of her affection in using the word 'Father' pierces his gaze, making him waver and avert his eyes, turning to hide behind the harsh persona he has fashioned as protection, one which mistreats all around him.

The sequences which follow their first meeting provide the strongest of all reminders of just how much Tavernier invests in the creativity of his actors. During the homecoming banquet, the celebration music stops as François throws the shameful truth of his 'exploits' back at those who clamoured for the tale, leading to the almost total silence which heightens François's confessions of disillusion to Béatrice, and her delicate attempts to help him out of darkness, in spite of his refusal to let her in. François is surely one of the most brutal and anguished souls depicted in the history of cinema, and his portrayal is an immense task for Bernard-Pierre Donnadieu, who was stretched further by Tavernier's need to dispense with the kind of character exposition which would have turned the film into the psychological study he sought to avoid. Tavernier's main interest in François was in his gigantic inner struggle, and Donnadieu created a man whose violence comes not from volatile anger, but seems to be almost forced out of himself in a desperate expression of nihilism. Pressed in public by Béatrice to tell the story of his exploits himself, François describes the chaos, greed, vanity and incompetence of the battle, in which he did not kill a single Englishman, but only his own men during a debacle which ended up with him being captured after returning to save Arnaud, who was sitting petrified and alone on his horse in a pool of his own stinking excrement. The shock of de François's story is amplified by the frighteningly measured calm of Donnadieu's drawn-out delivery, which suggests a buried fury, reinforced by the picture cuts which hold the character in almost every shot. Instead of cut-aways of shocked faces around the table, Tavernier concentrates on François, in line with his dangerous introspection. The impact of his words is built up slowly, first by the dying away of the music, then by the cumulative force of each new angle of the protagonist, reinforcing his cruel anger as he piles on detail after detail, debasing his own image in the shape of his son as well as himself, and completely destroying all illusions. By the end of his story, he is unable to contain his rage, smashing Arnaud's face down into his plate for continuing to eat after his father has finished, going on afterwards to rape the fever-suffering woman whom he has brought to the chateau with an almost casual contempt. He is not yet ready to strike out at Béatrice however, and their story is set out in the next scene.

The image of Béatrice's face and voice haunts François even before she comes up to the tower in whose corner he crouches, and tries to comfort him in his loneliness. The scene is at once tender and horrifying. Béatrice succeeds in getting her father to share his most intimate doubts: his confusion and horror at the end of an era, and the realities of a new type of war that exposed nobility to the arrows of 'murdering peasants'; the loss of everything he held dear, including his idea of his King, who had fled from battle, and God, who has deserted him, or worse. Béatrice has managed to get close to her father, but fails to persuade him to look forward, and he slips back into resentment of what is already done, bitterly observing that she should have been his son. His acknowledgement of her devotion and bravery is darkened by a fade-out on her face, just as with the earlier haunting image of her: as Béatrice is precious to François, his lack of belief in goodness can only place her in even greater peril. A premonition of their mortal combat comes in the form of a game of chess which Béatrice plays with her father to keep him company through the night, and which gives her the first hint of danger. François has to

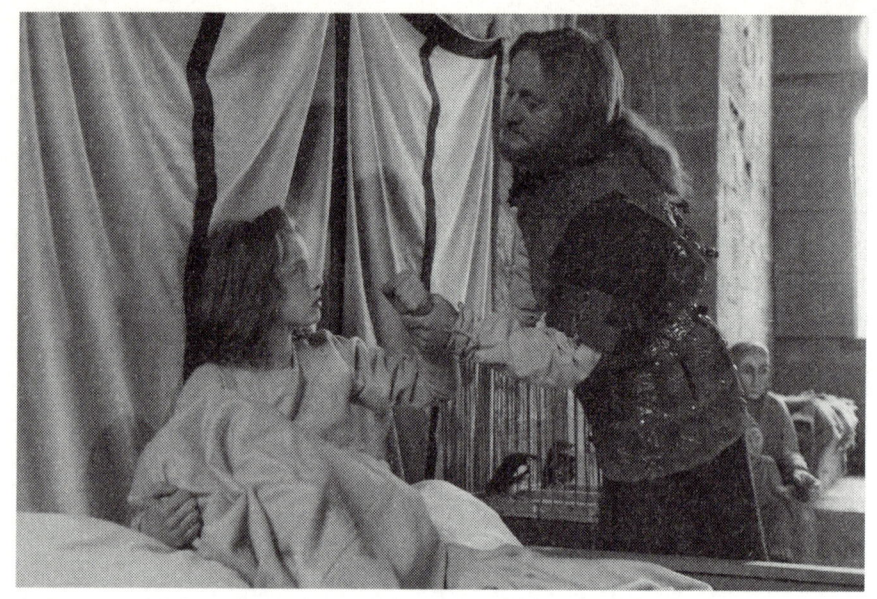

Deliberate destruction of love itself – François de Cortemart intent on dragging Béatrice into the Hell to which he has consigned himself.

instruct her to perform the checkmate which she had already thought of but resisted, as though frightened of his reaction. François releases her at the end of the game, when dawn arrives, but from that point on their relationship sours and disintegrates into a bitter struggle.

Béatrice's tenderness towards her father on that first night touched his heart, but he cannot recover his lost self-worth, and every facet of her goodness is doomed to remind him of his opposite nature. He begins by criticising unfairly her stewardship in his absence, then is jealous and resentful of her affection for the son he despises. His feeling for her changes into a confused, total madness which swings from love for her to a violent obsession to possess or destroy her. He tries to force a priest to perform a marriage between them, and tries to validate their relationship himself with pathetic gifts and rituals when the priest refuses. Even his reasons for raping Béatrice are confused in his mind, as he repeats the phrase 'God and my love don't exist' before the first violation, as if claiming justification, then saying, 'Now you too are a whore'. He can no longer disentangle his feelings towards the mother who betrayed his father, towards the God he dares not believe in, and towards his own children, whose very existence confronts him with everything that he has lost or hates in himself.

La Passion Béatrice is laden with dramatic detail which can be related to the themes of family, communication, madness and doubt explored in Tavernier's other works, from the religious doubt shared also by Philippe d'Orléans in *Que la Fête Commence...* to the similarities between the loss of François's wife and his subsequent brutalising of his son and the childhood memories of Lucien Cordier in *Coup de Torchon*. Its wide framing and camera movements, designed to emphasise its characters' searchings and wanderings, follow the principle which Tavernier had already well established. The only obvious departure from other dramas was the frequent use of dissolves and fades, occasional slight slow-motion and images such as a Béatrice spinning around or the depiction of a jackdaw's flight in a series of fragmenting jump-cuts. These effects clearly strengthen the film's important dream-aspect, but do not represent an essential change in approach. *La Passion Béatrice* is isolated only by the sheer depth of doubt and despair that it plumbs, and the confusion of love, anger and incestual violence which it dares to contemplate. Despite moments of light and hope, the film's darkness is so brutally challenging that it is equally hard to imagine how it could ever have been a major success. Death is not enough for François – it is the damnation of Hell that he seeks. While sacking a village, he attempts suicide by walking calmly into the inferno of a blazing cottage, only to be dragged back out by his comrade. This failure exposes his parallel failure to deny God totally. When he returns to the castle, his face charred, Béatrice screams in terrified disbelief, thinking him dead as a result of her own witchcraft with an effigy. When she insists, 'He is dead,' to the group she is with, her father calls her to him and makes her touch him as proof, in a perverse mirroring of the resurrected Christ's call to His doubting apostle Thomas.

The film's terrible dénouement brings no respite: François kills Béatrice's captured birds with his father's knife, in the action of an enraged child, provoking her to take up the bloodstained weapon herself. The father and daughter's final act is to pretend a total denial of any sort of love for each other in order to help each other commit the violence that will release them both. Tavernier voices doubts about God's plan through other characters, but François confronts the possible absence of God, first rejecting Him by deliberately embracing evil, then going on to deny His existence out of a terrible fear of the ultimate folly: love for someone who is not there. If the film does stand out from Tavernier's other work, the extremes of its fearful darkness can be read as a turning point. Doubt over God's existence have been at the heart of his work from the start, but it is impossible to imagine that he could ever take the theme to more painful limits than in *La Passion Béatrice*.

Michel Desrois[5] told Tavernier, while shooting the film on location, 'You make films purely to fight with the Minotaur who is inside your own Labyrinth. This time it has been an almighty battle.'

NOTES ON CHAPTER 14

1. Arnaud de Cortemart was the first major role which Tavernier gave his son Nils, casting him again as Vincent, the rookie academic police officer in *L.627*. Nils also played a comic role as Quentin in Tavernier's *La Fille de D'Artagnan*.
2. Colo had by then re-adopted her maiden name as part of her professional surname. As Colo Tavernier O'Hagan, she has written scripts and dialogue for other directors including Claude Chabrol (*Une Affaire de Femmes*, 1988) and Daniel Vigne (*Comedie d'Été*, 1989).
3. Asked whether or not he felt that *La Passion Béatrice* had been misunderstood by audiences, Tavernier said he did not, but felt that they found it too hard to accept the misogyny of the period that the film portrayed. In particular, he cited a scene where François de Cortemart comes across a woman who has strangled her newborn baby in the snow. When he asks about the sex of the infant, and the woman confirms that it was 'une garce' ('a wench'), there is almost total disinterest from the entourage, except Arnaud, who seems worried what his father might do to the woman. However, even Arnaud confirms that there is no need to bury the baby because 'wenches have no soul'. For Tavernier, the scene was crucial in setting out the beliefs of the period, but he suspects its typifies what caused audiences to reject the film. If he is right, *La Passion Béatrice* was doomed very early on with this scene, which marks the adult de Cortemart's first appearance in the film.
4. Interviewed, Tavernier recalled with great amusement the amount of (unidentified) praise he received for the period realism in *Coup de Torchon*, praise for art diretcion that he pointed out was 'totally invented'.
5. The famous 'Tonton' ('uncle') of Little Bear's production 'family', sound recordist on *La Passion Béatrice* and all of Tavernier's feature-films except *Un Dimanche à la Campagne*.

CHAPTER 15

LA VIE ET RIEN D'AUTRE (1989)

The effect on Tavernier of the mixed critical response to *La Passion Béatrice* and its failure at the box office seemed to resonate in the opening lines of his reflective television documentary *Lyon: Le Regard Intérieur* (1988), in which he speaks of his need to return to Lyon in 'moments of doubt, uncertainty and anxiety' and of 'rediscovering oneself'. Following his pattern of contrasting each film boldly, even violently, with the previous one, Tavernier replied to the extinguished faith of *La Passion Béatrice* with growth, renewal and an irrepressible affirmation of life in *La Vie et Rien d'Autre* (*Life and Nothing But*). The film was hugely successful in France, and is still one of Tavernier's best-known films internationally. French, British and American reviews typically assessed the film as representing the director's return to form, identifying it as a 'classic' Tavernier work, assisted by the presence of both Philippe Noiret in his first lead role for Tavernier since *Coup de Torchon*, and Sabine Azéma,[1] whose image was so strongly associated with her effervescent portrayal of Irène Ladmiral in Tavernier's biggest previous success, *Un Dimanche à la Campagne*.

La Vie et Rien d'Autre can be regarded as classical in many ways, both in terms of content and formal construction, but the film's visual style cannot be singled out as somehow essentially representative of Tavernier's work, since its consciously classical mise-en-scène is actually in contrast to most of his other films, including *Un Dimanche à la Campagne*, where melodic camera movement and narrative construction tend to favour the transitions between emotions over conventional types of continuity.

The element of *La Vie et Rien d'Autre* which can be identified as being close to a Tavernier archetype is without doubt the central Noiret character. Totally involved in a battle against state structures which constrain or disrupt his mission, Commandant Dellaplane is a truly classic Tavernier hero whose questioning of the status quo and stubbornness echoes right back to Michel Descombes's recognition of truth in *L'Horloger de Saint-Paul*, and whose stance can be compared to the rebellious beliefs and provocative activities of Philippe d'Orléans (*Que la Fête Commence...*), Sergeant Bouvier (*Le Juge et l'Assassin*), Bernard Rougerie (*Des Enfants Gâtés*) and Lucien Cordier (*Coup de Torchon*). At the same time, Dellaplane represented another important shift in direction for Tavernier, shaping the focus of Tavernier's interest which has most influenced his later films. The essential nature of the character and situation which most interested Tavernier is best indicated by his own description of his first encounter with the film's co-writer, Jean Cosmos:

I was working at the SACD [Société des Auteurs et Compositeurs Dramatiques], doing some work to protect the rights of directors and writers, and Jean Cosmos was part of that committee, where we work against everything which threatens artistic freedom, commercial freedom; against all the threats done by television, and Jean was one of the most influential fighters, and I liked him very, very quickly. I started to watch what he was doing for television and I loved what he was writing. He knew how to write about people with jobs. He knew their vocabulary. His judge spoke like a judge. His café-owner spoke like a café-owner. He knew how to write about somebody who is working, who has a small job, and he knew how to write about people who are poor, who are neglected, who are suffering, and there was a great compassion in his writing. A few times over the years, I gave his name to producers so they might hire him, but there is, contrary to England, a great frontier between films and television in France and there is a kind of snobbery which is totally, totally absurd. Nobody believed me when I recommended him, and when I tried to put him onto three or four projects, people did not even try to meet him. Then I found out the figures of the people who were missing in 1920, and I had an idea of making a film about the missing persons. I wrote two or three pages about the people who were missing – somebody who was trying to find the people who were missing, and somebody trying to find the Unknown Soldier. Those were the two elements which I had and I gave it to him and I said, 'Do you want to do a screenplay which will be your first film?'

Tavernier's 'adoption' of Cosmos into cinema feature-writing in the face of industry prejudice mirrors his decision to work with Jean

Mme de Courtil searches for clues about her missing husband, whom Major Dellaplane has agreed to completely devote exactly 'one 350,000th' of his 'stunning incompetence'.

Aurenche and Pierre Bost despite their having been written off by Truffaut, but his desire to work with Cosmos has less to do with his response to the bias of film producers than with his attraction to Cosmos's feel for the small player at work within a hostile society, and the dramatic nature of everyday work. In creating Dellaplane and the troubles which threatened his total commitment to his mission, Cosmos was instrumental in shaping the precise viewpoint of the political concern that drives Tavernier's later works:

> The theme of people working was not new, but it exists very deeply in *Life And Nothing But*. It is in many of my films: in *Spoiled Children*; the sense of people doing their jobs in *A Week's Vacation*, the doubt, the struggles of people working. The only film where people are not working is in *Sunday in the Country* and the rest, even *'Round Midnight*, are about people working, but in *Life and Nothing But* work really is the theme. In fact *Life and Nothing But* can be compared to *L.627* – there is exactly the same attitude in the film, concerning the fight led by somebody inside the system who is trying to do his job, according to some principle, some moral principle, and he soon becomes a problem for the whole system. It is as if the system didn't want people to work, or to work with moral principle. Lulu [in *L.627*] becomes a thorn to the system, a burden, in the same way that Dellaplane does, because they both have a liberated view of things. They are anarchistic, in a way, but they have moral principles.

Noiret's Dellaplane is a towering presence in the film, but a very minor individual to the system within which he operates, and it is his status as an individual struggling against the stupidies of officialdom which attracted Tavernier more than anything else. With the film's scathing exposure of the amoral posturing of the French military command, Tavernier took an important step towards the head-on indictment of contemporary official attitudes and government policies which would follow immediately afterwards in *La Guerre Sans Nom*, *L.627* and *Ça Commence Aujourd'hui*, all of which are specifically concerned with small players in their world. Again, empathy with a man who is at his core a worker exists just as strongly in *Capitaine Conan*. As well as fermenting Tavernier's increasing tendency to focus on life *as* work, the narrative construction of *La Vie et Rien d'Autre* demonstrates his continued pursuit of freedom from certain conventions, and in particular with the strongest cinematic convention of all, plot:

> It was interesting to do a subject like [*La Vie et Rien d'Autre*] which is about looking for bodies, for war casualties, but to do it with a completely different angle, in which a film would be not morbid, but would be a kind of hymn to life. I think it's interesting to approach a subject from an opposite angle from what you would expect — so you do a film about looking for the unknown soldier, counting the dead, and then in opposition try to make a story about a country and people learning how to deal with peace. What is consistent with the rest of my work is that on each film I try to find a principle which will be the dynamic of the film. *On Life and Nothing But* it was the style of the film, those long shots,[2] the very Fordian[3] kind of framings and the sense of collectivity. The fight, not for an individualistic hero, but somebody who is related to a community, and who is never an individual alone who is fighting against the world, but always belonging to a group of people. Noiret is almost never alone in the film — almost always in the shot with other people. In fact, from *Life and Nothing But*, and going on through to *L.627*, I was rewriting *Fifty Years of American Cinema*, and I was watching many, many American films for the book — discovering or seeing again, checking twelve hundred films — and I got a bit over-fed and exasperated with something in the American ideology in the films — the individualistical approach. The fact that you have to solve all the plot and all the elements in the film. The fact that the beginning and the end must be very precise in the story. And so I decided to do films where the beginning could have started earlier. *Life and Nothing But* starts like that. You discover that Sabine's character, Irène de Courtil, has been searching for two years; that Dellaplane is in the middle of his mission, everything has started, and there is no ending. The same goes for *L.627*. The film starts, and you have an impression that it could have started before, and it ends without having any conclusive ending.

La Vie et Rien d'Autre marked the development of another of Tavernier's important creative relationships, this time with Alain Choquart, who framed the film for him while Bruno de Keyzer remained as director of photography. Choquart would go on to work as combined director of photography and camera operator on *La Guerre Sans Nom*, *L.627*, *L'Appât*, *Capitaine Conan* and *Ça Commence Aujourd'hui*. Tavernier showed Choquart *She Wore a Yellow Ribbon* (John Ford, 1949) to illustrate the principle of mise-en-scène which he sought, pointing out that there are no close-ups of John Wayne until about 80 minutes into the film. In one interview for the release of *La Vie et Rien d'Autre*, Tavernier talked about 'creating intimate feelings in wide spaces',[4] in connection with the fact that there is no close-up of Noiret until the final section of the film, and the phrase provides the key to Tavernier's choice of 'Fordian' framings, as well as identifying the approach to mise-en-scène which is behind his preferred sparing use of close-ups, a tendency which he applied so pointedly in *La Vie et Rien d'Autre*. Tavernier's mise-en-scène used the 1:2.35 aspect ratio to exploit as much as possible art director Guy-Claude François's constructed devastation and cavernous interiors to create an intricate visual backdrop that in itself formed a portrait of an emptied, wrecked country, with its people rebuilding their lives. Alongside that, his priority was to have Choquart exploit the wide frame to ensure consistent visual form, expressing Dellaplane's dramatic inner struggle between obsessive commitment to his enormous task and his sudden, disorientating love for the troublesome and provocative Irène, who breaks into his world and into the defences of his preoccupations.

The story of Dellaplane, his operation and his relationship with Alice and Irène, women from opposite corners of French society who are looking for a missing fiancé and husband respectively, plays out against a background of incessant activity and the impression of people immersing themselves in work until they are strong enough to continue life consciously again: tilling shell-ridden fields, searching for relatives and lost possessions, beginning school classes again, clearing a backlog of bombardment ruins, teaching the injured to get around again, re-starting small businesses with meagre supplies, running cafés to keep the exhausted troops going, exploiting the immediate demands for statues, plaques and monuments.

The sense of life's shoots starting to push upwards again is driven further by Oswald d'Andrea's complex score, its central theme beginning with the low tones of strings which spill outwards threateningly, only to be gradually taken over and finally forced aside each time by the notes of woodwinds, clambering hurriedly in regular steps like people on the march. The theme envelops the more epic sequences showing the war survivors rebuilding activities, but the flourishing section also announces the first image of Irène sitting in her car on her search for her lost husband. Whilst she appears pensively detached and vulnerable, the music's counterpoint introduces her, underneath the surface, as the force destined to shock Dellaplane back to his senses and allow his life to move forwards again. The motif returns the first time that the very sight of Irène in her car makes Dellaplane stop in his tracks and salute her respectfully from a distance. Its melody is tied most of all to Irène, adapting to her emotions, its persistence drained of energy as she looks at the photo of her lost husband in her locket, as if hope has started slipping. The entire main theme's lyrical complexity reflects the range of conflicting emotions provoked in every lengthy scene between Dellaplane and Irène, as the momentum of their attraction is thrown by bitterness and selfish misunderstanding.

Tavernier's primary goal in framing the film, tending to favour wider long shots which frequently contain two or more characters, was to ensure that the narrative centre of Dellaplane and Irène's stormy journey from distant, resentful acquaintance into a consuming love, and her effect on Dellaplane especially, was related clearly to the commandant's dedication to his accepted duty: finding and identifying the 350,000 missing soldiers. The wider framing of Dellaplane integrates him with the constant activity that surrounds him, placing him at the centre of all events. Instead of close-ups which would emphasise Dellaplane's individual reaction to the world he inhabits, we see him framed again and again in medium-long shot,[5] dealing with, conversing or working on some pressing matter, with the events or people on the edges of the frame invariably on the point of requesting his attention elsewhere to deal with some new problem. This visualisation of involvement results in long shots that lend a heroic quality to the character, rather than weakening it within the frame's expanse. The wide frame also allows the physical distance between Dellaplane and Irène to be combined with explicit emphasis on Dellaplane's steadfast commitment to his mission, such as when we see him heading towards Irène in order to talk to her after arranging to have her provided with his plate and cutlery, but allowing himself to be diverted while approaching her, responding instantly to the needs of his officers.

Creation of this particular view of Dellaplane is also behind Tavernier's resistance of the use of any close-ups of Dellaplane's intense regard towards Irène, so that even when his attraction for her becomes clear there is never any visual suggestion that Dellaplane's fixation is holding his attention to the extent that the world and his task are being excluded. This framing, which underlines the commandant's deep involvement in the entire clean-up operation happening all around him, allows his growing interest in Irène to show clearly, whilst simultaneously suggesting that it is badly timed from his own point of view, something which proves to be the case later on when he is eventually faced with her direct challenge of love.

Mise-en-scène in the film's first half places a huge emphasis on the distance between Dellaplane and Irène, from their first fractious encounter, helped by the use of wide-angle lenses which stretch the foreground-background perspective as well as the anamorphic frame with its emphasis on spatial relationships. This concentration on spatial expression of their attitudes towards each other comes across most sharply in the consistent absence of close-ups of Dellaplane throughout the lengthy scene in which he calls Irène into his makeshift office and reprimands her for verbally abusing his officers. When he goes on to complain to her about the behaviour of her father-in-law, the Senator who plagues him with demands for priority treatment, his intense frustration could easily prompt cuts to close-ups, but the scene depicts a man whose passion is totally directed towards his work, and the director refuses to separate him from the environment which is his life. By consistently presenting Dellaplane against the background illustration of the post-war clean-up, Tavernier sought to construct intimacy in the proper broad sense of the word, rather than simply letting us get close to his face, insisting that we contemplate the whole world and human chaos that he is up against in order to have a clearer sense of the overpowering pain of his situation and therefore sympathise with the whole man. The expansive frames of *La Vie et Rien d'Autre* certainly focus more on the reasons behind the character's torn feelings for Irène and the milieu that she represents through marriage than the simpler intimate detail that exists in close-ups of facial expression.

The images of Dellaplane as a small figure in the idyllic landscapes representing his post-military existence at the end of the film reflect more eloquently than facial shots the environment and life that is behind his relative state of mental repose. Towards the end of the film, Tavernier finally does frame Dellaplane and Irène in close-ups when their mutual attraction comes out into the open at last, as they are having dinner together and in Dellaplane's car. There is little physical contact, and still some formality in their meeting, but a powerful feeling of erotic approach is generated in these final scenes because the closeness of view follows such a lengthy absence of visualised physical proximity.

The effect is similar to that created in the panic of the Grézancourt tunnel explosion in the film, presented using only 11 mainly wide shots for a scene lasting close to a minute. Tavernier's primary interest in creating scenes which have their own rhythm driven by characters, and which are then captured 'intact' by the camera, has ensured that he

'We've done nothing *but* keep quiet!' – after the Grézancourt tunnel explosion, Major Dellaplane refuses to hide his men's suffering in order to make Mme de Courtil feel at ease.

never seeks to create action sequences by constructing a series of fast and furious short close-ups for sheer energetic effect. The wide shots allow us to take in the sense of a people responding to the event as a group, in time with each other. At the same time, the image of Irène's personal reaction to the bang is particularly striking, despite her being framed in a way which still takes in the activity round her, simply because it is framed slightly closer within a small number of developing shots. Tavernier's distaste for images which tug at emotions too bluntly is behind his disinterest in showing such moments in close-up or big close-up,[6] but this shot is particularly important to the main narrative, since it represents her deep concern for Dellaplane as a milestone in their relationship, and its positioning in just a few longer and wider shots manages to lend this fleeting but pivotal image striking narrative impact, without the need for a full close-up.

Despite the plot being 'open' at both ends, the classical style of *La Vie et Rien d'Autre* is also supported by the narrative structure of Cosmos and Tavernier's César-winning original screenplay, which has a far more symmetrical construction than any of Tavernier's other films, including *Capitaine Conan*, which they also went on to create together. Its status as one of Tavernier's greatest successes has to be partly attributed to the warmth and charm of its characters, who drive the film's essential optimism, causing it to break through the blood-drained blue-grey impressions which de Keyzer created as his last photographic representation of Tavernier's emotional world. The film's end, carried by the healing truth of a profoundly intimate love letter, is expressed visually by the retired Dellaplane's rolling corn and vine landscapes, bathed in a light whose warmth only began to glow around Irène during their final dinner together. It is Tavernier's most unambiguously optimistic film ending. Even so, the film closes with a reminder and a strong sense of warning, as Dellaplane apologetically inflicts his last calculation on Irène in his letter, still trying to put the enormity of the war into some kind of form which can be grasped.

The last image of vines, anticipating the growth that will lead to the harvest, is tinted with a worried urgency as the camera accelerates alongside them, and the same music which opened the film reminds us of the terrible threat implied by its images of dangerous-looking stormclouds. At their last meeting, Irène had reprimanded Dellaplane and all his compatriots harshly, accusing them of being ready to go marching off enthusiastically into the next terrible battle at the first sound of a few rousing songs. The same violin-siren which suggested unknown dangers with the film's first images of the open sea now closes the film with the inevitable suggestion of World War Two, and every conflict afterwards. *La Vie et Rien d'Autre* certainly represented unfinished business for Tavernier, and Dellaplane's angry reply to Irène, following her suggestion that men should keep quiet about their terrible experiences in the war, was a prophetic announcement of the understanding which would lead Tavernier, three years later, to give a voice to the ex-conscripts of the Algerian war in *La Guerre Sans Nom*.

NOTES ON CHAPTER 15

1 Tavernier had in fact originally cast Fanny Ardant in the part of Irène de Courtil, but she subsequently had to pull out due to pregnancy. Azéma even offered to act as a double for Ardant in certain shots if Ardant could fulfill most of the shooting, until it became impracticable for the actress to fulfill the commitment at all, and Azéma replaced her completely.
2 The term 'long shot' refers to the framing of a human subject. In a long shot, the character(s) are presented full height in a frame which shows a considerable amount of foreground and background.
3 A reference to the Hollywood director John Ford, most famous for classic westerns such as *Stagecoach* (1939), *My Darling Clementine* (1946), *Rio Grande* (1950) and *The Searchers* (1956); other works, such as *The Grapes of Wrath* (1940), *How Green Was My Valley* (1941), the documentary *The Battle of Midway* (1942), *The Quiet Man* (1952); and a lengthy collaboration with the actor John Wayne.

4 Interview in David Thompson, 'Life and Nothing But', Preview, *Time Out*, 25 October 1989, p 79.
5 The medium long-shot is around three-quarter length, and favours the depiction of spatial relationships and physical interaction between characters. Within the wide frame employed for *La Vie et Rien d'Autre*, it also favours the involvement of background and surrounding action.
6 See endnote to the chapter on *Que La Fête Commence...* for explanation of close-up and big close-up.

CHAPTER 16

DADDY NOSTALGIE (1991)

Daddy Nostalgie (*These Foolish Things*) was Tavernier's third drama to be shot largely in English, following *Death Watch* and *'Round Midnight*, and bilingual communication, a long-standing aspect of his personal experience through both work and marriage, now appeared as a catalyst for the film's characters and their emotions. Tavernier has frequently stressed that all of his films have been highly personal projects which he wanted very badly to make. *Daddy Nostalgie* is a film which seems especially personal simply because it feels closer to home: the small joys, pains and truths of a bilingual, intellectual family were well within the scope of Tavernier's own experience, whether as son or father. The film is acutely personal also in that it represented a farewell to his own father, René, who died shortly before shooting began. Throughout the making of the film, Tavernier kept with him the letter from his father, written for his second birthday, quoted at the beginning of this book. Including the text in the official publicity for *Daddy Nostalgie*, Tavernier openly cited the letter as 'a foreword, and perhaps an explanation' of the film.

    Daddy Nostalgie formed the third and final chapter of his more conscious filmic message to his father, following on from the delicate reproaches of *Un Dimanche à la Campagne* and the gift to René of 'his own' film, of recorded memories and observations, *Lyon – Le Regard Intérieur*. Again, Tavernier's personal identification with the story seemed to be underlined by the presence of his own voice-over narration in the film, and the screenplay was written by Colo Tavernier-O'Hagan, Tavernier assisting in writing the dialogue on their fourth major collaboration. Colo based the film's English-French couple, played by

Dirk Bogarde and Odette Laure, on her own parents, including a clear reference to his mother's Irish, Spanish and English blood in one scene where Daddy teases Miche about her Catholicism, referring to the 'blood of the Spanish Inquisition still coarsing through her veins', and corrects her reference to Anglo-Irish religious violence. Colo also made the film's central protagonist, the young woman, Caroline, played by Jane Birkin, a drama writer who returns home to assist her mother during the convalescence of her ageing father following a serious heart attack. Colo was already writing *Daddy Nostalgie* at the same time as she was developing *La Passion Béatrice* with Bertrand: two family dramas which could hardly contrast more greatly in their human sentiment and visual tone.

In its essential preoccupations, *Daddy Nostalgie* is comparable most of all with *Un Dimanche à la Campagne*, consciously small-scale and equally intimate in its depiction of family communication. Typically, the film's concerns are carried directly through the anxieties of its characters. Daddy is less engaged with the larger-scale, philosophical questions concerning existence and creativity that affect Ladmiral, and his reflection is even narrower, more self-satisfied in its analysis. But it is also more in touch with the present, allowing him to achieve something which seemed to elude Ladmiral: some painfully revelatory self-awareness regarding the impact of his past selfishness on his own children, and perhaps on their children too. *Un Dimanche à la Campagne* contemplates the impossibility of balancing familial love with the need for self-fulfillment, whereas *Daddy Nostalgie* concentrates more sharply on the immediate effect and very nature of the quiet bitterness that grows secretly within family relationships, where buried resentment over ordinary selfishness orchestrates a quiet destruction of communication and, ultimately, of happiness. Tavernier's portrait of an injured couple and their daughter, who is torn between adoration and anger, grasping for a last chance to have answers before time runs out, stands out as his most acutely detailed observation of the delicate and bitter intricacies of intimate family relationships.

The film is remarkable for having attracted Dirk Bogarde out of virtual retirement from cinema acting to play Daddy. Bogarde had not made a film since completing *Despair* (Rainer Werner Fassbinder, 1977) twelve years earlier, although he had made three films for television. Tavernier's admiration of Bogarde as a film actor was long-standing, the detailed eloquence of Bogarde's face under the close gaze of cinema having inevitably come to his attention through the films he made with Joseph Losey, who was one of a number of directors who influenced Tavernier during the time he was working as an independent press

Insistent memories – thoughts of the past drag Daddy back yet again to question his life.

agent with Pierre Rissient. Bogarde first worked with Losey when the director was still blacklisted,[1] and during a two-part television interview on his career[2] Bogarde recalled his first reluctant meeting with Losey, the man with whom he would go on to make another four films, referring to him as 'my destiny'.[3] During the same interview, Bogarde also talked about fighting for the part of Daddy, which he feared was being handed to another actor, after having turned down the part a few years earlier.[4] Bogarde was still worried about being too sprightly for the part, but seemed ideal: a well-spoken, refined Englishman who was, like his screen character, 'retired' in the South of France. As well as claiming to be never retired if given the opportunity to work for Tavernier, Bogarde was keen to work with Birkin, who was by then already committed to the project. Coincidentally, Birkin's earlier work also included work for another blacklisted director who had attracted Tavernier's attention while working with Rissient: Abraham Polonsky, for whom Birkin made *Romance of a Horse-Thief* (1970), and to whom Tavernier had dedicated *Le Juge et l'Assassin*.[5] Bogarde's diary entry conveyed delight – 'Clearly this is not television. Thank God' – but also a hint of bemusement that Tavernier was shooting 'Just we three in a small villa in Cinemascope'.[6]

By now, this 1:2.35 aspect ratio, which he first employed for *Le Juge et l'Assassin*, was already becoming Tavernier's favoured compositional frame, regardless of narrative scale, and in *Daddy Nostalgie* the frame works to heighten the sense of isolation that exists in the film equally for all three characters, and to accentuate the constantly changing emotional distance between them. Loneliness was already the most common single theme connecting all of Tavernier's films, and the air of intimacy and affection created in the film exists within a mise-en-scène which is his most pointed visualisation of the essential isolation that delineates the human path, as Daddy, Caroline and Miche try to break out of the past and reach one another. We first see Caroline shut in her room alone, as her profession as a writer often demands, and throughout the film she seeks time on her own in order to recall her past and try to make sense of it. Increasingly, the impression is created that, regardless of family, work and a *joie-de-vivre* which Daddy compliments her on, loneliness is Caroline's natural disposition, a condition over which she has little choice anymore, and the one within which she was condemned to learn about the world as a child. Recurring flashbacks of Caroline seeking the attention of her father, viewed from the little girl's eyeline, isolate her in a crowded room of adults for whom she barely exists, the feeling of her detached reality heightened by the lens, which lifts her sharply out of the integrated softness of the rest of the room and the other people in it.

Daddy, Caroline and Miche are often pictured alone: lying in a hospital bed, wandering pensively along the shores and cliffs, praying alone in church or in a closed bedroom, small figures in a world whose silent expanse suggests insecurity exposed rather than freedom, but their loneliness is equally stressed in scenes where they are all together. In constructing the film's conversation scenes, Tavernier cuts between reverse angles of characters more often than he usually does, juxtaposing single-character shots and cut-aways with two-shots to emphasise the persistent and intrusive loneliness which grips them, sometimes suddenly, in spite of their close proximity and genuine love. The feeling is heightened especially by cut-aways which stress exclusion from an out-of-shot conversation, such as when Daddy slides into fear of death, as Caroline and Miche are busy looking over photographs of Caroline's son Martin, struggling to re-enter their space and ask, 'Is it cold?' seeking reassurance about the cause of the chill that he feels.

Daddy constantly drifts inside himself, barely aware of the present as he withdraws into his own thoughts about the past and his fear of the future. Caroline struggles to make contact with him, but the past has as much of a hold on her as well. 'Where were you?' she asks, pulling him back into the present. 'Miles away... Singapore,' Daddy replies, and the camera sweeps round to underline his emotional advance towards his daughter. Too late. Singapore, or something else, prompts the bitter childhood image of her failure to make contact with him. As Daddy arrives, Caroline has gone, and this scene, which first introduces the song 'These Foolish Things', represents the film's essential sadness: Daddy, Caroline and Miche never totally give up trying, with light words or innocent gestures, to make contact and send messages of reassurance that everything in life has not been wasted, but constantly keep missing each other, through reticence or introspection. Every attempt at lightness and joyful reminiscence brings bitterness in its wake, with every image in the film warm but tinged with pain, like the image of a flock of pigeons painting sweeping lines across an idyllic sea view to the strains of the last tinkling flourish of the song of love that, for Caroline, is a reminder of love's absence.

Tavernier's adoption of the film's theme song as its English-version title clearly indicates the centrality of its importance to the film's emotion. The references in the lyrics to images, sounds and objects which set off memories of life's most meaningful moments mirror the second paragraph of René's letter to his son, which acknowledges the richness and importance of those everyday things that are both an influence on us and a reflection of what we become. After the film's time-lapsed opening image of Paris apartment buildings which establishes a sense of moments that pass too quickly and of time running out, Tavernier's voice-over describing Caroline's dream features the souvenirs of Singapore, Hong Kong and New Delhi which they have hung on branches. As the dream continues, the camera tracks slowly through Caroline's apartment to introduce her through the photos, books and momentos which fill her room and, as with everyone else, help to give definite shape to her sense of self.

Daddy and Miche also rely on objects as symbols that provide them with the feeling of security which they need in order to continue with life, like Daddy's absolute insistence on a hankerchief which matches his tie, and Miche who clings to the use of the last three pieces of family-crested silver teaspoons at the breakfast table. Miche also clings to her Coca Cola and her cigarettes, like a child consoling herself with sweets, whilst Daddy's hunger, more immediate, has become one for photographs that will recover those memories which might convince him once and for all that life has been as perfect as he insists it has been, to anyone who will listen to him. Daddy likes to think of himself as liberal, and even something of a non-conformist, making self-congratulatory comparison between his own wonderful choices in life and 'those thousands of retired businessmen who live in those dreary little bungalows outside Brighton', but his superior attitude is rooted in a basic conservatism that is perhaps more educated than Miche's but just as reactionary. He sets himself above those 'loathing all bloody foreigners', proudly claiming enlightenment, but laments the passing of customs and traditions purely on his own terms, profoundly insensitive to the needs of people outside his class in society, whom he views in a stereotypical manner. Caroline attacks this element of sham in his stance, her left-wing beliefs always happy to challenge the right-wing view of history, but the most serious hurt she feels is the result of the chasm between her own memories of childhood and Daddy's insistent romanticising of his own past, separate viewpoints which are the inevitable result of lives that were, in truth, lived apart from each other.

The repetition of 'These Foolish Things' creates the nagging sense of something wrong with Daddy's 'truth', as its very constancy fuels the sadness that centres around the fear that things can never be changed. Each time the song recurs, its soothing melody becomes increasingly jaded, and its words grow more ironic when interlaced with Caroline's growing hurt and final acceptance of the reality of the past that throws into question the recollections of a father she has idolised, and still does. Colo's screenplay served Tavernier's desire to escape from goal-centred linear narrative form, at least in that its most striking dramatic climax occurs at its centre, with an intimate chat between Daddy and Caroline over a glass of wine in a café. This is derailed into minor political bickering between them and spontaneously descends into an outpouring of resentment in which Caroline finally attacks Daddy with all her pain, demanding that he confront the truth of his failure as a father. It is the film's most painful moment of revelation, and ends with Caroline's brutal accusation that his absent son is heading for as selfish a life as he has had, barbed with a cutting reference to the familiarity and predictability of Daddy's disparaging phrase 'Deeply boring', and hinting at a failure on his part which spans years. The moment is shocking for Daddy and cathartic for Caroline, a small drama which affects them both without being a revolution. It neither changes the past nor determines their future, but is nevertheless important, proving that life can still progress.

The relationship between such modest occurrences and the enormous drama that ultimately constitutes any individual human existence is at the heart of *Daddy Nostalgie*. While 'These Foolish Things' and Daddy appear to be overly taken with the superficialities of life, the film simultaneously rejects any value judgement which equates trivia and ordinariness with meaninglessness. The film's treatment of its settings and characters may be the strongest example of Tavernier's compulsion to subvert simplistic psychological assumptions about his characters and their behaviour, evident largely through the amount of unknowns that exist in the film concerning every character. The precise nature of

Daddy's prior occupation is not totally clear, nor is the exact meaning of how 'Things have changed' as he says of his relationship with Miche. Little is known about the background to Caroline's divorce, and Miche is ready to talk about almost anything concerning the present, but cannot face talking about the past, having become naturally secretive about her feelings. When Caroline presumptuously encourages Miche to talk to Daddy about the past because 'It will bring him pleasure' she is not prepared for Miche's response that doing so would cause her pain, and this reminder to Caroline that there are things she does not understand is also directed towards the audience throughout the film. We do not know what has passed between Daddy and Miche, but that is irrelevant anyway.

The fact that Colo's script does not provide explanations puts it exactly in tune with Tavernier's direction, which rarely seems to imply that total understanding is even possible. As the opening words of René's letter suggest, it will never be within Daddy's, Miche's or Caroline's grasp to experience life from each other's point of view, and the best they can ever hope to do is understand the small parts of their existence which overlap. Other than the theme of loneliness, the film's connection with Tavernier's other work can be traced back to *L'Horloger de Saint-Paul* in that it is not simply about Caroline and her father but is about the relationship between generations. In this instance, the focus is on the suppressed anger directed not just at specific grievance but at ageing itself. Caroline is angry with Daddy's blindness to his own insensitivity, but she is also angry with her parents simply for growing old, and this produces a hurtful outburst in which she reprimands Miche, as though she were a child, for the smudged lipstick on her teeth, then for her clinging behaviour on an earlier occasion, again caused by her failing eyesight. *Daddy Nostalgie* is essentially a poignant tragedy, but its pain, like Daddy's, is never immune from being pushed aside by little successes, where real communication momentarily breaks through once more: Daddy admits to Caroline, without resentment, 'I've been a terrible father'; when Caroline tells her mother, 'Your parents were fools,' after asking her to 'Have a good cry', she acknowledges the difficulties which have afflicted Miche's own life; Miche's fragile sense of closeness to Daddy still manages to appear occasionally, allowing her to ask him, 'Any news?' in English. The end of the film offers no earth-shattering revelations about Daddy's own past that might allow Caroline to understand why her father has let her down, just his faltering 'I love you' answer-machine message, which is enough for her under the circumstances. Acceptance without explanation, despite the prospect of future unhappiness, is the minor victory that ends the film.

Past the hardest truth – following Caroline's bitter accusations over his past selfishness, Daddy suppresses his own hurt for a moment in order to comfort his injured daughter.

The film's close concentration on life in and around Daddy and Miche's villa happens against constant reference to travel and distance, themes which are never far away from the very opening, with Caroline's dream about pushing Daddy in a wheelbarrow. Travel is the emblem of Daddy's past, and it brings him the most comforting sense of a life lived to the full, and the film's images of travel create an aura of inner loneliness. The first image of the empty tracks outside a Paris railway station terminus lead us towards the first sight of Caroline working alone. Then there is a telephone call which she answers off-camera, close by but just out of reach, as she is for Miche, who is distressed on the other end of the line. Her arrival in the Midi sees her step off a coach, her solitariness standing out as she passes a young woman meeting her lover off the same bus, then walk on, her detachment effected by a tracking and panning camera which leaves her and finally rests on rows of parked, empty yachts. The image of the boats introduces the atmosphere of closure which dominates the film, sometimes reflective and even restful, like the first quiet evening drink which Daddy and Caroline enjoy sharing in a cosy little club bar, other times more suggestive of loss and emptiness, like the end-of season quiet of the cafés where they go for their daytime chats, or the deserted 24-hour petrol station where they share feelings that are more open than ever, assisted by the darkness. Distance in various forms is constantly suggested throughout, from the distance of time, memory and longing for the past evoked by sea to the physical distance reinforced by all the dealings with telephones and answering machines, which if not bearing bad news act as blunt reminders of the absence of close contact, and the work commitments which wrench Caroline away from her family, reluctantly despite all her resentment at having to be the dutiful daughter in a crisis.

Distance is also the driving force behind most of the film's camera movement, which often moves between the characters 'unmotivated' by movement, but drawing lines between characters. The effect is slightly restless, supporting all the images of Caroline wandering near the sea which in turn reflect Daddy and Miche's preoccupation with the past, but the camera movements also literally connect the characters, a style which strengthens the suggestion of a desire for closeness whilst inevitably heightening the distance between them at the same time. Their need to make contact, never quite abandoned, is too frequently let down by clumsiness or delay, and the camera moves which draw them together are set against a lilting, regretful score by Antoine Duhamel that is above all hesitant in its style, each phrase as tentative in execution as the last, as though testing the water, fearing risks. Like the film's main characters, Duhamel's music never stops moving for long, but remains contained, never quite breaking off in any new direction.

The last image of Caroline walking away from the camera along a quiet Paris street serves as a reminder of her loneliness, but also introduces the final rendition of 'These Foolish Things', a light and airy studio version sung by Birkin herself which both hints that enough was resolved for Caroline to at least reduce the destructive capacity of any hurt she feels and serves to widen the film's resonance, reminding us that Daddy, Miche and Caroline are just examples of any number of others struggling to make the best of what life has ill-prepared them for. Near the end of *Daddy Nostalgie*, Tavernier includes one other detail which serves to open up feelings for humanity beyond the film's characters. When Caroline arrives back in Paris she notices an old man stopped in a Métro corridor, watching her as she sings absently, and smiles at him. The old man is played by Louis Ducreux, who was the old painter M Ladmiral in *Un Dimanche à la Campagne*, and as Caroline glances back at him for a last look, Tavernier's cinematic farewell to his father seems complete, leaving Caroline to take life forward.

NOTES ON CHAPTER 16

1. *The Sleeping Tiger* (1953), which Jospeh Losey directed under the pseudonym Victor Hanbury.
2. Broadcast in the UK on Channel 4 in 1992.
3. The other films which Bogarde made with Joseph Losey were *The Servant* (1963), *King and Country* (1964), *Modesty Blaise* (1965) and *Accident* (1966).
4. Dirk Bogarde first related the story in an article 'Take Three, In Splendid Cinemascope' for the *Independent*, 28 January 1990. The story is also documented in his book *A Short Walk From Harrods*, from his autobiographical series.
5. The lyrical scenes of Bouvier's wandering in the Ardêche in *Le Juge et l'Assassin* can be compared with the atmosphere in some of Polonsky's work, such as *Tell Them Willie Boy is Here* (1972).
6. Quoted from the article transcript in the press release for *Daddy Nostalgie*, Little Bear, 1991.

CHAPTER 17

L.627 (1992)

L.627 was the first film since *Des Enfants Gâtés* whose exterior scenes Tavernier had to shoot entirely on the streets of Paris, and the film's scenario, portraying the everyday work of a Paris drugs squad team, prescribed a far more complicated shoot, with nine major acting roles, nearly 80 smaller parts, most with dialogue, and many complicated scenes in difficult street locations, often involving vehicles and crowds. Any trepidation which Tavernier's memory of his first experience of shooting in Paris provoked was, however, superceded by his desperation to make the film. *L.627*'s characters, events and moral viewpoints form dozens of narrative parallels with any of Tavernier's previous dramas, and it follows Tavernier's central concern with characters who are both empassioned and haunted by work, but the film's electric atmosphere of urgency and near-relentless tension was unlike anything which Tavernier had created before. The film's central character, Lucien Marguet, or 'Lulu' (Didier Bezace),[1] is shaken by doubt, but there comes a point in the film, where doubt gives way to a fixation with work and the immediate struggles involved in trying to get a job done properly. Lulu's worst doubt – whether his work is really futile, and whether he even has the strength to carry on – is really a symptom of the real problem, terminal frustration with the system within which he operates.

The other Tavernier hero who seems most like Lulu in his obsession with work is Commandant Dellaplane in *La Vie et Rien d'Autre*, although the lives of some others have been equally haunted by the professional dilemmas which confront them, as well as being regularly thwarted by external factors: the educational fads and politicians' platitudes which fuel Laurence Cuers' uncertainty in *Une Semaine de Vacances*, and the endemic cowardice and corruption which convince Lucien Cordier that it is not even worth trying to do his job properly in *Coup de Torchon*. Tavernier had also considered crime and justice in *L'Horloger de Saint-Paul* and *Le Juge et l'Assassin*, but with more of an emphasis on the judicial process. *L.627*'s focus on the situation of the police themselves was new. The theme of justice exists strongly in all of Tavernier's work, in every context from social attitudes to family communication, and in *L.627* the question of justice confronts the criminal imbalance between two contrasting levels of commitment and integrity: that of Lulu, Detective, Second Class, and that of the government, in particular the Ministère de Justice, which seems to exist in order to prop up the systematic barriers that prevent Lulu from achieving what he believes is attainable, and to create the culture of defeatism which gnaws at the professionalism of the drugs squad. When Lulu cracks as a result of years of frustration at every turn, the result of petty bureaucracy and rules imposed by the authorities, his fury is born of a simple desire to be allowed do what, theoretically, he is employed to do by the state: 'If we want results we act illegally twenty-four hours out of twenty-four, Vincent! We've got no money, no means, we've got nothing! We do what we have to do. You think what you like. You think I like beating up Arabs? You think I vote Le Pen? Go ahead – think what you like – I just want to do my job!'

Vincent, the young trainee detective who challenges Lulu's tired experience with naïve trust in academic procedure is played by Nils Tavernier, who had already worked with his father on *La Passion Béatrice* as the brutalised son Arnaud de Cortemart, and performed key roles in other films.[2] Tavernier dedicated *L.627* to Nils, who had suffered from some drug-related problems a few years earlier, and acted as the catalyst in the film's conception. While spending time with the police to research an acting role,[3] Nils met Michel Alexandre, the drugs squad police officer who later co-scripted *L.627*[4] with Tavernier. Fascinated by Alexandre's talk of his personal experiences as an ordinary detective working on the streets, Nils introduced him to his father. Tavernier was immediately taken by Alexandre's passion for his work and the wealth of first-hand experience he offered, and suggested that they collaborate on a screenplay based on his everyday life. Tavernier encouraged Alexandre to note down every event which interested him, and Alexandre eventually brought him 400 pages of material to put into shape:

a sequence of facts, situations, anecdotes shedding light on all kinds of contradictions, anxieties and frustrations. In short, a whole complex social fabric that is seldom tackled or analysed in film. From that starting point, I tried to find a light, open and undemonstrative dramatic line, dictated not so much by psychological motivations as by the nature of the job itself. I needed a structure that did not seem constructed, which would remain 'accidental', raw.[5]

The central principle which Tavernier adopted in constructing the screenplay from Alexandre's testimony was to concentrate on those events which depicted the day-to-day, typical aspects of work in the drugs squad, and leave aside the more unusual occurrences, regardless of any convenient high drama. Tavernier's fixation with remaining faithful to Alexandre's depiction of what was simply everyday toil, and the reality which he subsequently saw for himself while researching *L.627* over several months, impelled him to create a work which rejected dramatic intrigue as the driving force behind plot construction. The film is not anti-drama, however. Its drama resides almost totally in its response to immediate events, rather than being fuelled by the building of linear intrigue towards emotional climax. In the conventional sense, *L.627* has no beginning and no end. Lulu is seen to survive an endless stream of destructive problems, including the desire to give up a frighteningly impossible existence, but nothing has changed at the end of the film: he is exactly where he was at its start, in an unmarked stakeout van, on a job, after which there will be another. His 'climactic' violent outburst, in which he attacks the small dealer Miloud then launches a tirade of frustration at Vincent, is a minor event sandwiched between other upsets, giving the impression that it is little more than an inevitable release of tension which could have happened at any time in the film, and has probably happened before. The same applies to Lulu's most critical moment of personal decision, when he confides in his wife Kathy (Cécile Garcia-Fogel) that nothing can be worked out, and he seems close to giving up everything. *L.627*'s absence of developing intrigue goes against the *policier* genre as much as any. Ironically, its feeling of sheer tension is an element exploited as a matter of course in almost any detective drama, but the film substitutes the usual tension of visual anticipations constructed around identification with the cop against the thug, with the inner tensions and fears of its hero Lulu.

Lulu's vexation is very clear from the many dialogue sequences involving complaints about working conditions, sometimes mocking, at other times despairing, and *L.627*'s framing style externalises tension visually, maintaining the constant presence of Lulu's simmering state of mind. The mise-en-scène is a classic example of Tavernier's concern

Totally committed, surviving in chaos – Looping, Lulu, Vincent and Marie, all making do within a corrupt system, and inside squalid, prefabicated offices.

over cinematic point of view and morality. While seeking to avoid all the visual clichés associated with the *policier* genre, Tavernier also wanted to avoid his commitment to realism turning the film into a drama-documentary offering a more journalistic viewpoint, illustrated with consciously descriptive compositions and reaction shots. His primary intention was to allow the audience to remain with Lulu's viewpoint as much as possible, and most importantly in terms of event discovery. Combined with the script's rejection of parallel action, this formal decision ultimately removed any risk of intrigue diluting the representation of Lulu's position. Tavernier's approach to camera concentrates on events in terms of their direct impact on Lulu himself, although he is actually surrounded by colleagues most of the time, and despite the absence of choreographed emotional build-up it often supports the feeling of shock and cumulative disbelief.

Curiously, the shock effect is reminiscent of that created in *Chinatown* (Roman Polanski, 1974), Polanski's way of staying with J.J. Gittes, the camera often near the detective's shoulder, being similar to Tavernier's accompaniment of Lulu. However, *Chinatown* creates shock by using plot-intrigue very consciously as a way of challenging audience expectations of the technique, whereas Tavernier's method is directed more at the integrity of his subject. The question of how to take *L.627*'s vision of ordinariness to an audience did worry him at the outset, and at one stage in post-production the structure and approach he had chosen did provoke deep doubts in him about how the film would come across.[6] The marriage of camera to protagonist resulted in the film's visual sense of urgency, taken to the level of intense panic at times, and Tavernier chose Alain Choquart to execute his vision's nervous rapidity. Tavernier had used Choquart to both light and frame his previous documentary project, *La Guerre Sans Nom* (1992) about the forgotten conscripts of the Algerian war, but *L.627* was the first of his dramas on which he was both Director of Photography and Camera Operator,[7] a combination of roles which tends, among other factors, to speed up the shooting process. Being able to work quickly was a talent of Pierre-William Glenn's which Tavernier had favoured and, like Glenn, Choquart prefers to combine the two roles. The difficulties of shooting on the streets of Paris made Tavernier especially keen on Choquart's way of working.

Tavernier adopted the Steadicam image again extensively in *L.627*, though not as a constant effect, as he had done in *Coup de Torchon* with Glenn. The difficult and sometimes dangerous nature of the real locations, often with minimal production control, excluded the possibility of laying tracks and heavy dollies. In many scenes, Tavernier favoured Steadicam work over hand-held cinematography, which would have been the most rapid and flexible method, preferring a fluid image-movement which both avoided a total documentary look and added a quality of tense uneasiness to the frame that is closer to the sense of instability to be found in *Coup de Torchon*. The camera never gives Lulu's precise point of view in the conventionally constructed sense – close facial shot followed by a cut to what he is looking at. Instead of mimicking his physical viewpoint, the element of identification with Lulu is created by the camera staying with him as events develop, often with him in the frame. When he races out of a Lycée classroom vantage point with his colleague 'Looping' (Philippe Torreton), to join a drugs bust unfolding in a park, the Steadicam shot pans to follow them, then tracks in rapidly to follow and catch up with Lulu, favouring him throughout the blazing row which ensues, over a lack of interest in targeting dealers by another colleague, Dodo (Jean-Paul Comart). The effect is like racing to accompany Lulu, without creating the suggestion of an additional character. Another sequence shows the visual frame seemingly locked to Lulu's train of thought. Following the next drugs-bust, when Lulu explodes and attacks Miloud during his interrogation, the camera swings violently to frame a photo of an overdosed girl pinned to the wall before Lulu shoves Miloud's head against the image and forces him to look at it, reflecting Lulu's volatile thought process instead of following physical action in the classic manner.

Alexandre, on whom Lulu was based was also well-educated, and remained an unpromoted ordinary class detective. Another important detail which Tavernier retained was that Alexandre had taken the entry examination for the Paris film school IDHEC around the same time as ones he sat for entry to the Police Inspectorate. In *L.627*, Lulu tells Looping about his failed attempt to get into film school when they are hiding in a blacked out observation van and he is videotaping drugs deals taking place in rue Myrra. When a young junkie collapses pitifully in a heap, Lulu points his VHS camera downwards, saying 'That, I don't film', prompting his colleague's expression of disappointment. At that moment, Lulu communicates Tavernier's discomfort with exploitative voyeurism, a worry which was the heart of *Death Watch* and can be detected in every film, at moments of violence, emotional pain and sexual intimacy. Lulu films his targets, but the sequences he watches serve to increase the extent to which he is haunted by images of the work which obsesses him. His involvement with the squad's mission is so intense that his family life suffers, and the weddings that he videotapes in order to boost his income seem to bring him no satisfaction, his creative impulse having been reduced to little more than a necessity for survival as well as creating in him the empty feeling of being a temporary observer and outsider in the other ordinary dramas of family life. Lulu talks of nothing other than work to his wife Kathy, and listening to his jaded disillusionment about the wedding films he edits at home almost seems like the nearest thing that she has to respite from his otherwise total involvement in the drugs squad.

We see Lulu's baby girl Karine just once, very briefly, as he kisses her and Kathy before running for a bus to work. Later, his words, 'Our baby is asleep,' represent all that we learn about his involvement with her, and it is Kathy who expresses fear for their daughter, making Lulu promise that they will leave Paris when Karine is eleven. Like Commandant Dellaplane in *La Vie et Rien d'Autre*, Lulu is totally devoted to his work, but his dedication has reached a level where it prevents him from living fully in other ways, and leaves his own family unable to get close enough to him. Lulu's preoccupied silence as he sits in a restaurant with Kathy, at his most troubled, contrasts with the attention which he gives to Cécile (Lara Guirao), the junkie prostitute he has 'adopted'. Lulu cannot let go of Cécile, obsessed with saving her as if she represents the way of proving that his incessant struggle is capable of achieving something tangible. Lulu may never have been fully involved with Cécile sexually, but he is betraying Kathy through the friendship all the same, shutting her out of a deeply personal aspect of his life which defines who he is and his relationship with the world. As with the petty dishonesty which Lulu engages in to make ends meet, Tavernier never seems to impose judgement on him about letting Kathy down, allowing the strong impression to come across that Lulu has his reasons, even though these are only hinted at. There is no clear indication that Lulu himself understands, just that he is aware of the nagging sense that something is wrong; something that it is even more threatening than the obvious wrongs of the world around him.

Tavernier's reluctance to judge individuals is obvious from the sympathetic light in which he shows those around Lulu, despite their flaws, but it it his sympathy for Lulu that is firmly at the centre of *L.627*'s emotion. He uses Philippe Sarde's music mostly to express the nervous emotions and consuming anxiety of Lulu's predicament. From the opening titles, which suggest frantic pursuit and combine the impression of constantly changing direction with the feeling of going into a tunnel, Sarde's music heightens the impression of desperate chase thwarted by chaos, and its attention to Lulu in particular is never stronger than the sequences which portray him in his most precarious state of mind. 'You need to clean out your head, or…' Lulu's colleague Marie (Charlotte Kady) warns as she sees he is retreating inside himself over his worries about Cécile, just before we see him visit his paralysed mother in hospital. Lost for words while feeding her, he lies to her about how well his work is going. All Lulu can do is stare downwards at the hospital bed, and as the pain of their distance takes hold of him, a twisting, perturbed violin insinuates itself into the air. The music refuses to let go. Cut to the persistent attack of a stream of roof lights inside a road tunnel. Emerge into daylight. While Lulu and Kathy's car travels across a river bridge in Lyon, the music will not leave, like an unwelcome memory or a dreadful realisation which cannot be shaken off. The same theme occurs earlier on, when Kathy asks Lulu to assure her that he is going to leave Paris, and he confides in her that he is as frightened as she is. Once again, the troubling, stubborn theme carries across well into the subsequent stakeout scene, giving the distinct feeling that Lulu's anxiety is like a chronic illness, never far away, although the music's attachment to an image of children playing in the waste-ground in front of decaying apartment blocks and the wide framings of the Paris streets also create the haunting sense of a society in danger.

Tavernier's disengagement with the conventional approach to audience identification in the *policier* is most acutely apparent through *L.627*'s uncompromising portrayal of the work of the drugs squad, which ensured the controversy that fuelled the film's considerable success at the box-office. As well as Lulu, his brigade colleagues Dodo, Marie, Antoine (Tonio, Looping), Manu and Vincent, and others such

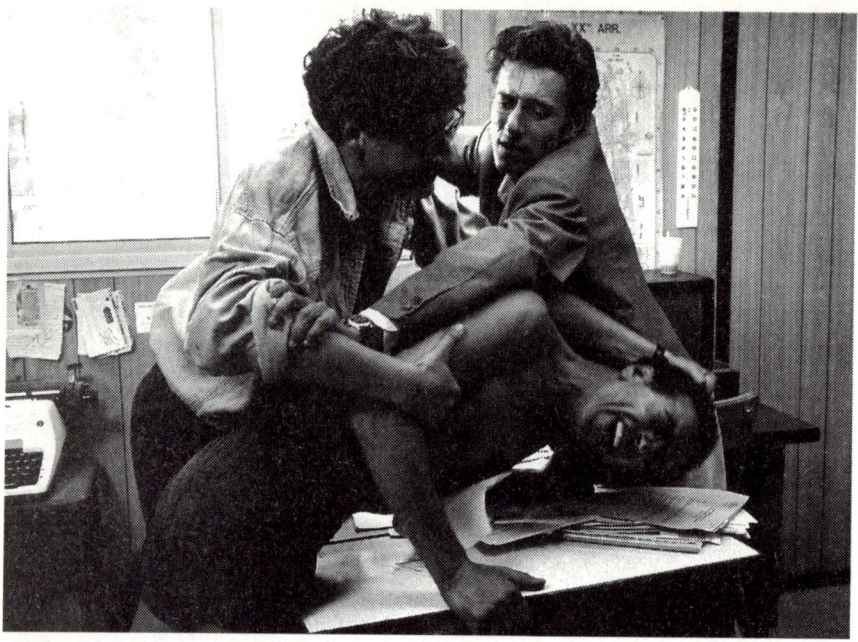

Displaced anger – Lulu's frustration with state bureaucracy and his own professional impotence finally explodes, finding only Miloud, a petty drug dealer

as his superior and mentor Adore (Claude Brosset), are all depicted with a level of character and situational detail that results in the film's two dynamic angles of approach on the drugs squad: confronting the often questionable, and at times reprehensible, activities and attitudes of the police, whilst exposing equally the culpability of those powers who are a source of their disillusionment by depicting the shocking conditions and system of regulations under which the police are forced to work by the state. The film conveys Lulu and his colleague's maddened impatience with the wilful laziness of other, bored members of their service who refuse to answer telephones and whose deepest commitment is to their lunch hour. This is also illustrated with a catalogue of minor bureaucratic idiocies: the police garage insistence on their checking in with a full tank in a van with a fuel leak; the automatic delivery of pencil erasers which are not needed while at the same time there is no carbon paper; Lulu's enforced participation in courses on mundane tasks which he has been doing for years, and could do with his eyes shut. Dodo fills much of his time with infantile practical jokes and board games, while Manu (Jean-Roger Milo) is frequently drunk on duty and regularly jams the telephone line making porn calls, and their ingrained racism is revealed mercilessly from the outset. Whilst *L.627* paints a deeply unflattering portrait of the police, Tavernier's diary covering the film's early stages of production and post-production through to its release referred to the widespread police view of the film's accuracy and gratitude for its exposure of their working conditions, in spite of all the racism and other negative facets of the portrayal.[8]

The film's anger, expressed through Lulu, is not directed essentially at the failings of Dodo or Manu, but at the system which has made them what they are and which effectively rewards them for remaining unchanged. The root of the increasingly volatile arguments between Lulu and Dodo is the Ministère de Justice's convenient system of statistical analysis, which prescribes that convicting a small pusher for selling five grams of cocaine brings as much credit as convicting a major dealer, logically resulting in Dodo's refusal to hold out for larger, more difficult hauls, and his selfish betrayal of the brigade's informants. Failure is guaranteed by the policy-driven culture, of which L.627 — the pitifully ineffectual Public Health Code regulation stipulating statutory medical check-ups for narcotics offenders — is an example. Dodo's position as head of Lulu's group — and the accompanying water pistol games and primary dedication to producing the reports that fulfill his superior's quotas — is simply another example of the system's corruption, ensuring that those who obediently ignore reality are rewarded. Compared to Dodo, the academic Vincent is totally dedicated, and still full of integrity, but already risks going the same way, drilled into blind acceptance of the Ministry's suffocating status quo. Vincent is in moral danger from his reliance on authority, but in personal danger from his own lack of humour — Alexandre's stories about his work inevitably reminded Tavernier of the tactics employed by Hawkeye and Trapper in *M*A*S*H* (Robert Altman, 1970), and humour is something which *L.627* also depicts as literally essential for survival. Vincent seems isolated from the rest of the team, out of touch through his inexperience, but he is the one who launches the film's essential accusation during the rue Stevenson raid debacle: 'I didn't join the police for this!' He stands with the screaming of a crack cocaine addict's baby ringing in his ears during a raid in which their squad is thrown at insignificant victims of the drug culture whose lives they can only make worse. The horrifying waste implied by his remark is stirred further by Manu: 'Show some charity,' he calls to Dodo, whose harsh taunting of one woman about the likelihood of her ending up in prostitution is finally too much for him. The survival of this side of Manu's nature, in spite of everything we have seen from him earlier, creates one of the most moving moments in the film, a sense of buried humanity coming through. Manu may be the most disgracefully unprofessional member of the group, but he has his own wisdom and logic, is knowledgeable about the effects of drugs, and is too appalled by the destruction of drug addiction to accept even Looping's gallows humour when they come across an overdosed girl, whom they at first assume to be dead.

The secondary involvement of Manu in the drama belies the importance of the role in building the film's emotion through an accumulation of detail unconnected to a dramatic line, also exemplified in Marie's exasperated intelligence and judicious sensitivity towards those who need it and Vincent's compulsion to give some money to an addict who is being discharged without the means to buy something to eat. The tragedy of *L.627* presents an image of squandered humanity that ultimately questions even Lulu's ability to maintain his commitment to his work.

The first words Lulu speaks in the film are 'Laisse tomber' ('Drop it'), a phrase which he uses several times to calm down hot-headed colleagues. Kathy has helped Lulu through his deepest moment of doubt, but there is no suggestion of a let-up in the systematic attack on his morale. *L.627* ends with Lulu having failed to get Cécile's address after finally finding out that she has a baby, is off drugs for the moment and is getting out of Paris. Lulu, however, has not yet found the route out of the city that Kathy asked him to find. The last image shows Lulu travelling towards his next job. Despite the optimism of his chance meeting with Cécile, Lulu's feeling of loss at her departure ends *L.627* with a deep sense of uncertainty, providing no guarantee of how long Lulu can be expected to continue, before he too decides to 'Laisse tomber'.

NOTES ON CHAPTER 17

1 Before playing the lead role in *L.627*, Didier Bezace was best known as a theatre director in France.
2 Notably including *Une Affaire de Femmes* (Claude Chabrol, 1988), opposite Isabelle Huppert, as Lucien, her collaborator lover; and in *Valmont* (Milos Forman, 1989), adapted from the novel *Les Liasons Dangereuses*, as second knight of the Maltese Order.
3 The role of Didier Theron in *Sale Comme un Ange* (Catherine Breillat, 1990).
4 Michel Alexandre was still working in the drugs squad while writing the script of *L.627*.
5 Bertrand Tavernier, 'I Wake Up Dreaming: A Journal for 1992' in Boorman and Donohue (eds), *Projections 2*, London, 1993, pp 253, 370.
6 Ibid., p 281.
7 Choquart had worked as camera assistant to Pierre-William Glenn on several films, including Tavernier's *Coup de Torchon* and *Pays d'Octobre/ Mississippi Blues*, then camera operator on *La Vie et Rien d'Autre* with Bruno de Keyzer.
8 Bertrand Tavernier, 'I Wake Up Dreaming', op. cit. p 370.

CHAPTER 18

LA FILLE DE D'ARTAGNAN (1994)

La Fille de D'Artagnan (*D'Artagnan's Daughter*) came as Tavernier's biggest surprise since *La Passion Béatrice*. Following a long record of making films which seemed especially difficult to pigeonhole because they subverted the usual expectations of genre, came the first film which could be easily categorised: a light-hearted, swash-buckling comedy adventure, its classical credentials further validated by the very presence of Dumas's famous musketeers. In fact, *La Fille de D'Artagnan* is totally unique within Tavernier's body of work, being the only film he made which he never intended to direct himself. He had taken over the film from his friend Riccardo Freda, reluctantly and out of a sense of obligation. Freda gave Tavernier his first real film production job following his two shorts for Georges de Beauregard, writing a few scenes and some of the dialogue for his *Coplan Ouvre le Feu à Mexico* (1967).[1] Tavernier admired Freda as a master of cape-and-sword, 'historical' adventure and horror films, beginning with *Aquila Nera* (Black Eagle, 1946) and remaining prolific throughout the 1950s and 1960s, directing films mainly for the Italian production house Cinécitta. Freda's output reduced to a trickle during the 1970s when his type of flamboyant adventures became unfashionable, and he had not directed a film since *L'Ossessione Che Uccide* (Delirium, 1980) when Tavernier invited him, out of respect, to join the production of *La Passion Béatrice* as technical advisor in 1987, the film having started out as a remake of Freda's own *Beatrice Cenci* (1956).

The history of *La Fille de d'Artagnan* can be traced back to 1949, when Freda directed *Il Figlio de D'Artagnan*.[2] He was not happy with the film, after having failed to obtain the Italian star Vittorio Gassman for the lead role because he was too expensive, and in the end regarded the completed film as 'unworthy of Dumas'.[3] Eventually, it was another admirer of Freda from Tavernier's press agent days, Pierre Rissient, by then working as artistic consultant with the Paris production house Ciby 2000, who got the project which Freda had conceived with Eric Poindron off the ground. With the apparent rediscovery of French audiences' appetite for costume and myth in the wake of the success of *Cyrano de Bergerac* (Jean-Paul Rappeneau, 1990), Ciby 2000 agreed to have the eighty-three-year-old Freda direct *La Fille de D'Artagnan*, with Little Bear involved in production and Tavernier serving as 'patron' to the venture. The writing credits are complicated, with the scenario based on Freda and Poidron's idea credited to Michel Léviant, the screenplay adaptation credited to Léviant, Tavernier and Jean Cosmos, and the dialogue to Léviant and Cosmos.

When shooting got underway, *La Fille de D'Artagnan* soon ran into serious difficulties, when the actress playing the title role, Sophie Marceau, did not get on with the director, who had never been known for his respect for actors, or those in cinema he disagreed with: 'Lynx-eyed and viper-tongued, this fanatical artist of popular cinema spent the essential part of his career voicing everything bad that he thought of actors and Hollywood directors ('That fool De Toth[4] was incapable of placing the camera or conceiving a movement!') or neo-realists ("Profiting from everything pitiful that life offers, as De Sica[5] did, has always revolted me!").[6] Marceau had little faith in Freda's direction, and eventually threatened to quit the project unless he was replaced, until Tavernier reluctantly agreed to come and co-direct the film with Freda. Ultimately, Marceau refused to continue with Freda, who left Tavernier to direct the project on his own. Ironically, 20 years after his intention to film Dumas's *La Fille du Régent*, Tavernier found himself being handed the task of directing a film about Éloïse D'Artagnan, daughter of the most heroic of the musketeers, but had to see the project through with a bitter taste in his mouth, knowing that despite his reluctance to take over completely, the friend he had admired for so long had left feeling betrayed.[7]

It would be wrong to assume that Tavernier in some sense simply went through the motions of directing the film. His personal commitment to the film was already very strong when the project was being set up for Freda, and ultimately he took on the task of directing the work with the relish of a film-maker given the chance to make and pay homage to the kind of film which drew him into the cinema during his youth.

Moments of comedy have consistently lifted the spirits of Tavernier's work, but *La Fille de D'Artagnan* is his only straight comedy, his only

LA FILLE DE D'ARTAGNAN (1994)

Beautiful, feisty heroine – Élöise D'Artagnan in full flow, true to the cape-and-sword genre.

other comic work being the despairing and blackly funny *Coup de Torchon*. As well as its tone and the frequency of humour, Tavernier kept the film true to its genre, filling the film with many of the expected ingredients: an innocent and rebellious heroine of stunning beauty, often wearing men's clothes; a cruel and beautiful noble counterpart; scheming nobles and idiot servants; lengthy, bloodless sword-fights won by super-human heroes very heavily out-numbered and cornered; fights which reach their climax on balconies, battlements and roofs; spectacular horseback escapes across a banquet table, the horse crashing through a sugar-glass and balsa-wood window; the heroes' main foe dressed in black, in possession of the popular blend of malevolence, eccentricity and stupidity; the interweaving of subplots about conspiracy, disapproved love and misunderstandings, whose unfolding creates the fleeting exchanges between friends and foes during the pauses in épée-work. At several moments, the film revels in gentle parody of the genre and self-mockery: when the musketeers board an anchored galleon preparing to depart for America with its cargo of kidnapped nuns, after repeated shots – emphasised in slow-motion – of the cavaliers' steeds leaping spectacularly from the quay onto the ship, Aramis comments, 'Herioc, but absurd...' before slashing a rope allowing the drawbridge to come clattering down. The sub-plot about deportation to America recalls the events depicted in *Que la Fête Commence...*, and Tavernier also referred mischievously to his own earlier venture into the eighteenth century, notably in one scene where the Duke de Crassac (Claude Rich) gleefully shares with his mistress, 'Woman in Red' Eglantine de Rochefort (Charlotte Kady), his excitement over the power which his scheming will bring him while her stockinged thighs are draped over his shoulders, an image virtually identical to the scene between the similarly conspiratorial Abbé Dubois and his whore in *Que la Fête Commence...*

The fact that Tavernier remained within such conventions of style and structure in *La Fille de D'Artagnan* was certainly a departure from his usual goals, but his basic fidelity to the genre was simply further confirmation of his belief in respecting the integrity of the authors of source material, whether it be the atmosphere and feeling evoked in a novel, as with *Coup de Torchon* (*Pop. 1280* by Jim Thomson) and *Un Dimanche à la Campagne* (*Monsieur Ladmiral Va Bientôt Mourir* by Pierre Bost), or the first-hand, everyday experience of drugs squad officer Michel Alexandre in *L.627*. Tavernier remained faithful to Freda's intentions, but at the same time was able to make the film his own, helped by the fact that the scenario covered many themes common to his 'own' films, and which had long interested him. D'Artagnan (Philippe Noiret) is yet another paternal figure at the human centre of the drama, and once again the father in the story survives alone without his wife, regretting her absence. This same situation was first handled by Tavernier with Michel Descombes in *L'Horloger de Saint-Paul*, a predicament that is central also to the emotional make-up of the father figures in *Un Dimanche à la Campagne* and *La Passion Béatrice*, despite the huge differences in the nature of their troubled minds. The scene in which we first see Éloïse and D'Artagnan meeting up is like a reverse image of the moment when François de Cortemart returns home to be greeted by Béatrice in *La Passion Béatrice*. Like their doomed counterparts, D'Artagnan and Éloïse have also been apart for years, but by contrast their own reunion is filled with joy, and this time it is the father who is overwhelmed into one-word utterances at the sight of his daughter: 'Constance,' is his first response, mistaking Éloïse for her long dead mother. Later, when D'Artagnan slaps Éloïse for persistently calling him an 'unworthy father' in front of his friends, her bitter remark, 'And I dreamed of finding you...' comes closest to recalling the disappointment and pain which Béatrice experiences at the reality of her father's return.

Loving as it is, the relationship between Éloïse and her father is not an easy one. The distance between them has left D'Artagnan out of touch with his daughter's maturing sensibilities to the extent that he has great difficulty in understanding her needs; this results in frustration on both sides. The reason for the difficulty which D'Artagnan has in accepting Éloïse's needs seems due to the fact that she is simply moving on, as her generation must. When he behaves selfishly and stubbornly towards her, wanting to send her back to the convent at the first sign of her recalcitrance, he is fighting to maintain the stability of old beliefs and structures he understands. D'Artagnan is virtually in retirement when we find him, smoking his pipe as he coaches young swordsmen lazily from a seated position, and all the confidence and up-to-date knowledge which Éloïse throws at him increases the sense that he is being left behind. *Que la Fête Commence...* was charged with fears of the unknown, introduced by the knowledge that an entire era was coming to an end, and the story of the retired musketeers shares some similar concerns, although they are treated on a more humorous, modest and less anxiety-ridden level. The irritation with which the older generation receives the fashions of the younger one is treated humorously: Cardinal Mazarin (Luigi Proietti) tries to explain away the apparent senselessness of the conspiracy-code poem by citing the contemporary penchant for idiotic lyrics in modern songs.

The film ends with D'Artagnan and Éloïse continuing an earlier argument about her plans for the future in which he complains that she does not know how to sew, cook, embroider or make jam, all the things a woman who wants to settle down needs to know. She counters that she wants to work for the King as a specialist in foiling conspiracies, but the friction between them has dissolved into light-hearted banter by the time we see them ride off into the distance through the woods, still casting their retorts at each other, but with their earlier animosity replaced with energetic *joie-de-vivre*. This scene is a typical example of the general gaiety created in *La Fille de D'Artagnan*, sustained mainly by the film's acting style, informed in turn mainly by the script's enthusiasm for words as weapons in energetic conflict. The characters' word-play seems to mirror the showmanship of the film's frequent sword-play, the combination creating an atmosphere which prevents the film's intrinsic violence from becoming too dark. Further protection against this is the film's slapstick humour and farce, including D'Artagnan's expert dropping of the trousers of his daughter's impudent suitor Quentin (Nils Tavernier) with a flick of his sword and his own clattering, ignominious descent through a chimney stack, emerging covered in soot to confront the future King, whom he finds *in flagrante delicto* with a young woman he initially mistakes for Éloïse.

More than the mere distance between one generation and the next, the theme of ageing itself is a strong element in *La Fille de D'Artagnan*. One of the first things D'Artagnan informs Éloïse about is how badly Planchet (Jean-Paul Roussillon) has aged, and he goes on jokingly to blame his own ageing for his inability to 'stoop' to the young King

Élöise's stubbornness confronts D'Artagnan with the rebellious energy that he has lost.

Louis XIV, whom he does not respect, before describing how he confronted the king face to face about his shortcomings and had to resign his royal commission.

D'Artagnan's direct concerns with ageing are not pursued as part of the film's comedy, but form the main aspect of its more serious contemplation. The most biting moment of cynicism comes when D'Artagnan and Éloïse sit on a staircase observing, from a distance, the aftermath of their defeat of Crassac. '…and the court returns to its King like pigs to the trough,' comments D'Artagnan at the sight of Eglantine de Rochefort, Cardinal Mazarin and others queueing to swear allegiance to the king because he still holds the power and wealth. Behind all the comedy lies an attack on Tavernier's most consistently and violently attacked target: greed for power, the main vice in *Que la Fête Commence...* and *Le Juge et l'Assassin*, also coming under fire less directly in works like *Death Watch* and *Ça Commence Aujourd'hui*. 'Ah well, I'm worn out,' is D'Artagnan's resigned response to the spectacle. His joy at the battle they have just won is overshadowed by his tired understanding of predictable human failings: another war seems inevitably lost, and his age makes him more susceptible to defeatism. For a moment, D'Artagnan voices Tavernier's fears and warnings through straight pessimism, although its depressive effect is reduced by the film's comic atmosphere and the prospect of an energetic successor to D'Artagnan in the shape of his irrepressible Éloïse.

La Fille de D'Artagnan has to be singled out within Tavernier's work also for its treatment of death. The director's usual tendency to place violent death off-screen was clearly incompatible with his desire to handle the genre faithfully, at least in overall tone, and in keeping with tradition, the film's sword-deaths are as anaemic as they are frequent. However, his discomfort with trivialising death, and even depicting it on screen at all, has a notable impact on key scenes all the same, harnessing the film's few close-ups to strengthen the impression of human pain as an intrinsic aspect of death. Many of the fencing deaths occur at the edge of the frame, with the victim's back to camera, or obscured by their killer, but the first spectacular battle in which D'Artagnan and Éloïse fight against a large group of Mazarin's cavaliers ends with Éloïse killing her first enemy, seen face-on as she pushes her sword into his stomach. The shot is followed by a cut to Éloïse in close-up, which holds on her face for several seconds in almost total silence as the enormity of her action wells up inside her, eventually making her turn away and hide her face in her hands. D'Artagnan enters the frame and takes hold of her, turning her round to face the man she has killed: 'Don't turn away my little girl – look'. Her father's voice wavers with emotion as he encourages her to toughen herself up while she is young, signalling again the weariness that his age has imposed. He goes on to remind her of the need to retain an inner sensitivity at the same time: 'We are truly good and generous when our eyes become dry, but our heart remains gentle'. The film's first close-up of Éloïse is also motivated by her contemplation of death, when Mère Thérèse is lying on her death-bed, giving her final requests and advice to Éloïse.

In Mère Thérèse's last words, she tells Éloïse that she has information which will put the 'Woman in Red' in prison, and the character of Eglantine displays Tavernier's need for ambiguity in all his main players, including those representing the forces of darkness. Light and shade are seen in those on every side of the battle for justice over exploitation and violence. Eglantine's ruthlessness is apparent right from the film's aggressive opening tracking sequence, in which an escaped black slave is pursued, but her later conversation with her prisoner Éloïse informs us of events from her past which at the very least provide some degree of mitigation of her personality and actions. Éloïse's cocky remark that perhaps Eglantine should not have poisoned M Labédie is met with a shocking reply: that Labédie was a 'monster', and that he had once raped her. 'My dreams are worse than my life,' Eglantine says when Éloïse asks her why she does not sleep, in order to rest or dream, and their conversation continues with Éloïse suggesting that Eglantine misjudged Mère Thérèse's feelings for her. Like François de Cortemart in *La Passion*

Béatrice, Eglantine is kept awake by her inner fears, and whatever she is guilty of, she has apparently already been condemned to unhappiness. The dark thoughts which keep her awake surface again later. When Elöise pleads with her to reject her wicked intentions, suggesting that people can change, Eglantine stares into space, haunted by her own view of things: 'I know the world too well. There are the good and there are the wicked. It sometimes happens that the good become wicked. Never the contrary.' Eglantine seems gripped by sadness as she voices her pessimism, but Éloïse refuses to accept her suggestion that her situation is irreversible, and in challenging the possibility that Eglantine might lock her up in a cloister, to be forgotten, she identifies the core of Eglantine's vulnerability: 'No, you won't do it. It's too late. Before, things were simpler: humiliation, vengeance, poison... but now you are lost. You are frightened... If you help me, you will be less lonely'.

Eglantine has been ready to marry the Duc de Crassac for his proximity to the throne, without love, and in her loneliness shares the Achilles heel which is shared by more of Tavernier's characters than any other: the desire to counter feelings of isolation with something tangible, in her case power. Such aspects of *La Fille de D'Artagnan* make the work one that Tavernier can still regard as personal, but they exist as humanising moments, rather than as the core of the film's expressive atmosphere. Regardless of Tavernier's renowned eclecticism, its sheer escapism is a curiosity in relation to his increasing concerns with modern society. Given the unusual circumstances under which Tavernier directed the film, it seems unlikely that he will make anything quite like *La Fille de D'Artagnan* again.

NOTES ON CHAPTER 18

1. Riccardo Freda directed *Coplan Ouvre le Feu à Mexico* (1967) under the name Robert Hampton, and the film was released in Italy as *Entre las Redes* (1966).
2. *The Son of D'Artagnan* – in Freda's film D'Artagnan's heir was male.
3. Jean-Luc Douin, *Tavernier*, Paris, 1997, p 90.
4. André de Toth, the Hungarian director who began in Hollywood as a protegé of Alexander Korda. Best known as a director of westerns such as *Ramrod* (1947), *Last of the Comanches* (1952), *The Bounty Hunter* (1954), and *The Indian Fighter* (1955), as well as *House of Wax* (1953).
5. Vittorio de Sica, the influential Italian neo-realist director whose work includes *Sciuscià* (*Shoeshine*, 1946), *Ladri di Biciclette* (*Bicycle Thieves*, 1948) and *Il Giardino dei Finzi-Continis* (*The Garden of the Finzi-Continis*, 1970).
6. Jean-Luc Douin, *Tavernier*, op. cit., p 89.
7. Ibid, p 91.

CHAPTER 19

L'APPÂT (1995)

Tavernier was already developing *L'Appât* (*The Bait*) with Colo Tavernier-O'Hagan while making *L.627*, and although his decision to follow his realist police drama with the joyful medieval fantasy *La Fille de D'Artagnan* seems consistent with his previous record of contrasting adjacent films, his next project was originally intended to be *L'Appât*. Shooting, planned for November 1993, was postponed when he was forced into taking over *La Fille de D'Artagnan* from Riccardo Freda. With *La Passion Béatrice* and *L'Appât*, Colo was responsible for two of Tavernier's darkest works. *L'Appât* is as pessimistic as *La Passion Béatrice*, and the films stand together in their almost total lack of humour, an aspect which contrasts even with the bleak *Coup de Torchon*. However, in contrast with attitudes to *La Passion Béatrice*, French audiences seemed far more willing to accept Tavernier's hard-hitting pessimism when he rooted it firmly in contemporary France, and *L'Appât* was very successful at the French box office. Having seemed especially concerned with bringing 'forgotten' subjects to his audience, the director chose to deal with a story which was already planted in the French public consciousness.

L'Appât is based closely on Morgan Sportès's book of the same title about a news story which shocked France in 1992, and became known as 'the Valéria Subra affair': a beautiful young woman acts as 'bait' for an affluent lawyer, tricks her way into his apartment and ensures access for two male friends, who burst in on the 'couple', pretending to be total strangers conducting a burglary. Hoping to gain access to a safe, the two young men torture the lawyer, then beat and stab him to death, leaving with only a couple of thousand francs from his wallet. After failing to obtain the wealth that they seek, the three choose another affluent victim from the young woman's notebook of 'contacts' and commit an identical crime, involving torture and ending in murder, again gaining only a negligible quantity of cash and valuables before being arrested, tried and imprisoned for the crimes. Colo Tavernier-O'Hagan followed the entire trial, mesmerised by the apparent notion of three young people who as individuals would not do any harm to anyone, yet together proved capable of commiting such obscene acts. When Colo bought the rights to the book, she wrote a first draft screenplay of *L'Appât*, combining her own impressions with Sportès's precise detail, then got together with Tavernier to write the second version of the script, which became the film. Tavernier began production of the film even before he had even completed *La Fille de D'Artagnan*, stressing the urgency he felt in getting the film moving, fearful that his passion for his subject might start to dissolve after the delay in starting the film. Comparing his 'need' to make the film with that which he felt concerning *L.627* when Michel Alexandre showed him the pitiful prefabricated offices used by the police,[1] he also pointed out the direct connection between *L'Appât* and *La Guerre Sans Nom*, which also contains sections dealing with torture.[2]

Disturbed and fascinated by the notion of the most ordinary people drifting off the rails to inflict terrible cruelty on other human beings, the drama of *L'Appât* appalled Tavernier more than anything he had dealt with previously: where the French conscripts of the Algerian war who proved capable of committing torture did so under violent and extraordinary circumstances, like Lulu's vicious outburst in *L.627*, the three adolescents in *L'Appât* committed their atrocities without any direct pressure to perpetrate violence, identifiable mainly by their ordinariness and that of their social circumstances. Two came from relatively privileged family backgrounds, and the three lacked any criminal or violent history. Without the mitigation of some extreme influence on them, their single motivation, the desire for material reward, was frightening in its ordinariness.[3]

Tavernier first expressed his dismay at the role of the media (especially French television) in pushing materialism in *L'Horloger de Saint-Paul*, and seemed to imply that the situation had deteriorated further in *Une Semaine de Vacances*, as well as attacking the relationship between television voyeurism and commercial ratings directly in *Death Watch*. With *L'Appât*, he focused completely on creating a detailed portrait of the attitudes of the adolescent generation of the 1990s, and used the tragedy of Nathalie (Marie Gillain), Eric (Olivier Sitruk) and Bruno (Bruno Putzulu) to mount his most devastating attack on the

Seduced by instant gratification and by Hollywood – Eric enjoys posing in front of Bruno with their newly-acquired 'passport' to quitting France for guaranteed quick riches in America.

alliance between commercial television and American capitalist culture, depicting a society in which the saturation of French youth with Hollywood's message had created a generation whose identity relied totally on beliefs formed through conformist materialism masquerading as individualism. Nathalie is incapable of defining herself in terms of what she is, able to see herself only through her possessions, validating her existence through the criteria of those 'approved' brands and labels which confirm her proof of status: Mont Blanc pen, Piaget watch, Mercedes car, first class air ticket, Hèrmes scarf.

The film opens to find Nathalie talking to her friend Karine about Isabelle Adjani and Julia Roberts as they sit in the Paris Métro waiting for a train. Nathalie brushes aside a reference to Adjani's beauty, far more interested in assessing her through her acting fee, dismissive of the 10 million francs she commands per film, compared to Julia Roberts's $10 million. When they reach the club which Nathalie frequents in order to seek rich and successful men, contacts who might provide her with a quick route to affluence or fame through television, she reprimands Karine for gulping her 'Carlton Pêche' thirstily, embarrassed by the idea that her friend is not aware of what is the 'done thing' with the fashionable cocktail. As with her eager absorption of the invented statistics on people's sex lives in the magazine she read on the Métro, Nathalie's thinking is funnelled by her commercially synthesised notions of social acceptability. She can only conceptualise success through her detailed knowledge of what is 'in' or 'out' within the affluent circles she frequents and hopes to enter fully – information which substitutes for her own lack of imagination. What Nathalie represents is the appalling logical conclusion of that insidious conformism which disturbed Laurence Cuers so much about her pupils in *Une Semaine de Vacances*, although she herself never contemplated just how far the brain-washing of a generation might go.

Tavernier was developing *L'Appât* during a period when he was also preoccupied with the prospect and progress of the *GATT* negotiations, attending seminars and involved in campaigning for solid quota agreements across the European audio-visual sector which might offer some protection against the United States' intention to control and dominate the film and television distribution market throughout Europe. One of the elements which Tavernier specifically added to the real story was the extent to which America featured in the protagonists' fantasies, and the world depicted in *L'Appât* reflects many of his fears about Hollywood's increasing hold on young film audiences, the designer-label idolatry of wealth and the Americanisation of French society in general. Nathalie's boyfriend Eric deals with his frustration at his standard of living in France by channelling his energy into a clichéd fixation with America as the land of opportunity, convinced that he could easily run a chain of businesses there successfully because the country is free from French bureaucracy. Nathalie and Bruno are equally obsessed with the idea of great wealth and the status conferred by its acquisition. The society they survive in is infested with a commercial ideology that equates success with the possession of specific items, driving French youth to buy, wear, eat, drink and watch, in particular, American goods, under the clear advertising warnings that lacking them represents a failure to acquire the only image which confirms your position as an accepted member of society. As if to back up Eric's constant assertion that the way everything is done in America is better, Bruno drinks Budweiser; they would rather watch a dubbed video of *Scarface* (Brian de Palma, 1983) or hire almost any American movie in preference to anything French ('bound to be rotten'),[4] settling in the end for *Nightmare on Elm Street 6* and the latest Steven Seagal film purely because it is in the video Top 10. Posters for American films adorn their walls, as well as the home of Alain Perez (Richard Berry), their second victim, and the game-shows which frustrate Bruno with the knowledge that he could have won a jackpot feed the public obsession with the status signalled by enormous film budgets: 'What was the budget of Terminator 2?'

The most excruciating reminder of the degree to which they have been anaesthetised by their cultural diet comes when Nathalie asks the police officers arresting her if they have a warrant, and one points out with a degree of embarrassment at her naïvety that they are not 'in an American TV movie'. Tavernier's interest in the three's desire to emulate everything American – from Eric's half-baked business plans to his congratulatory 'high-fives' with Bruno and Nathalie's quotes from the French translation of Al Pacino lines – is in the flight from reality that their behaviour represents. Nathalie and Eric have succeeded in convincing themselves that they are justified in petty theft from an employer or deliberately bouncing cheques, two of a stream of examples of words and deeds which confirm the ingrained lack of integrity that is the natural by-product of their inability to deal with any reality which includes the needs of other people.

Tavernier encapsulated the shocking tragedy of *L'Appât* with a single image that persists long after it has disappeared from the screen: Nathalie is sitting on a big leather couch, outside the room where Bruno is killing Antoine Jousse behind closed doors, feverishly scrabbling for her mini-earphones, putting them on, switching on dance music, turning it up and pressing the earphones against her ears so that she can shut out the sound of the lawyer screaming. Eric has explained to Nathalie that they have to kill Antoine because he could work out that she was an accomplice, and she knows that he is being murdered, but she will not open the door and look into the room where the event is taking place. She sits immobile, letting the insistent beat and tone of the music drug her. Within a few moments, she is able to converse with Eric about cigarettes when he asks her for one, as if nothing was going on. When Eric and Bruno come out of the room to say that they have finished Jousse off, the music seems to have taken Nathalie far enough away for her to accept the event passively.

The next scene brings the terrible truth: on the drive home after this first murder, Nathalie expresses surprise at the comment that Jousse wore a wig, her readiness to lapse back into her predictable preoccupation with image confirming her inability to grasp the enormity of the man's death. With her reaction comes the sombre, staccato violin chords which are Nathalie's own theme as she gazes out at trees, covered in white Christmas lights, which line the avenue they are travelling along. Nathalie's step across the terrible threshold is linked to all the mixed emotion associated with Christmas, a time when vulnerability to feelings of loneliness is heightened, and a festival whose significance as a religious symbol of hope is also being suffocated by the cynicism of commerce. Immediately afterwards, her dismay at the tiny sum of money they obtained is directed at the trouble they were put through, rather than the price paid by Antoine for their gain.

The ease with which Nathalie manages to cocoon herself from the terrible nature of their crime is followed by several examples of the three literally blocking out their own guilt with the images that feed their illusions. The sound from a music video playing on the second victim Alain's own giant video projector is enough to protect Nathalie's sensibilities from his cries while Eric and Bruno are torturing him, and when Bruno insists that it is Eric's turn to do the killing this time, he too deliberately turns up the volume on the video-projector to drown out his screams. The three also seek out clubs straight after committing their crimes, in order to lose themselves in dance music and conversations about obtaining wealth and jokes about rich people.

The impression created in *L'Appât* is that Nathalie, Bruno and Eric are desperately seeking to fill their lives with material pleasures as a consolation for their inner emptiness, exemplified by Nathalie sitting alone at night in a darkened kitchen, spooning Nutella into her mouth like some medicine which will dull the pain of her feelings of rejection resulting from Eric's angry disappointment in her, and her own disappointment with the level of attention she receives from her parents. Nathalie may be the bait of the title, but so equally is the seductive culture of instant gratification which engulfs her and her generation, having succeeded in slowly building up her childish greed into a full addiction over the years, encroaching almost unnoticed, like the creeping red lines of the film's opening graphics, which close in like the bars of a cage to form the main title.

Themes relating to night, darkness, loneliness and fears exist throughout Tavernier's work, from the night train which leads us past a burning car at the start of *L'Horloger de Saint-Paul*, to the nocturnal traumas and doubts that grip Philippe d'Orléans (*Que la Fête Commence...*), Sergeant Bouvier (*Le Juge et l'Assassin*), Katherine Mortenhoe (*Death Watch*), Laurence Cuers (*Une Semaine de Vacances*), Dale Turner (*'Round Midnight*) and Commandant Dellaplane (*La Vie et Rien d'Autre*). *L'Appât* is Tavernier's most nightmarish film: in it the darkness of night dominates the lives of the main characters more than in even *Coup de Torchon* or *La Passion Béatrice*. When daytime comes, it never seems able to lift their spirits, bringing only transitory sensation with no sense of engagement with the present, all thought taken up with looking ahead or planning the events of the next night. They are in a permanent state of dissatisfied anticipation, never living, just waiting, like Nathalie sitting outside the room where Jousse is being killed, shutting out the present and hopeful only for the future. She has neither enthusiasm for nor commitment to her job, and lives for the night when she can stalk the clubs. Eric and Bruno are unemployed, and their lives are spent largely indoors watching television and videotapes, day barely distinguishable from night. They plan their robberies at night and in the darkness of their basement, are forever hanging around in the dark in their car for Nathalie to arrive with their prey, and when they commit the crimes even their victims' apartments are dimly lit. The light generated by the video-screen is stronger than the lamps in Alain's apartment, bathing Bruno and Nathalie in the projected video images as he loses his temper and shakes her for accusing him of lying about his disadvantaged past. When Nathalie comforts herself in her mother's kitchen at night, her sister comes in afraid of the dark because of the 'beast under the bed', just as Laurence tells Anne about the nightmare in *Une Semaine de Vacances*. Eric welcomes the darkness, knowing that it will hide the blood-stains on Bruno's jeans when they go to Niels club after the first murder in order to have an alibi. The day has no sense of beginning, being just an echo of the previous night, bringing Nathalie the cold reality of Bruno's blood-stained jeans lying soaking in the bidet.

As well as failing to drive away the spectre of night, the little daytime in *L'Appât* is additionally stifling because its landscape brings no respite from the film's physically oppressive, claustrophobic atmosphere. The first time we see them together, Nathalie complains about having to share space with Bruno, and the three spend their lives constantly shut inside: bedrooms, basements, bars, garages, telephone boxes and cars. The image of nearby closed doors hangs heavy on the iconic image of Nathalie with her earphones. On one very rare occasion when we see them in the streets during the day, when we first see Eric going to visit Nathalie's place of work, the street is crowded with the activities of low-grade commerce being set up for the day, with no view of the horizon and no sense of space. The shop where Nathalie works is a typical low-quality, high-turnover outlet with little space between the crowed racks of badly displayed clothes, where commercial pressure literally takes over every available space in order to cram in the stock and shift as much as possible. The cramped interiors and absence of exterior space combine with all the closed doors of *L'Appât* to express the sense in which the three are themselves shut out from life, without any meaningful relationship with the wider world. The film's heavy sadness is directed mainly at the awful sense that none of them is even searching beyond the narrow confines of their existence. Nothing between one place and another matters – they are only engaged with the sterile ambition of filling up the interiors they inhabit and a few vague dreams, like Nathalie's suggestion that she might like to be an actress, or maybe a singer. It hardly matters which, uninterested as she is in the nature of the work itself, seeking only the trappings.

Forever waiting for life to get better – Nathalie sits in the hall outside the lawyer Jousse's living-room, about to scramble for her earphones.

Nathalie, Bruno and Eric share a fundamental impatience at the root of their volatile natures, and the constant hurry they are in motivates the forceful camera movements that switch from the static frames of the three in attendance to reactive pans, expressing impatience more aggressively than the urgency projected in *L.627*. The frame's impulsive, second-guessing coverage of the protagonists' actions, executed by Alain Choquart, addressed Tavernier's specific request to marry the expressive quality of camera movement to their personae, rather than using it to dynamically heighten action and physical violence. Tavernier also pressed Choquart into following principles directed at avoiding audience superiority:

> Don't judge the characters. Neither gaze at them like strange animals, insects that we dissect, from afar. Avoid the detached report just as much as the thesis or the explanation. Flee condescension like the plague. Never be superior to them. Think that they could resemble us. And also that they are trapped. Just as their victims are. A few films which avoid these traps: *Badlands* [Terence Malick, 1976],[5] *Honeymoon Killers* [Leonard Kastle, 1970], *Thieves Like Us* by [Robert] Altman [1973]. There is a reference film-maker for you, as is [John] Cassavetes. Altman knows how to show maladjusted, even stupid characters, whilst avoiding sniggering, better than anyone.[6]

Tavernier's determination to refrain from adopting positions of judgement in the *L'Appât* is behind the film's consistent frame, which favours moving with the characters, cutting back out only when necessary so as to avoid dispassionate distance. At this level, Tavernier's attitude to Bruno, Nathalie and Eric is similar to his treatment of the police in *L.627*, parallel to his dogged fidelity to Lulu's situation, and rejection of the drug dealers' point of view. *L'Appât* stays close to its doomed protagonists, including only one short scene of police investigation towards the very end of the film, rejecting the drama of the chase.

Nathalie's arrest comes without any build-up of tension, its lack of drama matching her own inability to contemplate the terrible nature of what she has been involved in. Any question about whether or not she and her friends will be caught faded long before anyway, its certainty ensured by their failure to make the connection between events, and therefore to recognise others' ability to do so. Nathalie's obsession with image was bound to catch up with her, and the arresting officers are first seen framed in one of the shop's dressing mirrors. *L'Appât* comes to a close with a last desperate attempt to force Nathalie to face her actions, the film's most powerful moral voice coming from the furiously insistent detective in charge of the interrogation: she must stop blocking out the reality of her complicity in the murders. Outraged by her denials in the face of a deluge of incriminating evidence, the young detective grabs Nathalie and shakes her, insisting that she look him in the eyes while he describes to her the appalling reality of the deaths of Antoine and Alain, inviting her to look at photos of the tortured bodies he had inside a brown envelope.[7]

Having refused to have Choquart's camera stare in close-up at the men's worst state of fear and pain, Tavernier places his trust in the ability of the emotional conviction of Philippe Torreton's performance[8] to ensure that outrage at the shocking brutality of what was done to Antoine and Alain is expressed properly, being integral to the film's tragedy. Torreton's portrayal of the detective, racked with fury at the fate of the victims while remaining concerned for the naïve girl in front of him, lets the film's emotional moral voice burst forth, like a release. Nathalie realises enough to confess, but not yet enough to change. She cannot stop herself from asking if the pen which the detective hands her to sign her confessions with is a Mont Blanc, and the last thing she asks is if, now that she has told him everything, will she be allowed to go home by Christmas, barely having been relieved of the stolen jewellery which Alain had wrapped and placed below the Christmas tree for his family. The only glimmer of hope at the end of *L'Appât* – and it is a tiny one – comes from the discomfort which Nathalie shows in response to the silence with which the detective meets her question. Possibly she has the potential to understand, to learn, but nothing is certain.

NOTES ON CHAPTER 19

1. Interview in press release notes to *L'Appât*, Little Bear, 1995 (interviewer anonymous).
2. Ibid.
3. Ibid.
4. According to producer Frédéric Bourboulon, this was a comment that he had overheard in a video store with Tavernier which they could not resist using.
5. In terms of atmosphere, *Badlands* and *L'Appât* might hardly seem further apart, in terms of their protagonists' sheer naivety and utter failure to deal with reality: it can be noted that Nathalie, Eric and Bruno are in fact very similar to Holly and Kit.
6. Notes from Bertrand Tavernier to Alain Choquart for the shooting of *L'Appât*, reproduced in press release notes to *L'Appât*, op. cit.
7. The detective who made Valéria Subra 'crack', played by Philippe Torreton, was the only person involved in the case whom Tavernier met personally. The detective did challenge Subra to confront photos of her victims, but bluffing – the envelope he offered her was empty.
8. Frédéric Bourboulon recalled that Tavernier was especially interested in seeing Torreton's portrayal of violent anger, already having the actor's commitment to play *Capitaine Conan* in his next film.

CHAPTER 20

CAPITAINE CONAN (1996)

When Tavernier completed *La Vie et Rien d'Autre* in 1989, he intended it to form the first part of a trilogy dealing with the aftermath of the First World War and its impact on those who fought in it, or were close to those who had. Pleased with the experience and results of his collaboration with Jean Cosmos, Tavernier asked his screen-writer if he had any other projects which they might work on together, and by then Cosmos knew very well the great importance the First World War in the director's mind, as a defining event of the twentieth century:

'The climate of the 1914–1918 war was something which haunted Bertrand; this conflict which people were beginning to forget, and which had been pushed into the background by another one. He is really searching for his personal memory, but also – and very much so – the collective memory.'

Cosmos told Tavernier that he did have an adaptation of *Capitaine Conan* (*Captain Conan*), the prize-winning novel by Roger Vercel which was well known in France. The book, awarded the prestigious French literary Prix Goncourt in 1934, is set during the conflict which dragged on in the Balkans for over a year after the general armistice of 11 November 1918. Cosmos's original adaptation was intended for television, eventually drafted as a six-part series, but the project ultimately languished at the production development stage. Tavernier had read Vercel's book decades earlier, and was immediately interested in tackling the work, remembering several aspects of the anti-war novel which were of great interest to him. He sensed that had it been made a couple of decades earlier, his own *La Vie et Rien d'Autre* might well have suffered the same fate as *Paths of Glory* (Stanley Kubrick, 1959), which was banned in France until the 1970s for its exposure of an uncomfortable chapter in French military history. A great admirer of Kubrick's indignantly anti-militaristic film, set in 1916, which depicted a shameful incident of exemplary court-martials and executions for cowardice, Tavernier was equally interested in some of its main themes. *Capitaine Conan* similarly examines the contrasting points of view and lives experienced by the various classes of soldier caught up in war, from the aristocratic career generals to the worker-conscripts who fought and died in the squalor and carnage of the trenches and battlefields, but Tavernier's main interest in the novel was Vercel's tragic evocation of the sheer brutalising impact of war on those condemned to fight and kill, and the long-lasting emotional and spiritual problems facing those who survive beyond the establishing of 'peace'.

Tavernier's wish to document the testimonies of the French conscripts of the Algerian war in *La Guerre Sans Nom* was driven by his sense of terrible injustice at the plight of the men and their families who had been suffering in silence for decades. Conveniently buried away and forgotten by French official history, left to struggle alone with their bottled-up memories in homes, offices, factories and farms all over France, their situation represents the vital link between *La Guerre Sans Nom* and *Capitaine Conan*. Despite their contrasts of form and historical setting, the shared emotional and moral concerns of the two films render them inseparable in creative terms, at least as close in motivation and feeling as any of Tavernier's thematically-connected dramas. Both works' sympathies lie with soldiers who are repaid for their sacrifices by being forgotten, in the case of Conan and his comrades, before their return home. Tavernier and Cosmos worked for nearly five years, going through ten different drafts of *Capitaine Conan* in the process of turning the six-hour television adaptation into a two-hour screenplay, dispensing with Vercel's device of first-person narration by Norbert, the central character invested with the work's authorial voice. Norbert is a young, educated officer who admires and sympathises with Conan, but violently opposes his warrior philosophies at the same time. Philippe Torreton was playing the energetic and impatient squad member 'Looping' in *L.627* for Tavernier in 1992 when the director asked if he would play Conan, and it was in October 1995 that shooting for the film finally got underway in Romania, the largest-scale project of Tavernier's career to date.

From the outset, the production was fraught with enormous practical difficulties, and the experience of shooting the film in the dreadfully impoverished post-Ceaucesceau Romania accenuated Tavernier's natural doubts, to the point where he began to question not only the film but the very meaning of his work as a director. The repeated failure of promised crucial production requirements to materialise properly obliged him repeatedly to contact Cosmos to discuss short last-minute rewrites and scene additions, and on one occasion, at his lowest ebb, he admitted to Cosmos that he was contemplating aborting the entire project. Tavernier directed the gruelling twelve-week shoot in winter under a constant threat of failure which seemed truly tangible this time, and the completion of *Capitaine Conan* stretched both the dedication and skill of his beleaguered production team to their limits. The end result is probably Tavernier's most potent synergy of visual and aural expression, as if his own and his crew's determination to overcome their problems had somehow reinforced their singular grasp of a truly drama-centred goal, the basic challenge facing any film *auteur* with a creative team. Tavernier and his editor Luce Grunenwaldt (who also edited *La Guerre Sans Nom*) shaped their gathered elements of cinematography, performance, sound, music and art direction into a sensual portrait of constantly shifting internal and external conflicts, laden with an atmosphere swaying between fear, frustration, incomprehension and despair.

The film begins in September 1918, with Conan's regiment of the French Armée d'Orient embroiled in the battle of Dobropolje, then undertaking their final assault on Mount Skopol, backed by the British and the Serbs in the last definitive battles of the Great War. The army's success leads to the capitulation of the Bulgars, precipitating the armistice signed in Rethondes, but the agreement to lay down arms leaves Conan's regiment forgotten by the official peace, the only French soldiers not demobilised. Forced to remain in place as a military presence intended to form the guard against the feared spread of the Russian Revolution, Conan and his men are transported to the capital of their Romanian allies, Bucharest. Stranded in a lycée commandeered as a makeshift billet, in a state of fear and doubt, neither at war nor at peace, Conan's men soon slide into violence again, having become, literally, trained killers. In the absence of an immediate enemy, it is the local people they are meant to protect who pay a dreadful price for their disorderly brutality, the consequences of which splinter the fragile relationships between Conan and the only two officers he has any respect for: Lieutenant Norbert (Samuel Le Bihan) and Lieutenant De Scève (Bernard Le Coq).

The film's moral point of view is expressed via the complicated sympathies and disagreements between these three very different characters. Conan is a conscript, a brave and immensely clever fighter who considers himself a 'warrior' rather than a 'soldier', referring to the

Courage, but with eyes open – Conan assesses the risks ahead around Mount Skopol.

career military brass whom he despises almost without exception, both for their sheer stupidity and for their lack of any true sense of justice or morality. De Scève is the only officer of that tradition whom Conan respects, he being a Viscount who follows the traditions of his lineage with a military career, but voluntarily rejects the privileged position of cavalry officer that befits his rank in order to join the infantry. Nevertheless, De Scève's view of the world and the men around him is strictly bound by his traditionalist, aristocratic concepts of honour and class. Norbert is, like Conan, another conscript, but from a completely different background, a well-educated man of letters whose republican allegiance puts him at odds with De Scève, but whom Conan respects for his integrity and strong sense of right and wrong. In turn, Norbert lives in high admiration of Conan's total and apparently fearless dedication, fascinated by the ordinary Breton craftsman's single-minded commitment and personal sense of fairness, whilst not sharing or always approving of his ruthless approach.

The impression of an internal struggle to know the right way to act, in the face of impossible situations, is channelled mainly through the stormy development of the central relationship between Conan and Norbert, who start out as friends but come into conflict when Norbert is cajoled and coerced into serving in the regiment's court martials, first as a defence advocate, then as prosecutor. Their relationship deteriorates until they become violently opposed enemies when Norbert agrees to prosecute some of Conan's men who have killed and maimed two women during a masked robbery of a town café. Whilst at the lowest point in their relationship Conan feels hatred for Norbert and makes violent threats towards him, their friendship is never really destroyed, and communication never breaks off completely as they continue to argue over each other's stance, as if simply sharing their passionately opposed beliefs mattered. Eventually, after pleading successfully for the lives of Conan's convicted men, Norbert is charged with the task of prosecuting Erlane, a terrified young conscript who strayed behind Bulgarian lines while carrying despatch orders. Despite his official position, Norbert finds himself on the same side as Conan again, as they search together for a way of preventing the pitiful Erlane from being executed for letting intelligence reach enemy hands.

Vercel's novel was intended to express his profound horror of war and the extent to which the brutality of conflict is capable of poisoning the spirit of an ordinary man like Conan, and Tavernier's desire to convey Vercel's message with integrity resulted in his creation of his most violent film to date, by far. The cancerous nature of the violence created and nurtured inside men by the proponents of war is the central theme which shapes the film's outraged viewpoint, but the obvious logic behind the sheer volume and explicit severity of the violence in *Capitaine Conan* does not remove the surprise of Tavernier's willingness – not present in previous films – to portray maiming, torture and killing with remarkable frankness. Tavernier still refuses to have his camera gaze in close-up at the visceral signs of human pain, but the shockingly primal nature of the fighting is important to the integrity of his anti-war sentiments. During the fierce battlefield scenes which show Conan and his men on the attack, Tavernier's emphasis is not on the horror of anonymous killing – men mown down by the machine-guns of an unseen enemy – but on the appalling reality of the vicious hand-to-hand combat that was an inherent feature of the theatre of war portrayed. Without resorting to gut-wrenching special effects, the film depicts the savagery of fighting at close quarters, in which enemies are killed with a bayonet in the stomach, a knife in the throat, or by having their head smashed repeatedly against a stone wall.

The fact that ordinary men, who might never normally have hurt another person, could be made to behave with such ferocity is important to Tavernier's film, but showing the especially extreme evils of hand-to-hand combat is not the point he makes. On the contrary, the film's concern with the question of individual responsibility rejects any such judgement, and an exactly opposite view is taken by Conan himself. Conan has utter contempt for the abilities and performance of his professional soldier superiors, and at the same time despises their working methods. He displays a pragmatic approach to the violence he commits, admitting to Norbert that his men deliberately cut enemy throats in order to generate maximum fear in their surviving comrades and encourage their surrender. He contrasts the willingness of himself and his men to go to the limits of physical violence with what he regards as the weakness and moral cowardice of those who rattle off machine guns from a distance. Conan's thoughts recall the words of conscript Jacques Bec in *La Guerre Sans Nom* about his involvement in the violence in Algeria: 'It is politicians who make people fight in wars. If they don't want atrocities, they shouldn't make wars'.[1] Conan and his band have to be close enough to look into their enemies' eyes in order to kill them, and he has more respect for his enemies as human beings, in spite of his brutal determination to destroy them in order to survive and win.

Alongside the film's loathing of war lies Tavernier's refusal to simply condemn Conan's attitude towards violence. One of the emblematic images of the film comes during the last battle: Conan careering frantically down grassy slopes at the head of the group of reinforcements he has liberated from the regiment stockade; like a band of street fighters, clutching hastily gathered small arms as they race to save their comrades from the surprise river attack launched by the Russian army. 'Anti-hero' is a fair term for Conan, whose human morality is as confused as any of Tavernier's other most troubled protagonists. He is genuinely heroic in his brave commitment to his men and the goals he has been set, and challenges the folly of his superiors by avoiding any suicidal manoeuvres which he knows cannot succeed anyway, but he is also the stubborn soldier who defends his own blindly, including his comrade who killed a café cashier for money by smashing her head down on a desk, one of the most shocking moments of the film. However, too tied to the individualist doctrine prevalent in American cinema, and which Tavernier has sought to avoid since *La Vie et Rien d'Autre*, the 'anti-hero' label fails to convey the importance of the fact that thousands of men like Conan share his desperate plight. Conan can be admired for his heroic conduct, but the bravery of his actions does not alter the fact that he has been forcibly dragged into playing his own part within a gigantic evil over which he has no control, and from which he will emerge with absolutely no prospect of success.

In the diary he kept intermittently during shooting, Tavernier wrote that he derived his formal inspiration for the emotional feeling of *Capitaine Conan* from *The Battle of Saint Pietro*[2] (John Huston, 1945), drawing parallels between that work and the overall philosophy he

Blind loyalty – Conan threatens Norbert if he crosses him by prosecuting his comrades.

adopted, and indicating its influence on his approach to the film's battle scenes:

> I want small, discontinuous actions that come to nothing. We must never get the impression that the soldiers reach any goal, that they are caught up in some vital situation. That forbids us from using certain framing, certain camera moves [reverse tracks].[3] We must never precede the soldiers, just stay with them. We have to avoid imposing a unique point of view, whether it be that of the hero or of the director. Replace that with a kind of collective point of view, which avoids any individualist vision.[4]

Tavernier did end up using some hand-held and Steadicam reverse tracking shots, similar to those which proved indispensable for the conversations held while walking along the trenches in Kubrick's *Paths of Glory*. Tavernier sacrificed this detail of principle in order to support his primary consideration of mise-en-scène, which was to have the camera follow the actions of his characters in movement as much as possible. After the title sequence of flames in darkness tinted with the sound of a Romanian lament sung by a solitary young woman, the action begins with a long travelling shot:[5]

> Close-up – an officer writing a personal letter. An explosion is heard. Dirt falling. The camera follows the soldier as he puts down his pen and walks out of the candle-lit bunker and along the trenches to play down the event and reassure his men that the small explosion does not signal a serious attack, and is nothing to worry about. Suddenly, he turns around as a group of men start to drop down into the trenches from the darkness above.

Their bereted leader speaks, boasting about the silence and efficiency of his commandos, discusses tactics, then heads back out into the night again with his men.

The brusque, confident young lieutenant was Conan, and the undramatised, anonymous nature of his arrival is followed up by the film's avoidance of any tightly composed visual dramatisation of the central character. Tavernier needed the power and determination of Conan's persona to be expressed directly through Philippe Torreton's performance, allowing him to concentrate his mise-en-scène on emphasising the image of a man who is defined by the world he inhabits and who is in own mind, above all, accountable to those close to him. The 1:2.35 frame which Tavernier adopted once more is essential to his desire for a collective viewpoint in the film, shaping images which always favour the impression of individuals as members of groups, whether they be in alliance or in opposition, as with *La Vie et Rien d'Autre*. The emphasis on collective tragedy is served also by Tavernier's formal concern with the notion of an integrity of viewpoint. In the same way that the police are excluded from the most part of *L'Appât*, *Capitaine Conan* does not contain any shots which show the enemy's point of view. Tavernier considered his rejection of shots which serve only to create dramatic tension and intrigue as essential to the film's empathetic principle, with precisely the same regard for the integrity of cinematic viewpoint which found him in admiration of *The Thin Red Line* (Terence Malick, 1999) and slightly critical of *Saving Private Ryan* (Steven Spielberg, 1998), in their approach to battle scenes.

Tavernier's own approach aimed specifically first to introduce the physical nature of the theatre of war Conan's men inhabit, then remain close to the soldiers at all times. The hand-held and Steadicam forward and lateral tracking shots reflect the anonymous viewpoint of an integrated and ordinary soldier in their midst. Tavernier has often avoided using wide establishing shots – as he has avoided – so many systematic conventions – but he wanted the imposing presence of Mount Skopol – steep, arid slopes spiked with steel-grey boulders and stone outcrops – to symbolise the unyielding cruelty of the troops' existence, and to enhance the sense of men removed from the rest of the world through the sight of landscapes which contrast dramatically with all the familiar emblematic images of mud and trenches and flat fields.

Capitaine Conan was the fourth of Tavernier's films to be shot by Alain Choquart, and the director's desire to integrate the camera with the soldiers' experience, and the soldiers with their environment, placed huge demands on Choquart, the complexities of the wide frame compounded by the intricacy of the scenes of carnage and Tavernier's adherence to his style, which resists fragmentation of the internal rhythm of motion within the frame and performance. Reflecting the fate of the regiment, the camera is constantly on the move. The scenes of assault on the hills are laced with rapidly panning shots of the details that build up a human disaster, piece by piece, but with no time to stop and help, never mind gaze. Tavernier's interest in the metaphysical context of the drama and his dislike of conventional cover[6] and the trickery of ultra-rapid cutting for action sequences inevitably resulted in Choquart having to frame extremely complex foreground and background mise-en-scène, often on the move. Pushed to his limits by the urgency of the circumstances of shooting, Choquart achieved Steadicam images for Tavernier which are crucial to the emotional quality of the violent chaos of the hillside assaults, riddled with point-of-view glances that create the nervous atmosphere of panic and incomprehension. Movement itself increases the sense of tragedy unfolding, as we see a large group of soldiers standing still, being administered with a general absolution[7] by their padre in a rare moment of pause, while the moving frame opens up, sickeningly, to reveal the threatening slopes behind them and troops already heading towards their inevitable task. Perpetual movement is what characterises the men's nightmare, most forcefully lamented when Oswald d'Andreá's music theme of fearful warning from *La Vie et Rien d'Autre* is reprised for the melancholy images of the regiment boarding the train to be taken to Bucharest, marrying the films' respective concerns with the living and the dead.

The tragedy for Conan himself is that while his furious bravery keeps him alive, the same violent preoccupations of his army life distract him from sensing the death of his natural humanity until it is too late. When Norbert visits Conan years later, he finds a broken man, facing an early death precipitated by his alcoholism. Conan is hardly able to face the friend whose visit both moves and pains him. While he explains the state his life has reached, he faces out of a grilled, prison-like window, standing on the edge of an empty frame with nothing behind him but darkness. When Conan finally reaches the end of the conflict he is promoted to captain and laden with military decorations. In the end, his medals are all he has to leave Norbert, the legacy of his redundant training as a ruthless combatant being inner emptiness and a destroyed self-esteem. Although the terrible war has long since passed, Conan is incapable of shaking off his inbuilt concern for his own men. 'Take a good look,' he urges Norbert, referring to all the other ex-'commandos' that he knows, 'They are all just like me'.

NOTES ON CHAPTER 20

1 It must be noted here that Jacques Bec's words were made in the context of what is probably the most extraordinarily candid interview of *La Guerre Sans Nom*, during which he relates his actions and motives for sanctioning violence against captured enemy soldiers. As he talks in detail about events and his involvement in them, the similarity to Conan's feelings is extremely striking, far more than may be conveyed briefly here.
2 John Huston's documentary short covered a battle in which approximately 1100 American soldiers died while taking the town of San Pietro from the Germans, in order to clear a path for the Allied invasion of Italy.
3 A reverse tracking-shot is one in which the camera moves in reverse at the same pace as the subject(s) walking towards it. (Not to be confused with 'tracking-out' which means pulling back from a basically static subject). The technique is typically used to maintain the framing of moving conversation scenes, allowing a clear view of the characters' faces. Strictly speaking it refers to a set-up in which the camera is actually on tracks, but is sometimes applied loosely to Steadicam or even hand-held camera work.
4 Bertrand Tavernier production diary for *Capitaine Conan*, reproduced from press release notes for *Capitaine Conan*, Little Bear/France-Inter, 1996.
5 General term for a relatively lengthy take, in which the camera is in motion, usually following a moving subject.
6 The term 'conventional cover' refers to a formulaic way of constructing scenes: establishing the scene in wide/long shot, then moving in closer to medium shots and close-ups for the dramatic climax, perhaps even coming out to a wide shot again for closure.
7 The general absolution (from sins) is administered to Catholic troops during wartime during moments of collective and immediate danger.

CHAPTER 21

ÇA COMMENCE AUJOURD'HUI (1999)

Black screen. Sound: A teacher getting a class settled for activity.

Fade up: A young teacher, Daniel Lefèvre, sits facing his class of three- and four-year-olds who sit in a loose semi-circle, and he starts to lead them in chanting a nursery rhyme:

There was a little man, pirouette, peanut!
There was a little man
Who had a funny kind of house,
Who had a funny kind of house!

Cut to: Daniel's point of view, through a window. Early morning. A fragile, old woman, wearing her dressing gown, steps outside of her house, carrying a pail of smouldering cinders and empties them outside.

Daniel (voice-over): The length of a story is like the length of a dream. We don't choose the moment we fall asleep, nor the moment when we wake up. And yet we advance, we pass by.

The 'little man' of the classic nursery rhyme is an echo from the childhood experience of millions of people throughout France, and it is the teacher Daniel Lefèvre's status as a 'little man' which interested Tavernier most, persuading the director to place him at the centre of his seventeenth full-length drama. With *Ça Commence Aujourd'hui* (*It All Starts Today*), Tavernier created another intimate study set in contemporary France, with the hope of offering some insight into the real human drama created by the burden of problems facing society's small 'insignificant' players. In this sense, the subject of the film seems to prove that Tavernier's focus has remained unchanged, reminiscent of his first concern for the sudden plight of an almost anonymous watchmaker, quietly pursuing his craft in a back street of old Lyon; but in other respects the two films seem worlds apart. *Ça Commence Aujourd'hui* is another passionate reinforcement of Tavernier's political concern with the society he was born into, a factor which was already clearly explicit in *L'Horloger de Saint-Paul*, and therefore coming as little surprise, at least in terms of its subject matter. The film's most striking significance within his body of work is arguably its rich embodiment of the cinematic 'emotion through movement', the element which was also apparent in his first feature but which marks the later part of his creative journey especially.

The film with the most obvious connection with *Ça Commence Aujourd'hui* within Tavernier's own work in terms of script construction and characterisation is *L.627*, largely due to the parallel circumstances of the films' conception. In the same way that Michel Alexandre's first-hand description of his police work prompted Tavernier's desire to take his situation to a wide audience by making *L.627*, the story centred around Daniel stemmed from a dinner conversation with the film's co-scriptwriter Dominique Sampiero, who had been introduced to the director by Tiffany Tavernier. Like the character Daniel, Sampiero was both teacher and headmaster in an *école maternelle* (infant school), and was also a writer, in the habit of expressing his emotions through poetry. Tiffany recalled the detail which seemed to spark off her father's anger and make him determined to create a film that would help project the reality of a shameful situation that existed in his country: Sampiero's story about a mother who had explained to him that she did not have the 30 francs due quarterly to the school to help pay for special treats, because 30 francs was all that she and her four children had to survive on for the coming week. The story went into the film exactly as Sampiero remembered it, as a scene between Mme Bry and Daniel.

Tavernier asked Sampiero if he would like to write him a script based on his professional experiences, and the writer, who had never written for the screen before, agreed to do so, with Tiffany's assistance. By the end, the two had produced hundreds of pages of script, consisting of plotted-out scenario, anecdotes resulting from hours of interviews with the local population of the area where Sampiero worked, and his poetic writing, with all the main plot described in the first person by Daniel, a style which Sampiero felt assisted him in retaining the authenticity of emotion born out of his own experience as a teacher. At that stage, Tavernier sat down with the two and began shaping the mass of material into a two-hour screenplay. He had concerns about certain aspects of the script, especially the important use of Daniel's poetic expression in a series of voice-overs which mark the film's narrative

'There was once a little man...' – Daniel Lefèvre soaks up his small triumph that brings a ray of light into a community burdened by relentless problems and endemic poverty.

development. He was worried about combining what he regarded as two very different but very lyrical art-forms, fearing a mismatch of emotional styles, but in the end he was convinced that it was right to retain 'Daniel's' poetry, because its basis stemmed from the personal truth of Sampiero's own written thoughts, rather than being a synthetic dramatic device. In the end, it is the contrast in tone between those sequences combining poetry and landscape images and the tough realism with which Daniel's pressured work is portrayed which takes the audience closer to the central character. The different shades of communication which Daniel employs play a very large part in defining his personality, and these contrasting sides to Daniel's character are simply a more revelatory example of Tavernier's already well-established tendency to shed light on the hidden sides of his characters' humanity. In this respect, Daniel's creative release represents a hidden characteristic which exists throughout Tavernier's work, comparable with Michel Descombes's story about rebelling against a superior officer in *L'Horloger de Saint-Paul*, Marguet's secretive need to maintain contact with Cécile in *L.627* and Mancheron's admission to Laurence Cuers that he sometimes writes poems in *Une Semaine de Vacances*. Daniel's poetry exemplifies Tavernier's personal attitude towards every character who exists in his films: there is more to them than meets the eye.

The film's embrace of dream-like literary expression is combined with a very strong impression of the documentary: Tavernier's camera seems to see and just manage to catch seemingly unconstructed events to a greater extent than in any of his other films. *L.627* is the closest of Tavernier's dramas to *Ça Commence Aujourd'hui*, but in its precise scope of human concern there is an ever stronger connection between Tavernier's search into the lives of the disadvantaged population of the fictional town Hernaing and his 1997 television documentary *De l'Autre Côté du Périph'* about the residents of the Grands-Pêchers housing project in Montreuil in the outer suburbs of Paris. Tavernier described Cédric, one of the 'stars' of *De l'Autre Côté du Périph'* whose monologue opens the film, as 'looking like someone who had stepped out of a film by Ken Loach', and *Ça Commence Aujourd'hui* is the clearest creative reminder of his admiration for Loach's work. His esteem for the director was already suggested when he quoted Loach's personal response to his *La Guerre Sans Nom* in the film's television introduction in Britain, and Tavernier has been a strong admirer of Loach's dedicated and realist cinema ever since discovering the socialist film-maker's provocative works.[1] It is not difficult to draw a parallel between the work of two directors who seem to be so close in their common concern with the plight of individuals who are often weighed down with the harsh pressures of uncaring mechanisms of state and society, but *Ça Commence Aujourd'hui* represents the closest creative link between them. The injustice hanging over Hernaing's cradle of poverty and rejection is certainly akin to Loach's natural film territory, to the extent that it is very easy to imagine Loach picking up the script for the film and making the film just as readily as Tavernier did. Tavernier acknowledges the link between *Ça Commence Aujourd'hui* and Loach with reference to his decision to employ a mix of professional and non-professional actors for the film, a method which Loach used naturally throughout his career.[2]

Tavernier's record of providing actors with their first screen role was already very considerable, helped sometimes by a very specific wish to avoid faces that were well-known or associated with a particular genre, as with *L.627*, but *Ça Commence Aujourd'hui* involved his most substantial reliance to date on non-professionals. The experience of spending months with the people living in Grands-Pêchers increased Tavernier's confidence in working with large groups of non-actors, whilst simultaneously fuelling his desire to find another way of giving a cinematic voice to people who were at least as disadvantaged as the unjustly maligned residents of Montreuil. His decision to include in *Ça Commence Aujourd'hui* many of the local parents, teachers and helpers from the real *école maternelle* in Anzin, the film's central location, was little different from the decision to cast Dexter Gordon in *'Round Midnight*, instead of seeking a film actor. In both cases, justification is directly related to a need for physical and emotional authenticity.

Tavernier shares Loach's belief that there is no fundamental difference between directing professional actors and non-professional actors, and in this instance their inclusion was crucial to Tavernier's ideal of reflecting reality. The large numbers of Anzin's residents with small or walk-on parts ensured a substantial degree of visual and aural authenticity for the film's canvas, whilst at the same time integrating the creative process into the world of its subject as a way of strengthening its contact with reality. Tavernier never normally uses a casting director, insisting on casting even small roles personally, but in this instance decided to hand the task of casting many locals in minor roles to Tiffany,[3] in recognition of her involvement in the film's conception. It is often hard to distinguish between the professional actors and the 'acting residents' in *Ça Commence Aujourd'hui*, even in some scenes involving small but nevertheless crucial roles demanding great emotional intensity: examples are the stifled bitterness of the admission of Mme Bry (Nathalie Desprez) to Daniel over the 30 francs, and the shocking clash of anger and resignation expressed by Mme Féron (Sylvie Delbauffe) when she is confronted by Samia (Nadia Kaci) over her failure to care for her own baby.

Another critical factor which allowed Tavernier to breathe life into the fictional lives of Daniel (Philippe Torreton), his friends and colleagues was his decision not to individually select the children making up Daniel's class, instead casting a pre-existing class in its entirety. Daniel's class were aware that they were making a film, but their role certainly did not require any acting in the usual sense, except for one or two of them, like those who played Mme Henry's shy daughter Laetitia (Kelly Mercier) and Mme Gosset's battered son Jimmy (Matthieu Lenne). Reliance on the children's more natural behaviour, plus the large amount of sustained action which is set during Daniel's class time determined that Torreton had to become in effect a kindergarten teacher in a very real sense, with minimal pretence in his relationships with the class, whilst simultaneously playing out the gradual shredding of his invented character's energy and determination, as Daniel is crushed by the barrage of external attacks on his work and his integrity. The genuine nature of the dialogue between teacher and class helps create the film's impression of spontaneous reality, a dramatic necessity which is at the same time a benefit and an example of Tavernier's often-voiced search for 'a freer style' of film-making.

Inevitably, the presence of such young children in the film placed practical constraints on the production, including the greater necessity for rest breaks, a limit on the working day, and the need to keep shooting sessions short, with as few takes[4] as reasonably possible under simpler lighting set-ups. The high degree of flexibility required of the filming schedule made *Ça Commence Aujourd'hui* a demanding shoot, but the overall need to work quickly posed no problem for Tavernier, suiting his preferred working method, which is to use the maximum available time for preparation, then shoot rapidly. The need for flexibility also illustrated a crucial complicity between Tavernier and Alain Choquart in their primary artistic objectives, expressed in the precise nature of the director's praise for his cinematographer in connection with the film: 'He doesn't let technical considerations hold him hostage, which gave the cast the leeway they needed to feel comfortable'.[5] Choquart was already well attuned to Tavernier's dislike of framing images which appear too formally composed, and his own understanding of the drama's realistic core made him perfectly comfortable with downgrading the more technical servants of realism, such as precise lighting continuity; he concentrated instead on accommodating the often unplanned detail which came from the children in the classroom and playground.

Even leaving aside the documentary chase-and-catch visuals of the playground scenes, *Ça Commence Aujourd'hui* is shaped in dramatic terms by an extraordinarily rapid visual style constructed around the intensities of Daniel's professional life and his emotional state. Daniel works under an incessant stream of minor and serious crises, frequently forced to sacrifice his immediate attention as a class teacher in order to deal with problems brought to him as headmaster. The camera seems to be in almost constant movement, heightening the sense of pressure to hurry, and the focus of attention may never remain too long in one place. Like Daniel, the camera always reacts quickly to occurrences outside the frame or at its edge, whether innocent or troublesome, creating a sense of permanent nervousness, the point-of-view shots and over-the-shoulder shots reinforcing the film's portrait of a man constantly under siege, conditioned to expect news of trouble at any second.

The visually dynamic coverage of Daniel and his class forms one element within a wider dialogue of contrast between the different aspects of Daniel's life, emotional tensions which are supported stylistically by the cyclical alternation between the rapidly developing images and sequences depicting Daniel's chaotic life at school, and the more general stillness and slower pace of frame development when Daniel is away from his workplace. This aspect of the film's visualisation mirrors the duality in Daniel's professional and creative existence that is conveyed by his voice-over poetry. The stillness in these fixed images lends subconscious weight to a variety of emotions: a natural feeling of stability in the domestic scenes between Daniel and Valéria (Maria Pitarresi), even when there is distance between them; an uncomfortable sense of stilted communication and distance between Daniel and his brother Luc when their father is in the intensive care ward; an atmosphere of confinement and tension in the presence of the educational inspector Zeitek (Didier Bezace), who resents Daniel's challenge to authority. Stillness is essential also to the atmosphere of the images of the northern landscapes, to avoid the subjectifying tendency of panning movements, and underline instead the silent permanence of these natural symbols that serve as reminders of the personal attachment to social and geographical history that nurtures Daniel's writing.

The film's energetic camera is partly an inevitable result of the need to pursue the spontaneity of the children's natural behaviour, but it also results from the number of close-proximity images, which are unusually frequent for a director who has always been cautious of close-ups. The frequent appearance of visual closeness within the classroom mise-en-scène enhances the image of natural intimacy which is a prerequisite of Daniel's working relationship with the children, and the film's intimate regard for children singles it out from Tavernier's previous work. This is in total contrast with the long-shot views of children like the little girl in the train corridor who opens *L'Horloger de Saint-Paul* and the children in the streets who fascinate Katherine Mortenhoe and Roddy in *Death Watch* and Lucien Cordier in *Coup de Torchon*. Even in *Une Semaine de Vacances*, the children in Laurence's class tend to be set at a distance, with the exception of the painfully shy Lucie when she visits Laurence at her flat, in desperate need of close communication, to be nurtured with Laurence's reassuring advice that she needs as much of it as a new plant needs water. There is no question of Daniel withdrawing from those children who rely on him totally, sometimes even more than their parents. Nor is there time for reflection when Daniel is at school, and the combination of close-ups and moving shots that connect Daniel, the children and the contents of their classroom pushes aside detached observation in order to emphasise activity, above all.

Despite the distance from which Tavernier has tended to portray children, he has always lent dramatic weight to their presence, through their connection with his protagonists' state of mind, alongside a tendency to let their image linger on screen. During the making of *Ça Commence Aujourd'hui*, a clear impression of the near-reverence with which Tavernier seems to view young children came out when he came up against an element of Sampiero and Tiffany's scenario which troubled him far more than the integration of the poetry: the death of Laetitia and her baby brother, whom Mme Henry (Betty Teboulle) kills along with herself when the downward spiral of poverty and alcoholism finally seal her complete despair. Tavernier rejected the idea at once, refusing

Ready to throw in the towel – Valéria struggles to help Daniel after the death of Mme Henry, Laetitia and her baby brother.

to have the death of children in his film. In the end, he was persuaded that the event was crucial to the integrity of the story, as a basic recognition of the darkness that poverty is capable of creating, and he included the deaths, knowing that they would have to be shown with the emotional power that befitted the enormity of their tragedy. His treatment of the event is shaped by his grave reservations about using tragedy to milk audience emotion; it is deliberately executed with a rapidity that resists dwelling on the horror of the event. Nevertheless, it is carefully constructed to ensure that the family deaths impact on the narrative with terrible force:

> A joyful, intimate scene between Daniel and Valéria comes to a close with a picture dissolve into total disorientation – the rigid pattern of a brick wall seen in close-up, tracking left to emerge round the wall and face the sight of a decayed residential street now plunged into infamy and chaos. Too many people and vehicles. Children running as if excited about something, but something is wrong. Confusion rushes forward, deteriorating into a frame that rocks with running fear and panic, entering the open door of Madame Henry's house, past the face of a stunned-looking young gendarme. Hurrying through the house, dark with curtains closed, the camera discovers the worst – two bodies on the floor covered by a white sheet, one adult and one child, further in a smaller form draped inside a cot, a baby. An examining doctor attempts reassurance by saying that the level of drugs would have allowed little time for suffering, then it is all over.

Something close to a phobia of what he regards as emotional exploitation prevents the director of *Death Watch* from allowing his camera to pause and stare, but the lyrical tragedy of Choquart's hand-held plunge into the dreadful loss of Laetitia still generates a visual journey that is surely one of the most emotionally violent sequences of his career. Tavernier entrusted his camera operator with the task of carrying the scene's dark grief, and Choquart's stricken frame that he used to cover the scene is a classic example of the emotional painting-with-movement that is an essential element in Tavernier's cinema, albeit one of exceptional intensity.

Ça Commence Aujourd'hui frames many familiar themes: the difficulty of communicating directly across the generations; Daniel's troubled past relationship with his difficult father; a sense of anger at the absence of truth in society, viewed through the huge gap between the theorising of politicians and the imperatives for survival experienced by those 'on the ground'; the almost sacred importance of a rich education juxtaposed with a very jaded view of the motives and intelligence of educational policy-makers; a sense of deep responsibility towards children which is never far behind all other human concerns. *Ça Commence Aujourd'hui* also continues the powerful sense of urgency which increased markedly with *La Vie et Rien d'Autre*, linking Daniel especially closely to Commandant Dellaplane and Lucien Marguet, who also struggle against the enormous pressure to give up their moral stance. Tavernier provides some hints at his feelings, which partly motivate his films' growing sense of urgency, culminating in the extraordinarily rapid insistence of *Ça Commence Aujourd'hui*:

> It came from a kind of bitterness with what happened with Mitterand, the hope we had in '81, then the disillusion. The fact that the Socialist government was a great help for people playing the stock exchange, but not for the working class and for all the people who were very poor. The Socialists widened the difference between the rich and the poor, and we had not elected them for that. I think it's an unconscious evolution due to a reaction of anger, disappointment, of disillusion at what's happening in my country. When hope has been disappointed, you still have anger. What can we do? I don't want to make films which are hopeless. I want to leave, even if the situation is hopeless, the impression that people are still fighting. It was also a reaction against a generation of people whom I saw, who were very political in '68, who changed five or six times – they were Right-wing, then Communists, then Maoists and now they decide to be non-political, and to destroy anybody with political values – I mean those people who were labelled by George Orwell, when he said that it's always the people who swallowed the worst line of the Stalinist period who are now saying that you should not do anything political. In papers like *Libération*[6] or *Le Monde*, I have seen attacks on Ken Loach, on my films – anything that has a social meaning.

While *Ça Commence Aujourd'hui* shows Daniel suffering a catalogue of failures, Tavernier's commitment to some spark of hope is served by the film's wealth of unassuming visual and human detail: persistent impressions of colour and light and movement, from the arrival of daylight to the dazzling sight of a playground covered with plastic bottles filled with coloured water; a well of goodwill on offer, from the kindness and generosity of local people to the neighbour who takes Mme Henry's children on cold nights when the flat is without heating; the seemingly unquenchable spirit of the children who are totally absorbed in play and in creative learning. Alongside those music themes which create an impression of constant re-growth, much as in *La Vie et Rien d'Autre,* and the sheer vitality of the film's camerawork, it is the demanding charms of the children themselves which protect Daniel from the destructive force of his worst moments, like the doubt that descends on him when faced with the bitter recriminations of a distraught mother whose child has been taken into care. *Ça Commence Aujourd'hui* displays the ambiguities of character viewpoint that are an absolute prerequisite to the director's concept of dramatic truth, and Daniel does not have all the answers, but in Tavernier's eyes he remains, without question, a hero – if nothing else for his refusal to throw in the towel.

> None of the big problems is solved. You still have people whose electricity is cut off. You still have unemployment, kids who are underfed. The money problem with Madame Bry has not been solved. Jimmy, who is beaten up – that is solved, but is it solved in the best way? You don't know. I wanted to have that kind of ambiguity. When you hear the mother – did he do the right thing? You have the impression of having done something which was totally justified, then suddenly there is doubt. For me it seems to me the only honest way to approach a subject – never give all the rights to one character. I wanted, like *L.627,* music which would give me at least two or three themes which give the impression that it never finishes, always starting again, a kind of rhythm of tango, or waltz – the waltz is always starting again. The music reflects what is the hope of the film. The light. The fight of the people. The smile in children's eyes – things like that. But the big issues are not solved. He has not received more money to do real social work. And he will always have his guilt with Madame Henry. I would say that it is a bleak film, with a few optimistic notes, one of them being that he will go on fighting – but for how long?

> The school fête. In bright sunshine, Daniel dances in circles to the music of a local brass band, holding a little girl from his class in his arms. The music recedes. A voice takes over:

> Daniel's mother: There are things they can never raze here. It is in the flesh. It speaks. It is in the earth.

Cut to: A tidy, faded room lit only by sun through drawn curtains. Daniel's infirm father lies on top of his bed, leaning back on pillows, half-listening as Daniel's mother sits beside the bed, reading from their son's poetry writings.

Piles of stones placed one by one.
By the hands of our fathers and our grandfathers.
All their patience accumulated, to resist the rain, the horizon,
Building little piles against the night
So that the moonlight could attach itself to them.
To be upright.
To invent mountains and go sledging.
To believe that we had reached the stars.
We will tell our children...

Her voice recedes, and Daniel's voice crosses through hers then takes over. He repeats her words as silent images appear and disappear: the headlights of Daniel's in the winter-blue countryside; a woman in bright red smiles down at an opening car door; another woman holds her hooded winter coat to her face; groups of people talking, waiting in the streets; another woman crosses a footbridge; Daniel talking to children in class; talking to them in the playground. Daniel's voice finally reaches his mother's last words and continues on.

Daniel: ... we will say to them that it was hard
But that they were lords, our fathers,
And this is what we inherited from them:
Piles of stones, and the courage to lift them.

Cut to: Children approach the camera, murmuring, laughing, playing. The camera pans, settles and focuses, trying to catch them. Finally, a girl who is still. The camera finds her. She looks, hesitates, then walks to the camera. Looking straight into it, she crosses through the focus point. Freeze frame. Too late. The image is already blurred. Just beyond reach.

NOTES ON CHAPTER 21

1 Ken Loach's *My Name is Joe* (1998) was given a pre-release screening at the Ciné-Rencontres Festival in Prades in July 1998, one of a small number of films which Tavernier selected to run alongside the complete retrospective of his own work. Loach's other films include *Kes* (1969), *Family Life* (1972), *Looks and Smiles* (1981), *Hidden Agenda* (1990), *Riff Raff* (1990), *Raining Stones* (1993), *Ladybird, Ladybird* (1994), *Land and Freedom* (1995), and *Carla's Song* (1996).
2 Interviewed in press release notes to *Ça Commence Aujourd'hui*, Editions Gilbert Sachalas, Paris, 1999 (interviewer anonymous).

3 Tiffany Tavernier also took over as first assistant director during later shooting on *Ça Commence Aujourd'hui* when the original first AD was taken ill. The term assistant director is something of a misnomer, since the role does not include any decision-making regarding the directing of camera, actors or any aspect of production design. It is really more of a functional role that facilitates the (sometimes complex) practicalities of preparing for and 'going for' a take. Communication of the 'state of play' in production at any given time is fundamental to the task of the first AD.

4 Fortunately, it is well known by Tavernier's crew that he does not like to do many takes – not very surprising for someone who attaches so much importance to facilitating the creation of an impression of spontaneity.

5 Interviewed in press release notes to *Ça Commence Aujourd'hui*, op. cit.

6 *Libération* is known by those around Tavernier for almost guaranteeing a disparaging review of his films. In addition to the frequent word-play that flies around on Tavernier's set is the habit of putting a parody of the film's expected dire review in *Libération* on the production's daily call-sheets. Interviewed, Frédéric Bourboulon recalled the day he informed Tavernier that *Libération* had finally printed a good review of his work (for *La Guerre Sans Nom*): after a long silence on the telephone, his director finally responded… 'We'll sue them'.

CHAPTER 22

DIRECTING

SETTING THE SCENE

When talking to creative collaborators who have worked with Tavernier, contrasting and even contradictory images of him as a director invariably come up. Primarily, one receives the strong impression of a man who has the most definite and determined convictions about what he requires and does not want when it comes to performance and framing. Alongside this, the same artists consistently stress the high degree of freedom which Tavernier affords them in constructing their part in his overall his vision. Actors talk of feeling sometimes as if they have not been directed at all. These descriptions may appear paradoxical, but only if one has an impression of film-directing as an art whose process is characterised above all by precision, or if one equates the idea of a film *auteur* with single-minded control over all the visual, aural and dramatic expression. Theoretically, film-making can amount to the director having a vision fixed in such detail that it requires the crew and cast to operate purely as technicians, but such a scenario bears little relation to the realities of film-making, and it is the antithesis of Tavernier's directing method. Tavernier's aims are often very precise, epitomised by his exacting and often lengthy attention to script development, but they are balanced against his desire to achieve the sense of realism that stems from dramatic spontaneity. He combines a determined adherence to dramatic principle regarding camera, actors and point of view with a commitment to 'freeing up' the creation of the performance and the development of character-centred narrative during shooting. The energising effect on dramatic narrative that comes partly from his tendency to avoid formal, composed, overtly constructed images is pushed even further by his conscious liberation of his actors from the constraints of both technical precision and rigid psychological pre-determination of performance. Tavernier once said of Jean Renoir, 'He was putting his collaborators in a state of mind where they were bringing him things – and that's a great way to direct'.[1] Tavernier's own method includes great emphasis on the concept of creating the right conditions and atmosphere for people to give their maximum. In return, the feeling of creative freedom which his crew enjoys comes with the expectation that they immerse themselves totally in the film during production.

Frédéric Bourboulon, Producer:

> Bertrand is a film-maker who only likes shooting either abroad or in the provinces. He loves filming in the provinces, because there you have all the crew in the hotel. The film doesn't stop in the evening. In Paris, it is terrible for him because at six o'clock everyone has something they have to do. Somebody has to go to a dinner, another has to fetch his daughter from school. People are less accessible. He needs to take everything that people have to offer and to have an availability which goes beyond actual shooting. He wants people to himself for the sake of the film – he devours everything. When he is in the provinces with his crew around, he has the impression that the film doesn't stop. There is a kind of bubble with the film inside it and nothing else – not just for him but for everybody – the actors, the technicians. While shooting he wants there to be nothing but the film. In Paris, an actor has his family, his preoccupations, his bills to pay. That's why he detests filming in Paris. *L.627* was even worse because we were in the streets and in difficult areas with problems over permission. Everyday life took too much out of the filming's pace, that he felt a lot of useful time was being taken away from him – time which could have been spent talking. It is very important for him to say even just a few words to an actor in the evening, to see them after the rushes. That's what nourishes the film. It's total. I think he is right. When we shoot, we do nothing but shoot. We put our life into parentheses. Life becomes the life of the film. Like *Capitaine Conan*, when all life's experience can be used to benefit the film.

PERFORMANCE

Whatever the wider analyses of Tavernier's work are, there has never been any question about the quality of acting performance in his films. Every one of his dramas has awarded or nominations for Césars, and have collected many major international acting accolades, and the large number of awards given to actors and actresses in his films is something of which the director is openly proud. His work is filled with central and peripheral performances that project a level of truth for which he can usually enjoy critical praise, even when everything else fails. During the period from *L'Horloger de Saint-Paul* to *Coup de Torchon*, Tavernier's name was almost inevitably linked to that of actor Philippe Noiret, whose frequent portrayal of the director's protagonists[2] made him seem as integral to the emotion of his dramas as John Wayne was to John Ford's, or Robert de Niro to Martin Scorsese's. Tavernier has claimed that he would never have got his first film off the ground had it not been for Noiret, who acknowledges that he probably helped give the budding director confidence and prevented him from becoming discouraged, knowing that Noiret, who had already established a small name for himself with producers and distributors, was completely committed to the film.[3]

There was an immediate affinity between the two when they first met, and there seemed to be no doubt in Noiret's mind how it was that Tavernier succeeded in getting him to adopt roles which he would never have imagined himself in, like the regent in *Que La Fête Commence...* and Judge Rousseau in *Le Juge et l'Assassin*: 'I am completely free with Bertrand. I can do everything I feel, and I can try anything that I think of...'[4] Noiret has no interest in working directly on the script with a director through readings and rehearsals, regarding the script as an element which should be virtually settled by the time an actor is involved;[5] and Tavernier does not require actors to become involved in the formal rehearsals which seek to mesh writing and performance. Usually insisting on casting every part in his films personally, he does not believe in getting actors to read during auditions, preferring to seek out compatability indirectly, talking to them about their interests which may well have nothing to do with the film. Tavernier's ready praise of actors who have worked with him is noticeably dominated by his tendency to talk about directing actors in terms of accommodating different methods of preparation, or styles of performance, whilst often focusing on the most sensual and non-verbal aspects of their performance: '[Isabelle Huppert] imposes herself on a film in an odd way. She is a melodic actress. She imposes on a scene an almost musical rhythm, full of silences and emotion, out of which comes a sharp, almost dangerous quality.'[6] His description of Huppert typically reveals his particular interest in actors who bring qualities that reflect the mysterious, hidden side of human nature.

Tavernier has often deliberately employed actors as part of his way of subverting the expectations of genre and preparing the ground in order to facilitate the 'surprise' which he actively seeks from performance, casting either newcomers or relative unknowns in major rôles: Gerard Lanvin in *Une Semaine de Vacances*, Marie Gillain in *L'Appât*, Philippe Torreton in *Capitaine Conan*; or casting against type: Harvey Keitel in *Death Watch*, Isabelle Huppert in *Coup de Torchon*, Jane Birkin in *Daddy Nostalgie*. In the same way that he rejected the classifying snobbery of the French audio-visual industry, choosing to work with a television writer (Jean Cosmos) on *La Vie et Rien d'Autre*, he does not accept the existence of some fundamental distinction between theatre actors and film actors. Searching for new talent, he scours the French stage as much as the screen, and has cast several important roles with actors who have come directly from La Comédie Française in Paris with little or no film experience, most notably Philippe Torreton, who started out in *L.627*, going on to play a small but pivotal role as the cop who breaks Nathalie in *L'Appât*, having already agreed to play Conan in the film Tavernier was developing with Cosmos. Torreton's performance gained the Best Actor César, and his second major role for Tavernier as the beleaguered and angry Daniel Lefèvre in *Ça Commence Aujourd'hui* places him in a position comparable with that occupied formerly by Noiret. Tavernier's repeated work with Torreton is a reflection of his shift towards an interest in younger characters and the generation below him, whilst the feeling of urgency which Torreton's presence supports can be traced back to Noiret, who ushered in the intensified tone of his more recent work, as Dellaplane in *La Vie et Rien d'Autre*. Torreton is similar to Noiret in that he seems to work with a complete absence of professional ego, and his subservience to the task of creating a character comes with an open rejection of the ego-demands of 'method'. Torreton's most recent performance as Daniel, in front of a real class of infants, stretches the notion of dramatic authenticity to its limits, but in one respect his role was subject to one of Tavernier's working methods which affects all of his central players. The director's approach, remarked on by Dirk Bogarde during the making of *Daddy Nostalgie*,[7] places the greatest demands on film actors: he works using very long takes.[8]

FRAMING

Tavernier's habit of shooting lengthy takes addresses his wish to avoid the synthetic manipulation of the rhythm of performance as far as possible. He is more interested in the idea of an internal rhythm, human-centred and created within each shot. The unfragmented performances, assisted by long takes, reduce his need to resort to artificial emotion within scenes. The other concrete aspect of his mise-en-scène which opens up performance is his general approach to framing: shooting wide. Tavernier's marked use of wide framings is an inevitable part of his interest in drama that evokes the relationship between human nature, state of mind and the physical world. His desire to produce for lyricism is reflected in his special fascination with the physical nature of performance, and he uses wider framings as a way of liberating this aspect of his actors' dramatic expression. Michel Galabru's extremely physical performance as Sergeant Bouvier in *Le Juge et l'Assassin* provides a perfect example: all his intensity and manic-depression, so unpredictably expressed through his nervous movements and manipulations of his sticks, bags, accordion and hats, would have been constricted by tighter framing, and close-ups are rarely used in the film. When Bouvier and Rousseau are walking in the prison yard while the judge questions him about his letter to the newspaper, the open framing frees up performance within the reverse tracking-shot,[9] allowing it to accommodate more natural interaction between the two as they halt then move on, making it easier to shadow movements imperceptibly, and directly facilitating spontaneity. The space within Tavernier's wide frames also favours the expression of characters' feelings through direct contact with the external world, like Lulu's frantic, scrabbling attack on the objects littering Dodo's desk in *L.627*, the accusing silence hanging around a café after Francis has walked out on Sylvie in *'Round Midnight*, or Roddy's frightened reaching for a solid surface in Tracey's kitchen when realisation first strikes in *Death Watch*.

With Tavernier, shooting wider has often meant employing the wider 'cinemascope' aspect ratio as well as keeping the camera at a relative distance from his subjects. Both factors assist the integration of his characters with the décor of his films, emphasising people within spaces. At the same time, the wider frame is able to accommodate the presence of more than one character on screen, even when shooting in fairly close proximity. Directly related to Tavernier's dislike of the emotional artifice which it is possible to construct during editing is the wider frame's ability to keep intact the true physical dynamics of character interplay when scenes involve dual or multiple performance. Its effect is to allow the visible spatial relationship between characters to operate fully as a reflection or counterpoint to their psychological or emotional distance from each other. These forms of dramatic tension are absolutely crucial to the synergy of performance that is a defining aspect in Tavernier's films – an indispensible part of a cinema in which the pain of distance is ever present. It is perfectly possible to dispense with close-ups entirely when constructing film narrative, but Tavernier is not against close-ups as such. He is wary of them: for their aggressive intrusion; for their detachment from his characters' world; for their sometimes too easy and clichéd use to produce formalised emotion. Not least, his cautious use of them is ensured by his long-standing dismay over the 'televisualisation' of cinema, specifically caused by the self-perpetuating relationship between close-ups and cutting that stifles the very art of cinematic mise-en-scène. Inevitably, the effect of having few close-ups in his work is to dramatise those that he does employ, increasing his caution further. They are frequently used when direct expression of emotion is buried by his characters, and are motivated by his desire to create the feeling of closeness between audience and character. Tavernier does not like to use close-ups in the presence of extreme vulnerability or emotional outbursts. He avoids using them to reveal physical detail, and seems incapable of applying them to inanimate objects. Compare the image of Irène Ladmiral sitting in a tavern, grasping a brief moment of intimacy with her ageing father in *Un Dimanche à la Campagne* with that of Laurence Cuers, when she bursts into tears in her bathroom, suddenly overwhelmed with emotion in *Une Semaine de Vacances*.

CAMERA, MOVEMENT AND EMOTION

Avoidance of the systematic cutting that results from shooting closer will usually increase the need for camera movement as a way of keeping the rhythm of mise-en-scène intact. Tavernier's use of wide, open frames reduces this tendency to some extent, but he has always sought to use the moving camera as an extension of the drama which shakes his characters. The type of movement especially characteristic of his drama is not the purely functional pan or track which exists simply to cover action and maintain the aesthetic viewpoint of the character-in-shot, but the movement which connects his characters' crises with the physical world: 'I want [the camera movements] to be not parallel to the action, but either ahead or behind it. They should always aim to integrate a character with the décor... I like a camera that lingers, explores, discovers.'[10] His interest in the emotional nature of the moving camera was apparent right from the beginning, with the developing shots that connected an isolated watchmaker with the hidden side of his home town, Lyon. Ever since, the visual motion of his frame, creating either supportive or antagonistic expression of his characters' relationship with their world, has been a trademark of his fascination with people who are in constant motion: 'One of the themes which touches me the most is the difficulty of putting down roots, the perpetual errance of people who cannot settle down'.[11] His travelling camera expresses the soul of his characters' emotional displacement – they are people forever searching for something which they can never quite reach, and unable to rest, as if fearful that to remain still would allow doubt to take over completely.

The camera moves in Tavernier's films do not act as a formulaic comment suggesting environment as an explanation for characters' actions. The motion relates people and spaces in ways which vary enormously according to dramatic situation, informed by elements other than camera. Tavernier's words about integrating character with surroundings were made partly in reference to *Un Dimanche à la Campagne*, which also includes many moments when the camera moves between character and place without the conventional 'motivation' of a character's action or look. Compared with the developing tension between Michel Descombes and the city which represents everything he has taken for granted, the effect in *Un Dimanche à la Campagne* is almost the reverse, showing no sense of emotional detachment from the world, and the camera-moves show the characters and their environment in tune with each other. Whether the camera leaves M Ladmiral to pick up a painting, or moves away from his conversation with his daughter to watch people dancing in the background, characters and surroundings seem married to each other. Music reinforces this bonded feeling, the pace of the camera movements combined with the tone and tempo of Fauré's score forging an emotional link between people and place.

The feeling of metaphysical harmony is fractured within the visual similarity of the scene in *L'Horloger de Saint-Paul* in which Michel gets on the bus as the soundtrack seems to develop away from him, with city sounds rising to a shrill level, breaking images further apart. Subtle changes are enough to ensure that a unique feeling is created. *Une Semaine de Vacances* also includes a scene in which music dominates the soundtrack as the camera moves away from Laurence to the view from the window outside. This time the music and camera movement are independent of each other – the music has been played over most of the scene already, and this more visible move draws much closer attention to the new image found when the camera rests, of an old woman in her living-room in the next building. Rather than bonding the images, the way that the music Laurence is playing continues on 'away' from the pace of the camera move tends to increase the sense of distance between Laurence and the old woman, despite the sadness that seems to link the characters in their lonely state.

Camera movement across Tavernier's work often displays fundamental differences in approach that form the central basis of his idea of the dramatic principle used visualise his characters' dilemmas. *Un Dimanche à la Campagne* stands out in the way that the 'exploring' camera will move from the décor onto a character as easily as the reverse, enhancing the feeling of evenness in the character-environment relationship, whereas in *Coup de Torchon* the camera moves from surroundings onto character but almost never in the opposite direction, tending to stress the impact of the moral decay of Lucien Cordier's world on his own personal corruption.

One of Tavernier's most emotional visual 'marks' is the visually arresting rapid track-in[12] from wide-shot to medium-shot, but he uses this singular device to create an array of contrasting feelings. In *'Round Midnight*, the camera move lends Dale Turner's self-appointed minder, Buttercup, a very threatening air when she first makes contact with him in Paris; There is no such imposing presentation of Roddy when he spots Katherine Mortenhoe at the church refuge in *Death Watch*, despite important similarities in situation: in both cases, Roddy and Buttercup are seen making entrances as part of missions to spy on Katherine and Dale respectively. Roddy's disturbing function as a voyeuristic 'tail' on Katherine is intensified, but has an aura of slight sadness despite his predatory role. The visual effect is more aggressive on Buttercup than Roddy because the stark nature of her expanding image is heightened by being accompanied by a sharp sound then complete silence. The move on Roddy is made gentler through the even sound of people talking quietly in the background, and in particular a softly picked guitar works against any aggressive feel, and there is no feeling of him 'swelling up' in the way Buttercup's already sizable frame seems to do.

In *La Vie et Rien d'Autre* the same move is directed to de Courtil, whose doorway appearance is strikingly similar to Buttercup's, although the effect of the developing frame in relation to the subject is to give the impression of a feeling like a sudden rush of apprehension in her as she comes in to view a shell-shocked soldier, caused by the possibility that he might be her missing husband. In this instance, the track-in is preceded by a reverse-tracking shot of her approaching along a corridor, and the changing direction of motion between the two shots has a very disorientating effect on the latter one, creating a sensual evocation of the dramatic premise of apprehension and disappointment. The dramatic impact then spills into the next image, of an unidentified soldier, a perfect reverse camera move, rapidly tracking out. The disorientation is compounded, intensifying the impression of Mme de Courtil's inward fear at what she might find. Like Daniel's private poems in *Ça Commence Aujourd'hui*, the feelings that affect Tavernier's characters often represent a part of themselves which has been hidden or tempered. The camera in motion has always been at the dramatic core of Tavernier's work, essential to his way of externalising emotion in his characters. In its evocation of that which will not or cannot be spoken, its restless shifting and turning is at the very heart of the sensual elements of his cinema.

Pierre-William Glenn, Director of Photography/Camera Operator[13]

When I met Bertrand he was already open to the idea of a cinema other than that which was fashionable at the time, that is to say open to a popular cinema with social themes. In *L'Horloger de Saint-Paul*, there was already something which is in all his films, the idea of moving with the text. The difficulty was how to film something which was relatively static – things like people sitting eating – with a lot of written text and not much action. He spoke to me about hand-held camera and about developing-shots which would be long. He spoke to me about an idea which would be a constant in his work; an idea of tracking-shots that would accompany people – which is in all his films – and stay close to them. That set the visual construction of the film, having to light for the 360° movements we did when moving around the interiors. In a way it was very New Wave. The film stock was relatively insensitive to light, so I had to light to a high level, but without making it look lit, which is always the rule of the game with Bertrand – not seeing the way things have been lit. Another thing which was very important for Bertrand was to shoot with direct sound, so that the realism attained in the image was tied to the realism of sound. The complicity between myself and Michel Desrois was important, and against the convention of the period, I sometimes sacrificed the image for the quality of the sound. Bertrand has always accepted the discipline imposed on the photography by the continuity needs of the text. His interest is to escape from the text, that is to say that the method of filming has become more supple, intelligent and we forget the text in his films. In *L.627* we manage to forget that it has been written. I think that *L'Horloger de Saint-Paul* was very 'written', but already there was a desire to film – there are all those sequences which start and finish somewhere other than on the characters; there was already a text off-screen. It is very important for him to tie in the exteriors of places with the interiors – to have someone walking in the street then going inside a house. There was already the idea of material which moved quickly, people moving quickly, from outside to inside and outside again. The idea of a partly naturalist cinema that didn't look performed and was in some ways very close to documentary. In *L'Horloger de Saint-Paul*, he already had the idea of doing things which were not symmetrical. He did not like shooting dialogue scenes as reverse-angles. In his films you aften see the shot moving from one person to another but without cutting. When we did shoot reverse angles, he didn't like the shots to match. The opposite angles would never be taken in the same shot size.[14] Psychologically, he didn't want to place the characters at the same level. It was his way of thinking about the rapport between people.

Bertrand's contrary side, his refusal of convention, is one of the things which I like most. With *Que La Fête Commence...*, the interest for me was to do a historical costume drama in a way which was absolutely not academic. The film was almighty cheek in the method of realism, in the way it portrayed the parties, in its everyday treatment of the sordid, in its complete demystification – through the film's image – of royalty. With *Une Semaine de Vacances*, again, it was the idea of turning things upside down: taking a film like that – about psychological rupture – and filming it like a *policier*, with travelling-shots, coming out of sombre interiors into the streets, seeing someone running away from some danger, but we don't know what. It's the opposite of a psychological film, one where you are not installed in the film to engage in some debate about the human condition, but to try and find an equivalent with the geometrical camera movements around people who don't know where they are going, and creating a kind of danger with the lighting – the interiors lit like night. It's about creating, with the camera, a dramaturgy of movement which runs towards something invisible – a kind of anguish, or void; someone who is looking for a place, but wants to be elsewhere. The atmosphere of the town, the feeling of night creates anguish whilst being extremely surreal, with a lot of sensuality around Nathalie Baye. It is interesting when Bertrand talks about his feminine side in dealing with anguish. When he transposes the masculine personality onto the principal feminine character, like with Romy or Nathalie, something happens. I love *Une Semaine de Vacances* and *Death Watch* because there is a supplementary interpretation with them. I liked the idea of a psychological film done almost entirely in motion, particularly one film not stuck in a single place, although the film is very composed. The film only poses questions and doesn't reply to anything. It's interesting when a film doesn't pretend to have any answers.

In the book on [Michael] Powell,[15] Bertrand talks of him as a 'technician of the emotions' who could only engage with life as a film director, and who suffered dreadfully from that. I think that has always been the problem for Bertrand – the idea of someone who can only experience life as a film director. He talks of reality and he exists within a reality, but it interests him less than the way things are presented, and I can understand that – why, for a lot of people, cinephilia is a refuge. Equally, one understands why he gets involved in things: in social reality and all the political struggles; why he needs to have a political reality – because there is a real danger – that of heading towards completely derived interpretation where there is no reality left.

Bruno de Keyzer, Director of Photography:[16]

Bertrand is very curious about everything. He likes to take a risk with things, like the way he took me on for *Un Dimanche à la Campagne*. He is often in contradiction with things – like with the lighting in this film. In one way, what he wanted was something very aesthetic, with a lot of work on the special film process, mixing colour with black and white, which in terms of style was a very strong decision. In the meantime, he didn't want me to do anything like painting – very composed – and wanted me to shoot very quickly. In all his films he likes to mix different styles and to break the rules from the beginning. If we had shot *Un Dimanche à la Campagne* in a classical way, with establishing shot, medium shot, close-up, because of the process we used, it would have looked like painting. You have no choice with Bertrand – he breaks style in the way he works with the camera, which is always moving around. He likes to work with the actors and block the scene then wants you to be ready to shoot it, and doesn't like to wait because it will destroy the spirit. When you work with Bertand you need to be ready to change very quickly, and be especially prepared because he likes to get a scene in one shot.

Bertrand's approach to making films is not just visual. For me, Bertrand is – this is not negative – he is not a visual director. He has many ideas about visuals, but they are not his main concern in the film. He concentrates more on the story and the emotions of the actors. It's part of his generation: coming after the New Wave, many directors were critics, writers, journalists. It doesn't mean they have no pictorial culture. But in the *cinéma d'auteur* in France what is interesting is to tell a story. Visuals are not the main thing, but in one way it's good because you see so many films that look great but the subject is so empty and it looks beautiful but there's nothing... I have the same approach in films. I never try to create a beautiful shot. I try to follow the emotions of the actors. It's good if the emotion of the lighting follows that of the actors. The fact that Bertrand likes to shoot in real locations and is very precise about the locations he chooses means that 80 per cent of the lighting is done already. We had one main location for *Un Dimanche à la Campagne*, but the kitchen was too small and I think we visited 40 kitchens to find the right one. It's very important for him to find the real location. He treats location like the actors – its 'casting' is as important. He doesn't like the comfort of the studio, and the reason he is completely lost in the studio is because there is no feeling, no spirit. He likes to put himself and everybody in the real situation of the film. He likes the compromise of real locations, dealing with the problems. He organises everything and everyone on location to create something like a piece of life – then he has the opportunity to steal the best, the essence of things – what is important for the film.

Alain Choquart, Director of Photography/Camera Operator:[17]

You never really know where you are going with Bertrand. It's always something really new he asks you to do. You are like an actor in his films. The actors get their different characters and you get the camera and the light. It's somehow very precise but very difficult to explain. Bertrand never likes to give you a really strong direction, but he gives you the feeling of understanding where he wants to go. He knows that when we begin shooting, everyone knows very well what they have to do. I am not allowed to make any mistakes – I can't fail. We don't want to have retakes for a problem with camera – it's not our way of working. In a difficult, very aesthetic film like *La Vie et Rien d'Autre*, we shot all the rehearsals. I never had any rehearsal for the camera movement and very often we shot a rehearsal, one take, and that was all. Bertrand doesn't like to shoot many takes. It works because he gives everyone such a big part in the creativity of the film. He chooses the people he works with very precisely, technicians as much as actors. He communicates more through emotion than with technical terms. That's why I get on so well with Bertrand. If a director just tells you, 'Well, you're here with an 18mm [lens], on a low tripod, with two metres of tracking...' it's boring and restrictive. With Bertrand, we walk around together, watch the actors and move with the actors. Sometimes we don't even have to talk much during shooting. He never uses a storyboard.[18] And he never has the script on the set. I think it was on *La Vie et Rien d'Autre* that he stopped bringing the script anymore. He doesn't need to hear every word that was written in the script, or to get every shot. If he gets the emotion, he is satisfied with the day.

Bertrand doesn't like the precise homage, which is a way of reducing things. Sometimes he has an idea of a shot, before the film, but maybe just one. We didn't look at any films for *L'Appât* and anyway, it's never that precise. It's just a way of thinking about things, of beginning to work. We watched some John Ford films for the framing of Philippe Noiret like John Wayne, and to look at these western camps, made of wood, set in nature. What he likes is a kind of reference which is not too clear. Bertrand didn't really want close-ups for *La Vie et Rien d'Autre*. You had to stay a bit further away from people. Also, the close-up gives a real modernity in a film. You can of course make a modern film with a historical subject, but another way is to make you believe you are in this historical time. People at the time didn't touch easily, so if you also give this kind of shyness to the camera, you give something to the spectator which is a way of belonging to this time. Being closer doesn't mean seeing the face in detail. You don't need to be closer, except if you need to feel you are close. In *L'Appât*, the scene between Olivier Sitruk and Richard Berry – when he talks about the fact that he is Jewish – we first rehearsed it close, but not too close and when we looked at the monitor we agreed, 'No we're not in the scene'. They were so close that we needed to be closer. But we didn't shoot one, then the other, face-on, which is more about looking. We were in profile-profile. You don't need to see the eyes to be close.

The improvisation of *Ça Commence Aujourd'hui* was very exciting. It's as if you have the melody and you are writing the music. The film isn't meant to be a microcosm of life, with every person representing a category. That's why Bertrand didn't want to construct a realistic class of pupils. The fiction had to come from what we shot. That's why the way of filming never focuses on the main dramatic point of the scene. For example, with Madame Henry, who is going to kill herself and her two kids, the last shot of her is from far away. She just turns and leaves and very quickly we are on something else. A lot of directors would have done something closer, to give dramatic meaning to the way she leaves. The sequence where the Inspector comes to watch Daniel with the class is written very precisely as part of the story, but when Didier Bezace is watching Philippe Torreton with the pupils, nothing is written. Philippe had to try and get the kids to sing and recite poems while we tried to get fictional shots from something which was not documentary but... Didier Bezace was in the frame along with Philippe Torreton, so he had to react to what he was listening to and there was a strange feeling between the fiction of these two actors, who didn't speak to each other, and the whole improvisation with the kids. Bertrand doesn't like to know, too well, where he is going.

CINEMA AND LYRICISM

Tavernier's organic approach to directing, which has not changed fundamentally since he began making feature-films, has always been devoted to the vision of a cinema which is essentially lyrical, in a creative obsession that sometimes seems like a reaction against his own intellect. His notion of lyrical emotion centres around an awe-struck view of humanity that makes it impossible to separate the surprised gaze of his cinema from his way of making films, which pointedly seeks out the unexpected revelation that comes directly from his fundamental belief in opening up the creative limits of collaborators in front of the camera and behind it. His method of directing is characterised by a firm refusal to pre-empt the dramatic energy of performance on location, with a blue-print for camera that is already formalised in detail. Tavernier often talks about directing as if it were a fight against the imprisonment of inertia: his avoidance of shooting methods which 'freeze the actors'; a total dislike of the 'stiff and empty' results of cinema which mimics painting. The lyricism that he strives for represents his total rejection of any reductionist concept of cinema that idealises visual form whilst discarding what he regards as its essentially cinematic nature, the dynamic interplay between moving images and sound-track.

For Tavernier, exploring the lyrical possibilities in cinema has always involved embracing the emotional language of both the visual and the verbal. For him, it is a way of creating a new, more intensified, more complex melody. His frequent description of the elements that make up his films, and the construction of his films, in terms of music, constantly underscores the lyrical tensions between the defining nature of words and the expansion of their meaning through images and sounds, a defining aspect of his work. His cinema has always combined his deep-rooted pleasure in verbal language with the sense that lyricism is not about specifics. His consistently strong interest in spoken language does exploit the natural clarity of words to assist in shaping complex characters. However, he uses verbal language, especially voice-overs, for the way that the precision of words becomes softened and stretched when attached to the other expressive elements of film. Tavernier's voice-over in *Un Dimanche à la Campagne* accepts Pierre Bost's desire to give insight into a father's feeling for his daughter that is clear enough to allow identification, but its effect cannot be left there:

> Irène is momentarily lost in joyous play with her adoring nephews and niece. A counterpoint enters: a voice-over telling an unseen audience about the feelings created by her absence. All natural sounds fall away into the distance. The vitality of the scene dissolves into fragility, like life into old celluloid. Irène continues playing, soaking up life, while someone keeps talking about her as if she is gone already. The voice disappears, temporarily. Irène's life surges back with all the natural sounds as she runs indoors to gulp a glass of cold lemonade. In her thirst, oblivious to either past or future.

The explanatory nature of voice-overs tends to disguise their deeper impact, which is often essentially non-verbal, delineating the emotional connections between past and present, present and future, reality and desire, character and storyteller, storyteller and audience. Ironically, Tavernier's use of voice-overs are a crucial part of his desire to escape the literal and the real in his dramas, often an essential part of the cinematic dream-state created. Their impact on plot is less important than their creation of ambiguity. His interest in the lyrical over the literal is equally to be found in his treatment of the carefully-acquired sound, and he sometimes prefers to resist the seductive richness of a natural aural atmosphere, deciding instead to strip away reality and expose the sound which echoes the dramatic centre of a scene. Natural sound is as much a part of Tavernier's lyricism as his music, whether it be the incessant pattering of the rain which we can see pouring down the window behind Laurence Cuers, and whose relentless simmering sound becomes part of her dangerous, constant state of anxiety in *Une Semaine de Vacances*, or the heavy motorway traffic which screams in the background while Daniel stands in the cemetery in *Ça Commence Aujourd'hui*. The heightened sounds which help lift Tavernier's films out of naturalism and into lyricism are an important element in his attempt to break free from the constraints of plot – like the music he uses for inspiration, whilst striving for liberty, is part of a film's abstract nature.

Bertrand Tavernier:

> Jazz, for me, is my influence on film-making. When I am trying to solve some problems of narration, of construction, I very often think of music and of jazz – the relationship between the theme and improvisation, between the melody and the harmony, between the chords and melodic line. The notion of tempo, of rhythm. I find that direction has a lot to do with jazz. The relationship between direction and screenplay is a lot like the relationship in the treatment of some great melodies done by the great jazz players – I'm not talking about the moment where they improvise, although I could include that, but when they state some melody. Like Charlie Parker with Gershwin or Lester Young with *These Foolish Things*.[19]

You have the notes written there, but still it belongs very much Parker or Young. This is the mystery of jazz. With *These Foolish Things*, in a way Young goes beyond the melody, inside the melody, he even breaks it a little bit, but even when jazz players respect the melody, they give it a sound of their own. Jazz has taught me the meaning of freedom – not to follow the written words on the page. Especially since I have been producing my own films, I have allowed a long time for preparing my films and it is because of that preparation that I can be very free when I shoot. That preparation does not include storyboards and I never put out a list of shots. I want to be open, so the preparation gives me ideas, principles, and when I have those, I can start to direct without taking the screenplay with me. I know it – I have absorbed it during the preparation, so I can change things, I can be ready to accept a new scene. I have been able to change films on the set, to change the ending of *Une Semaine de Vacances* and *Un Dimanche à la Campagne*[20] because I was free enough to see what the shooting had brought to the film. The relationships between people had changed. The film had moved to a place I had not suspected.

NOTES ON CHAPTER 22

1 Interviewed in *Jean Renoir* (David Thompson, 1994), a documentary from BBC Television's 'Omnibus' series.
2 Michel Descombes in *L'Horloger de Saint-Paul* (1973); Philippe d'Orléans in *Que La Fête Commence...* (1975); Judge Rousseau in *Le Juge et l'Assassin* (1976); Lucien Cordier in *Coup de Torchon*; Commandant Dellaplane in *La Vie et Rien d'Autre* (1989). He also reappeared as Michel Descombes in *Une Semaine de Vacances* (1980) and played a cameo role as Redon in *'Round Midnight* and D'Artagnan in *La Fille de D'Artagnan* (1994).
3 Interviewed in Daniele Bion, *Bertrand Tavernier: Cinéaste de l'Emotion*, Renens, 1984, p 83.
4 Interviewed in Joseph Hurley, 'Tavernier et Noiret encore', *Films in Review*, vol. 34 no 3, March 1983, p 170.
5 Ibid. p 234.
6 Interviewed in David Overbey, 'Those Obscure Objects of Desire', *The Movie Orbis*, vol. 8 no 86, 1981, p 1712.
7 From Dirk Bogarde, 'Take Three in Splendid Cinemascope', press release notes to *Daddy Nostalgie*, Little Bear, 1991.
8 Bogarde's suggestion that long takes are demanding might seem odd, given that one of the special 'demands' of screen acting is to perform often in a very fragmented manner, out of sequence, during short takes, without the emotional momentum of the continuous action of theatre. He is addressing the fact that the sheer visual detail exposed on screen with film acting greatly increases the demands of visual perfection – anything that does not look quite right is magnified, and 'flaws' of visual detail which would not

be apparent on stage might be very obvious on the large screen, increasing the risk that lengthy (expensive) takes might have to be aborted.
9   See endnotes for chapter on *Capitaine Conan*.
10 Interviewed in Dan Yakir, 'Painting Pictures', *Film Comment*, vol. 20, Sep–Oct 1984, pp 20–1.
11 Bertrand Tavernier in Daniele Bion, *Bertrand Tavernier: Cinéaste de l'Emotion*, Renens, 1984, p 40.
12 Tracking-in means moving the camera (usually on tracks) in on a static subject. Tracking-out means pulling back from a static subject – not to be confused with reverse-tracking which is means moving backwards with a moving subject (usually someone facing the camera).
13 Pierre-William Glenn was cinematographer on *L'Horloger de Saint-Paul, Que La Fête Commence…, Le Juge et l'Assassin, Une Semaine de Vacances, Coup de Torchon* and *Pays d'Octobre/Mississippi Blues*.
14 See endnote to chapter on *Que La Fête Commence…* on 'matching reverse-angles'.
15 Pierre-William Glenn is referring to Michael Powell's autobiography, *A Life in Movies*. Tavernier wrote the preface to the edition published in France.
16 Bruno de Keyzer was director of photography on *Un Dimanche à la Campagne, 'Round Midnight, La Passion Béatrice* and *La Vie et Rien d'Autre*.
17 Alain Choquart was camera operator on *La Vie et Rien d'Autre* then cinematographer on *La Guerre Sans Nom, L.627, L'Appât, Capitaine Conan* and *Ça Commence Aujourd'hui*.
18 A pictorial representation of the key images that make up the scenes of a film. By it's nature, the storyboard approach tends to pre-judge the visualisation of a scene before arriving on set or location with actors.
19 'These Foolish Things' was the theme song used in *Daddy Nostalgie*, and was adopted as the film's English-language title. The music is by Jack Strachey-Lonk, lyrics by Eric Maschwitz.
20 In the final-draft script of *Une Semaine de Vacances*, Laurence and her boyfriend Pierre split up, but late on in the shoot Tavernier decided it felt wrong, and that they should stay together. The scripted ending of *Un Dimanche à la Campagne* has M Ladmiral walking into town the next day. When asked about his family's visit on Sunday, he refers to the pleasure of receiving a visit from his daughter Irène, but makes no mention of Gonzague and his family. Instead, Tavernier chose to show M Ladmiral contemplating his studio, and there is a hint that he is going to start another piece of work. It is interesting that in both these cases Tavernier opted to finish on a slightly more optimistic note than he had planned, although it has to be said that the endings in both films are typically ambiguous.

CHAPTER 23

THE FILM-MAKER OF LYON

Bertrand Tavernier's decision to set *L'Horloger de Saint-Paul* in Lyon – the city which held his fondest childhood memories within its streets and alleys and parks – is not difficult to understand, knowing how determined he was that his first feature-film would have a feeling of authenticity rooted in a strong sense of place. The quiet presence of the city itself forms an important part of the film's haunted atmosphere, but just as significant, is the very idea of needing to return to one's past. The sense of the young director taking steps towards his memories was mirrored perfectly in his protagonist Michel Descombes's need to return to old haunts in his attempt to make some sense of the present, and to locate some explanation for everything that has gone wrong with his son, and the great distance which marks their relationship. Tavernier had already made a second film in Lyon – *Une Semaine de Vacances*, in which the character of the city seemed to be a mirror to Laurence Cuers's troubled soul – when he decided to confront his own need to return to the city as a film-maker in his documentary *Lyon: Le Regard Intérieur*. Essentially made up of reflections on a city and its past by the director and his father, the film touches on many of the themes which have recurred along Tavernier's cinematic journey: the nature of memory and its relationship with reality and imagination; the invisible ties that connect people with places; and the quest to find a kind of truce with the memories of the past, through which an acceptance of the past and the pain attached to it is possible, despite limited understanding of its meaning, allowing life to begin moving forward once more.

Having always avoided carefully a tourist's-eye view of the places in his films, Tavernier allows himself for once to play the guide, and the film is a portrait of the physical nature of Lyon – although the tour shows the audience the everyday, secretive side to Lyon characterised by the labyrinth of low alleys, halls and high-ceilinged rooms. These hidden paths may impress the adult sensibility with their character, so suggestive of journey, but in childhood they represent a whole universe, in which every direction leads to the unknown, to the future instead of the past. The imposing presence of the dark corridors and the huge space of the shared hallways heightens human vulnerability, with the uncertainties of those searching or waiting within them inescapably contrasted against their calm strength and confident silence. The poignant nature of the empty halls and cavernous interiors exists beyond Tavernier's 'Lyonnaise pieces', echoing the fears that pursue Katherine Mortenhoe in *Death Watch* and keep Dale awake in *'Round Midnight*. There is nothing malevolent about these places, but their stillness tends to lay open or heighten the feelings that move their inhabitants. The same enclosed atmosphere that encourages little Mireille to steal a glimpse of what she will share later, out through the bedroom shutters, in *Un Dimanche à la Campagne* pushes Laurence to search inwards, deeper and deeper within herself, to the point of risking her very survival within their walls in *Une Semaine de Vacances*. The changes of time, like the rebuilding of Lyon's shattered bridges and the old buildings flattened to make way for the new in the name of 'progress', prompt consideration of past events; but feelings of permanence also provoke introspection. As with old Lyon, the constancy of a physical environment exposes and intensifies awareness of the changes felt by those who live there: whether they be part of the ageing process that confirms mortality, or the inner changes that shape life's meandering path from childhood into adulthood, now called into question.

Lyon: Le Regard Intérieur deals painfully with destruction, and the modern self-destruction which it laments projects the same concerns and outrage that existed in *Des Enfants Gâtés* over the wanton destruction of inherited wealth by commerce. The juxtaposition of Michel Descombes's world with the ongoing clearances that promise only more tasteless monuments to capitalism recalls the warnings hidden within *Death Watch* over the insidious marginalisation of a culture handed down through generations at the hands of corporate powers who evangelise the promotion of endless corporate growth. Tavernier's lament for the vandalised dignity of all the torn down buildings, including the old Tavernier family home that he had featured in *L'Horloger de Saint-Paul*, retains its most bitter sadness for what the physical destruction represents: the wilful destruction of the past, as if to deny its relevance to the present, and the debt owed to its influence. Tavernier's cinema has always been noted for its eclecticism, but there are common themes which run just beneath the variety of its time, place, colour and tone, and the most consistent and important connection between them all is the presence and treatment of history. A need to reflect on the events of the past informs the important documentary aspect that exists in all of his films, from the little-known medieval attitudes that appalled his audience in *La Passion Béatrice* to the unwrapping of sealed memories in *La Guerre Sans Nom*; from the poetic documentation of an artist's experience in *'Round Midnight* to the indignant rebuttal of officialdom's pat condemnation of a disadvantaged section of society in *De L'Autre Côté du Périph'*.

In his recollection of Lyon's past, René Tavernier refers to its history of questioning established order. Like the cultural resistance of René's magazine *Confluences*, the historical nature of Bertrand's cinema has always been motivated by his refusal to accept the official version of events, seeking instead to favour the victims of establishment with an alternative narrative. The anxiety in his work often stems from his distress at the prospect of the past being buried away, its meaning denied, along with the disappearing memory of its most generous players. In his fiction, the dead of *La Vie et Rien d'Autre* and the living of *Capitaine Conan* provide the clearest evidence of his fear, which seems particularly haunted by the enormity of the human losses of the First World War and the darkest side of humanity which it represents. In *Lyon: Le Regard Intérieur*, through the reminiscences of his father he enters the memory of another terrible period marked by almost unspeakable conflict: the Second World War, facing the emotional scars that remain in a town still darkened by the name of Klaus Barbie.[1] The nearest that Tavernier had taken us to the Second World War in his dramas was the loudspeakers bringing news of the impending carnage at the end of *Coup de Torchon*, and Tiffany Tavernier's reference to the time it takes her father to approach and confront the very worst aspects of the human soul makes one wonder if the anguish visited on the people of Lyon, and humanity in general, was still too painful for him to consider touching. In examining so much of the pensive feeling that exists throughout his earlier work, *Lyon: Le Regard Intérieur* is perhaps his most emotional film, and the sadness that it evokes is never deeper than during its contemplation of the wounds inflicted during the occupation. Tavernier seems to confirm the war's influence on his films that do not touch on it literally, using Antoine Duhamel's music for *Death Watch* over sections which deal with the war's aftermath in Lyon, but he leaves it to his father to put the audience in direct touch with the immediate reality behind the images of events that might seem distant – or perhaps just too enormous to comprehend fully and shape in the mind.

Standing among the trees of his old garden, wrapped in a long coat and scarf as protection from the cold of a winter morning, René faces the lights and reflectors of his son's documentary film crew, and tells the story of Eugène Pons, master printer, who committed *Confluences* to paper for him and his colleagues. He creates a visual image of the man who 'looked like a proud Gaullois', then describes Pons's deep conviction as a Christian and a Résistant, before moving on to relate the story of him being taken away and having to face Klaus Barbie following a Gestapo raid of his printing works in rue Vieille Monnae.[2] The faint strain of Duhamel's music, helping to spread the sense of fear caused by the very mention of Barbie's name, is all that breaks the stillness. René continues. His story develops into a quotation of the conversation between the two during Pons's interrogation. As if being pulled back into 1944, the past tense he has been using slips, and he plays out the final exchange between Pons and Barbie in the cinematic present tense, as if it were happening in his presence. The inner shadow that passes visibly over René's face on finishing his story prefigures the injured memories of the men interviewed four years later in *La Guerre Sans Nom*, recalling his son's voice-over from *Un Dimanche à la Campagne*: 'All sorrows resemble each other'. It would be difficult to find a better explanation for Bertrand's own *cinéma de résistance* than the filmed record of his father's recollection of Pons, whose small place in history belies the scale of his bravery and sacrifice.[3]

René's filmed rendezvous with his past contrasts greatly with the searching done by many characters in his son's films in that his sadness is communicated with a kind of peace, in near-reversal of the sense of anxiety and restlessness that they live with. In *'Round Midnight*, Francis's fears for Dale press him to get his hero out of Paris, the city that holds everything which is slowly destroying the weakened jazz player. Following a sequence which brings Dale's mortality closer by combining Francis's home movies of Dale playing in the club with 'real' shots of him rehearsing and recording, we cut straight to the image of Francis staring out of a train window as it races into the countryside. Francis may still be unsure what he is going to do in the long term, but at least he is travelling back to safety, for a time anyway; next, we are in Lyon, gazing at an image of the city and its rivers in total calm. Lyon brings Francis the chance to steal a few idyllic moments in the pleasure of sharing his own roots with Dale, but respite is short-lived for the weary musician: Dale can appreciate Lyon – he appreciates Francis's parents as people who 'like to live in harmony' – but the town cannot provide him with peace. Everything about the town that he can appreciate as beautiful is also helping to remind him that he is not home, and that he cannot escape facing his own past and future by hiding from the pull of New York City within Lyon's silent embrace.

In *L.627*, it is to Lyon that the exhausted detective Lucien 'Lulu' Marguet retreats, at the very point when he is becoming overwhelmed by the problems that beset his work in the Paris drugs squad, although, unlike Dale, Lyon does belong to Lulu's own past. Lulu's return to the city which is part of his family background is a necessary act, but rather than exorcising the anxieties which gnaw away at him, physical contact with the places that were part of the person he was before his work took complete control throw everything that is going wrong into relief. By the time Lulu reaches the fifth floor of the apartment building where his grandfather lived, he is in the very depths of depression, crouched in a corner like a small child again, in a dim and silent huge stairwell encircling an old cage lift. The old haunts of his childhood can push Lulu into searching within their confines and within himself for explanations as to why things have turned out this way, or even for the right course of action, but they cannot give him any clear answers. The intimate secrets between Lyon and Lulu expose his hurt more than his life in Paris does: the city is like a mirror to his own fears over his relationship with his wife Kathy, who has to live with everything that he is carrying.

Just four of Tavernier's 17 feature-length dramas portray Lyon, but the emotive idea of one's return to a familial homeland in times of doubt recurs powerfully in many of his other films. In *Death Watch*, the secluded country home where Katherine goes to visit her ex-husband Gerald allows her to bask in reminiscence of better times, as well as providing sanctuary from the predatory NTV. In *Un Dimanche à la Campagne*, a return to the idyll of their father's home brings both Irène and Gonzague Ladmiral face-to-face with the lost promise of the past, tying present doubts with choices made years earlier. Uncomfortable truths are also brought to the surface of family relationships when Caroline has to rush back home in *Daddy Nostalgie*. In *La Passion Béatrice*, homecoming entrenches François de Cortemart's total disillusion, bringing him only a sense of terrible distance between his recent experiences of war and the deceptive normality of home, blighted by a dreadful history. In *Capitaine Conan*, it is only after his return to the quiet ordinariness of his life in his Breton village that the brutalising experiences of war really begin to take effect on the charismatic young leader's will and ability to live. When everything in Nathalie's life seems to be going wrong in *L'Appât*, her immediate reaction is to return to her mother's home, although she finds little help there beyond the pitifully superficial comfort of some chocolate hazelnut spread in an empty kitchen.

Whatever consolation or pain the return home brings Tavernier's wandering characters, it always marks a hugely significant development. If nothing else, Lulu's trip to Lyon in *L.627* may have reminded him of Kathy's stubborn commitment to take the place of all the answers that will never come. At the end of the film, he discovers that Cécile's disappearance from the Paris drugs scene was the result of her decision to return to the Ardêche, where her family were from. The lack of substance attached to Nathalie's retreat home in *L'Appât* renders it more tragic than the journeys made by these other characters, hinting that the absence of any solid past may be playing its part in her inability to see the slightest meaning in the dreadful events that are leading to her inevitable downfall. When she is questioned by the police for the first time, Nathalie frustrates the detective taking her details by failing to decide whether she is from Neuilly or Levallois. Her conscious desire to bend reality towards the district which sounds more suitable to her image obscures the emptiness of the truth – that where she comes from seems close to irrelevant, given the failure of her past to provide her with even the most basic values that might have protected her from the moral cancer of empty materialism.

Nathalie's lack of an identity shaped by a sense of place and the past makes her one of Tavernier's rarer characters, the closest figures to her being Sergeant Bouvier in *Le Juge et l'Assassin* and Lucien Cordier in *Coup de Torchon*, whose errant nature stems at least partly from having been deserted or betrayed by the guardians or influences of his earlier life. More usually, Tavernier's characters are affected, one way or another, by a deep sense of belonging to the world of their past as well as their present, starting with Michel Descombes's silent search for truth within the secrets of his home town. Touching the prison walls after visiting Bernard, Descombes displays one of the most essential attributes of Tavernier's characters: being in real contact with their world. This element of the human condition – not always an easy one to live with – has continued to mark the people in his films, who always seem to be searching, like Dale in *'Round Midnight*, for 'harmony' within their universe. They might rarely enjoy a feeling of inner peace, and perhaps never experience a feeling of melodious unity with the world, but Tavernier's best hope lies in the real possibility that they will gain an awareness of their own place in it. The importance of awareness and reality is at the heart of his *De L'Autre Côté du Périph'*, his cinematic 'letter' to Minister Eric Raoult, whose assertions were destroyed more by the informed perceptions of the residents of Grands-Pêchers than anything else.

In *Ça Commence Aujourd'hui*, Daniel Lefèvre experiences terrible doubts over whether or not his existence is in real dialogue with his world, as he watches his best efforts demolished by remote authorities who regard distance as commendable, involvement as unhealthy. Whilst he is in real danger of being crushed, his strength comes from a commitment to the legacy of the past, an acceptance of a debt to the sacrifices of those who went before him, whom he detects everywhere in the surrounding landscapes. It is always through the places and objects of their physical environment that the past speaks to Tavernier's characters, even if the message is blurred or misleading in its presentation of recovered memories, like all the souvenirs and photos of travel which help an old man to create his soothing vision of past life in *Daddy Nostalgie*. In *Lyon: Le Regard Intérieur*, Tavernier talks of the delicate balance between memory, reality and imagination, unsure of exactly how much of what he reconstructs from his own memories really happened and how much is invented. Within his body of work, which has dealt so often with a deep sense of loneliness resulting from feelings of doubt, the one conviction which has always been projected with total certainty is the belief that the past is hugely important, that it is worthwhile to try to understand its relationship with the present, and almost unforgivable to deny its players their proper recognition and place in people's memories. Tavernier closed *Lyon: Le Regard Intérieur* with his father's explanation of the important place in his spirit occupied by those who have gone from his life, remembering especially that 'those who should still be here no longer are'.

Tavernier's cinematic journey to rediscover the Lyon to which he and his father belonged opens with images of the Paris–Lyon TGV[4] entering the city in the early morning, recalling the night-train that brought the 'inward regard' of its soul into his work as a film-maker. We can finish with another certainty: that the subjects and places to which Tavernier takes his crew of old and new faces may not be totally predictable, but somewhere along the line the soul of the Lyon that he has never really left will reappear. It will probably be found in many things, although to make predictions risks provoking the director's natural contrariness. Suffice to say that somewhere there might be a troubled character who feels the pull of a home and history which somehow communicates its insistence on a return journey, like Caroline in *Daddy Nostalgie*, barely conscious in her bewilderment as she finds herself back in the Gare de Lyon, Paris, hoping for a train home in the middle of a rail strike. Whilst the outcome is never certain, there is always the possibility – as with Lulu or Irène Ladmiral – that they will learn something that brings acceptance of the past closer, if not its full comprehension. Maybe the part of Lyon's nature which seems to have imposed itself most within Tavernier's work is its 'duality'. If there is one emotion which most defines his often deeply religious cinema, it is that of doubt. When talking about his work, his films and his characters, the word which keeps recurring is doubt. Yet when his daughter Tiffany tried to define her father's nature as a film-maker, what she talked about most was his faith. In Lyon, we could safely assume that they are both right.

NOTES ON CHAPTER 23

1 Klaus Barbie was the SS leader known as 'the Butcher of Lyon', because of the violent reign of terror he imposed on the city during the Nazi occupation.
2 The street was renamed rue René Lénaud, after another of René Tavernier's colleagues on *Confluences*. Lénaud was killed by the Germans during the war.
3 Lacking any hard evidence against Eugène Pons, Klaus Barbie told him he could go free, with a warning that he knew Pons to be guilty. Pons asked Barbie to free one of his colleagues from the printing works who had also been arrested, insisting that he was innocent. When Barbie refused to believe him, Pons said that if Barbie did not free his colleague, he too would stay. René Tavernier's story quoted Barbie as saying, 'Well, Monsieur Pons, you can stay'. Eugène Pons ended up in Buchenwaldt concentration camp, and died during deportation to Neuengamme.
4 Train à Grande-Vitesse (High-Speed Train).

FILMOGRAPHY

AS DIRECTOR
Short Dramas

Le Baiser de Judas (1963)
Sketch from *Les Baisers*; Producer Georges de Beauregard; Screenplay Bertrand Tavernier, Claude Nahon, Roger Tailleur; Camera Raoul Coutard; Music Eddie Vartan; Assistant director Volker Schlöndorff. Cast: Laetitia Roman (Tiffany); Judie de Carril (Sylve); Bernard Rousselet (Robert); William Sabatier (Inspecteur Bercy); Guy Saval (Stranger).

Une Chance Explosive (1964)
Sketch from *La Chance et l'Amour*; Producer Georges de Beauregard; Screenplay Bertrand Tavernier, Nicolas Vogel; Camera Alain Levent; Editing Armand Psenny; Music Antoine Duhamel. Cast: Michel Auclair (Lorrière); Bernard Blier (Camilly); Iran Eory (Sophie); Bob Morel, Gérard Tichy, Jacky Léonard, C.F. Medard, Antonella Campo di Fiori.

Feature-length Dramas

L'Horloger de Saint-Paul (*The Watchmaker of Saint-Paul*) (1973)
Producer Raymond Danon; Screenplay Jean Aurenche, Pierre Bost, Bertrand Tavernier, from *L'Horloger d'Everton* by Georges Simenon; Cinematography Pierre-William Glenn; Production Design Jean Mandaroux; Music Philippe Sarde; Sound Michel Desrois, Harold Maury; Editing Armand Psenny; Production Raymond Danon, Lira Films. 105 minutes. Cast: Philippe Noiret (Michel Descombes); Jean Rochefort (Commissaire Guiboud); Jacques Denis (Antoine); Sylvain Rougerie (Bernard Descombes); Christine Pascal (Liliane Torrini); Andrée Tainsy (Madeleine Fourmet); Yves Afonso (Bricard); Julien Bertheau (Édouard); Jacques Hilling (Costes), Clotilde Jouano (Janine Boitard); William Sabatier (defence lawyer); Cécile Vassort (Martine).

Que La Fête Commence... (*Let the Party Begin*) (1975)
Screenplay Jean Aurenche, Bertrand Tavernier; Cinematography Pierre-William Glenn; Production Design Pierre Guffroy; Costumes Jacqueline Moreau; Music arranged by Antoine Duhamel from the manuscripts of Philippe d'Orléans, Regent of France; Sound Michel Desrois; Editing Armand Psenny; Production Michèle de Broca, Fildebroc-UPF/Productions de la Guéville. 119 minutes. Cast: Philippe Noiret (Philippe d'Orléans); Jean Rochefort (Abbé Dubois); Jean-Pierre Marielle (Marquis de Pontcallec); Christine Pascal (Émilie); Alfred Adam (Villeroi); Jean-Roger Caussimon (The Cardinal); Gérard Desarthe (Duc de Bourbon); Marina Vlady (Mme de Parabère); Monique Chaumette (Governess Pontcallec); François Dyrek (Montlouis); Jean-Paul Farré (Père Burdo); Nicole Garcia (La Fillon); Raymond Girard (surgeon); Jacques Hilling (Abbé Grattelard); Bernard Lajarrige (Arnaud de Lambilly); Monique Lejeune (Mme de Sabran); Georges Riquier (magistrate); Thierry Lhermitte (Compte de Horn); Daniel Duval (Le Mirebalais); Michel Berto (Abbé de Louis XV).

Le Juge et l'Assassin (*The Judge and the Assassin*) (1976)
Screenplay Jean Aurenche, Bertrand Tavernier, from an idea by Pierre Bost and Jean Aurenche; Cinematography Pierre-William Glenn; Production Design Antoine Roman; Costumes Jacqueline Moreau; Music Philippe Sarde; Sound Michel Desrois; Editing Armand Psenny; Production Raymond Danon, Lira Films. 125 minutes. Cast: Michel Galabru (Joseph Bouvier); Philippe Noiret (Judge Rousseau); Isabelle Huppert (Rose); Jean-Claude Brialy (Prosecutor Villedieu); Renée Faure (Mme Rousseau); Cécile Vassort (Louise); Jean Bretonnière (Députe); Jean-Roger Caussimon (street-singer); François Dyreck (freed tramp); Monique Chaumette (Mme Lesueur); Yves Robert (Professor Degueldre); Lisa Braconnier (hospital nun); Arlette Bonnard (soup-kitchen woman); Jean Amos (chief gaoler); Aude landry (Suzanne).

Des Enfants Gâtés (*Spoiled Children*) (1977)
Screenplay Charlotte Dubreuil, Christine Pascal, Bertrand Tavernier; Cinematography Alain Levent; Production Design Jean-Baptiste Poirot; Costumes Jacqueline Moreau; Music Philippe Sarde; Sound Michel Desrois; Editing Armand Psenny; Production Alain Sarde Gaumont/Sara Films/Films 66/Little Bear. 113 minutes. Cast: Michel Piccoli (Bernard Rougerie); Christine Pascal (Anne); Michel Aumont (Pierre); Gérard Jugnot (Marcel Bonfils); Geneviève Mnich (Guite Bonfils); Arlette Bonnard (Catherine Rougerie); Georges Riquier (Mouchot); Gérard Zimmerman (Patrice Joffroy); Lisa Braconnier (Danièle Joffroy); Claudine Mavros (Anne's mother); Michel Berto (Muzart); Tiffany Tavernier (Rougerie's daughter).

Death Watch (*La Mort en Direct*) 1979
Screenplay David Rayfiel, Bertrand Tavernier, from the novel *The Unsleeping Eye* by David Compton; Cinematography Pierre-William Glenn; Production Design Tony Pratt; Costumes Judy Moorcroft; Music Antoine Duhamel; Sound Michel Desrois; Editing Armand Psenny; Production Janine Rubeiz,

Elie Kfouri, Jean-Serge Breton, Gabriel Boustani Selta Films/Little Bear/Sara Films/Gaumont/Antenne 2/TV 15 Munich/SFP. 128 minutes. Cast: Romy Schneider (Katherine Mortenhoe); Harvey Keitel (Roddy Farrar); Harry Dead Stanton (Vincent Ferriman); Thérèse Liotard (Tracey); Max Von Sydow (Gerald Mortenhoe); William Russell (Doctor Mason); Caroline Langrishe (girl in Bar); Bernard Wicki (Katherine's father).

Une Semaine de Vacances (A Week's Holiday) (1980)
Screenplay Bertrand Tavernier, Colo Tavernier, Marie-France Hans; Cinematography Pierre-William Glenn; Production Design Baptiste Poirot; Costumes Yvette Bonnay; Music Pierre Papadiamandis; Sound Michel Desrois; Editing Armand Psenny; Production Alain Sarde Sara Films/Antenne 2/Little Bear. Cast: Nathalie Baye (Laurence Cuers); Gérard Lanvin (Pierre); Michel Galabru (Lucien Mancheron); Anne (Flore Fitzgerald); Philippe Noiret (Michel Descombes); Jean Daste (Laurence's father); Marie Louise Ebeli (Laurence's mother); Philippe Delaigue (Laurence's brother); Genevieve Vauzeilles (Lucie); Catherine-Anne Duperray (Josiane); Jean-Claude Durand (Philippe); Jean Sourbier (André); Thierry Herbivo (Jean Mancheron); Nils Tavernier (Patrice); André Mortamais (client); Philippe Liotard (Docteur Sabouret).

Coup de Torchon (Clean Slate) (1981)
Screenplay Jean Aurenche, Bertrand Tavernier, from the novel *Pop. 1280* by Jim Thompson; Cinematography Pierre-William Glenn; Production Design Alexandre Trauner; Costumes Jacqueline Moreau; Music Philippe Sarde; Sound Michel Desrois; Editing Armand Psenny; Production Adolphe Viezzi, Henri Lassa, Les Films de la Tour/Films A2/Little Bear. 128 minutes. Cast: Philippe Noiret (Lucien Cordier); Isabelle Huppert (Rose); Jean-Pierre Marielle (Le Péron and his brother); Stéphanie Audran (Huguette Cordier); Eddy Mitchell (Nono); Guy Marchand (Chavasson); Irene Skobline (Anne); Michel Beaune (Vanderbrouck); Jean Champion (the priest); Victor Garruivier (Mercaillou); Gérard Hernandez (Leonelli); Abdoulaye Diop (Fête Nat); Daniel Langlet (Paulo); François Perrot (Colonel Tramichèle).

Un Dimanche à la Campagne (A Sunday in the Country) (1984)
Screenplay Colo Tavernier, Bertrand Tavernier, from the novel Monsieur Ladmiral Va Bientôt Mourir by Pierre Bost; Director of Photography Bruno de Keyzer; Camera Jean Harnois; Production Design Patrice Mercier; Costumes Yvonne Sassinot de Nesles; Music Gabriel Fauré, Louis Ducreux, Marc Perrone, adapted by Philippe Sarde; Sound Guillaume Sciama; Editing Armand Psenny; Production Alain Sarde, Sara Films/Films A2/Little Bear. 94 minutes. Cast: Louis Ducreux (M Ladmiral); Michel Aumont (Gonzague); Sabine Azéma (Irène); Geneviève Mnich (Marie-Thérèse); Monique Chaumette (Mercédès); Thomas Duval (Émile); Quentin Ogier (Lucien); Katia Wostrikoff (Mireille); Valentine Suard, Erika Faivre (little girls); Marc Pétrone (accordeonist); Jean-Roger Milo (fisherman); Pascal Vignale (waitress); Jacques Poitrenaud (Hector).

'Round Midnight (Autour de Minuit) (1986)
Screenplay David Rayfiel, Bertrand Tavernier, inspired by incidents in the lives of Francis Paudras and Bud Powell; Director of Photography Bruno de Keyzer; Production Design Alexandre Trauner; Costumes Jacqueline Moreau; Music Herbie Hancock; Sound Michel Desrois; Editing Armand Psenny; Production Irwin Winkler, PECF/Little Bear/Warner Brothers. 131 minutes. Cast: Dexter Gordon (Dale Turner); François Cluzet (Francis Borier); Gabrielle Haker (Bérangère); Sandra Reaves-Phillips (Buttercup); Lonette McKee (Darcey Leigh); Christine Pascal (Sylvie); Herbie Hancock (Eddie Wayne); Bobby Hutcherson (Ace); Pierre Trabaud (Francis's father); Frédérique Meninger (Francis's mother); Liliane Rovere (Mme Queen); Hart Leroy Bibbs (Hershell); Ged Marlon (Beau); Benoît Regent (psychiatrist); Victoria Gabrielle Platt (Chan); Arthur French (Booker); John Berry (Ben); Martin Scorsese (Goodley); Philippe Noiret (Redon); Alain Sarde (Terzian); Eddy Mitchell (drunk).

La Passion Béatrice (The Passion of Beatrice) (1987)
Screenplay Colo Tavernier-O'Hagan; Director of Photography Bruno de Keyzer; Camera Yves Angelo; Production Design Guy-Claude François; Costumes Jacqueline Moreau; Music Ron Carter; Sound Michel Desrois; Editing Armand Psenny; Production Adolphe Viezzi, Clea Productions/MLF/TF1 Films Production/Les Films de la Tour Little Bear/Scena Film. 132 minutes. Cast: Bernard-Pierre Donnadieu (François de Cortemart); Julie Delpy (Béatrice); Nils Tavernier (Arnaud); Monique Chaumette (Mère François); Robert Dhery (Raoul); Michele Gleizer (Hélène); Maxime Leroux (Richard); Jean-Claude Adelin (Bertrand Lemartin); Jean-Louis Grinfield (Maître Blanche); Claude Duneton (priest); Isabelle Nanty (wet-nurse); Jean-Luc Rivals (Jehan); Roseline Villaume (Marie); Maite Maille (La Noiraude); Albane Guilhe (La Recluse); Marie privat (Marguerite).

La Vie et Rien d'Autre (Life and Nothing But) (1989)
Screenplay Jean Cosmos, Bertrand Tavernier; Director of Photography Bruno de Keyzer; Camera Alain Choquart; Production Design Guy-Claude François; Costumes Jacqueline Moreau; Music Oswald d'Andréa; Sound Michel Desrois; Editing Armand Psenny; Production René Cleitman, Frédéric Bourboulon, Albert Prevost Hachette Première et Cie/AB Films/Little Bear/Films A2. 134 minutes. Cast: Philippe Noiret (Commandant Dellaplane); Irene de Courtil (Sabine Azéma); Pascale Vignale (Alice); Maurice Barrier (Mercadot); François Perrot (Perrin); Jean-Pol Dubois (André); Daniel Russo (Lieutenant Trévise); Arlette Gilbert (Valentine); Louis Lyonnet (Valentin); Charlotte Maury (Cora Mabel); François Caron (Julien); Thierry Gimenez (Adjudant du Génie); Frédérique Meninger (Mme Lebègue); Pierre Trabaud (Eugène Dilatoire); Jean-Roger Milo (M Lebègue); Michel Duchaussoy (Général Villerieux).

Daddy Nostalgie (*These Foolish Things*) (1991)
Screenplay Colo Tavernier O'Hagan, Bertrand Tavernier; Director of Photography Denis Lenoir; Camera Agnès Godard; Production Design Jean-Louis Poveda; Costumes Christian Gasc; Music Antoine Duhamel; Sound Michel Desrois; Editing Ariane Boeglin; Production Adolphe Viezzi Clea Productions/Little Bear/Solyfic/Eurisma. 105 minutes. Cast: Daddy (Dirk Bogarde); Caroline (Jane Birkin); Odette Laure (Miche); Emanuelle Bataille (Juliette); Charlotte Kady (Barbara); Michèle Minns (Caroline as a child); Sophie Dalezio (first nurse); Sylvie Segalas (second Nurse); Helene Lefumat (woman at hospital); Andrée Duranson (Yvonne); Raymond Defendente (Jimmy); Fabrice Roux (fisherman); Gilbert Guerrero (waiter); Louis Ducreux (old gentleman in Métro).

L.627 (1992)
Screenplay Michel Alexandre, Bertrand Tavernier; Cinematography Alain Choquart; Production Design Guy-Claude François; Costumes Jacqueline Moreau; Music Philippe Sarde; Sound Michel Desrois; Editing Ariane Boeglin; Production Frédéric Bourboulon, Alain Sarde Little Bear/Les Films Alain Sarde. 145 minutes. Cast: Didier Bezace (Lulu); Jean-Paul Comart (Dodo); Charlotte Kady (Marie); Jean-Roger Milo (Manuel); Nils Tavernier (Vincent); Philippe Torreton (Antoine 'Looping'); Lara Guirao (Cécile); Cécile Garcia-Fogel (Kathy); Claude Brosset (Adore); Didier Castello (Willy); Jacques Rosny (Tulip 4); Jean Oudatan (Mamadou Diop); Laurentine Milebo (Alimata); John Arnold (L.627 addict); Jeanne Dubois (Lycée director); Smail Mekki (Miloud Amrani); Isabelle Noah (Philomène).

La Fille de D'Artagnan (*D'Artagnan's Daughter*) (1994)
Screenplay Michel Leviant, Bertrand Tavernier, Jean Cosmos, from an original idea by Riccardo Freda and Eric Poindron; Director of Photography Patrick Blossier; Camera Nathalie Durand; Production Design Geoffroy Larcher; Costumes Jacqueline Moreau; Music Philippe Sarde; Sound Michel Desrois; Editing Ariane Boeglin; Production Frédéric Bourboulon Ciby 2000/Little Bear/TF 1 Films Production. 125 minutes. Cast: Sophie Marceau (Éloïse D'Artagnan); Philippe Noiret (D'Artagnan); Claude Rich (Duc de Crassac); Sami Frey (Aramis); Jean-Luc Bideau (Athos); Raoul Billerey (Porthos); Charlotte Kady (woman in red); Nils Tavernier (Quentin); Luigi Proietti (Cardinal Mazarin); Jean-Paul Roussillon (Planchet); Pascale Roberts (Mother Superior); Stéphane Legros (Louis XIV); Partick Rocca (Bargas).

L'Appât (*The Bait*) (1995)
Screenplay Colo-Tavernier-O'Hagan, Bertrand Tavernier, from the book *L'Appât* by Morgan Sportès; Cinematography Alain Choquart; Production Design Émile Ghigo; Costumes Marpessa Djian; Music Philippe Haim; Sound Michel Desrois; Editing Luce Grunenwaldt; Production René Cleitman, Frédéric Bourboulon Hachette Première/Little Bear/France 2 Cinema/M6 Films. 115 minutes. Cast: Marie Gillain (Nathalie Magnan); Olivier Sitruk (Eric); Bruno Putzulu (Bruno); Richard Berry (Alain Perez);

Philippe Duclos (Antoine Jousse); Marie Ravel (Karine); Clothilde Courau (Patricia); Jean-Louis Richard (restaurant owner); Jean-Paul Comart (Michel); Philippe Helies (Pierre); Jacky Nercessian (M Tapiro); Alain Sarde (Philippe); Daniel Russo (Jean-Pierre); Philippe Torreton (chief investigator); Francois Berleand (Inspector Durieux), François Levantal (policeman 2); Thierry Gimenez (policeman 3); Isabelle Sadoyan (Eric's grandmother); Laurent Arnal (Vincent); Jeanne Goupil (Nathalie's mother); Thierry Beccaro (game-show presenter).

Capitaine Conan (*Captain Conan*) (1997)
Screenplay Jean Cosmos, Bertrand Tavernier, from the novel *Capitaine Conan* by Roger Vercel; Cinematography Alain Choquart; Production Design Guy-Claude François; Costumes Jacqueline Moreau and Agnès Evein; Music Oswald d'Andréa; Sound Michel Desrois; Editing Luce Grunenwaldt; Production Alain Sarde, Frédéric Bourboulon, Les Films Alain Sarde/Little Bear/TF 1 Production. 130 minutes. Cast: Philippe Torreton (Conan); Samuel Le Bihan (Norbert); Bernard Le Coq (De Scève); Catherine Rich (Madeleine Erlane); François Berleand (Commandant Bouvier); Claude Rich (Général Pitard de Lauzier); André Falcon (Colonel Voirin); Claude Brosset (Père Dubreuil); Crina Muresan (Ilyana); Cécile Vassort (Georgette); François Levantal (Forgeol); Pierre Val (Jean Erlane); Roger Knobelspeiss (Medic. Major Cuypène); Frédéric Pierrot (adjudant train chief); Jean-Claude Calon (Gendarme Greffier Loisy); Laurent Schilling (Beuillard); Jean-Yves Roan (Rouzic); Philipppe Helies (Grenais); Tonio Descanvelle (Caboulet); Eric Savin (armoury corporal); Olivier Loustau (Mahut); Jean-Marie Juan (Lethoré).

Ça Commence Aujourd'hui (*It All Starts Today*) (1999)
Screenplay Dominique Sampiero, Tiffany Tavernier, Bertrand Tavernier; Cinematography Alain Choquart; Production Design Thierry François; Costumes Marpessa Djian; Music Louis Sclavis; Sound Michel Desrois; Editing Sophie Brunet; Production Alain Sarde, Frédéric Bourboulon, Les Films Alain Sarde/Little Bear/TF 1 Production. 117 minutes. Cast: Philippe Torreton (Daniel Lefèvre); Maria Pitarresi (Valeria); Nadia Kaci (Samia); Veronique Ataly (Mme Lienard); Nathalie Bécue (Cathy); Emmanuelle Bercot (Mme Tiévaux); Françoise Bette (Mme Delacourt); Christine Citti (Mme Baudoin); Christina Crevillen (Sophie); Sylviane Goudal (Gloria); Didier Bezace (school inspector); Betty Teboulle (Mme Henry); Gérard Giroudon (mayor); Marief Guittier (Daniel's mother); Daniel Delabresse (Marc); Jean-Claude Frissung (director's colleague); Thierry Gibault (police detective); Philippe Meyer (Municipal official); Gérald Cesbron (M Henry); Michelle Goddet (Jimmy's mother); Stefan Elbaum (Jimmy's 'uncle'); Nathalie Desprez (Mme Bry); Françoise Miqhelis (Mme Duhem); Frédéric Richard (M Bacheux); Johanne Cornil-Leconte (Mme Bacheux); Sylvie Delbauffe (woman with baby); Lambert marchal (Rémi); Kelly Mercier (Laetitia Henry); Mathieu Lenne (Jimmy); Rémi Henneuse (Kevin).

FILMOGRAPHY

Feature-length Documentaries

Philippe Soupault et le Surréalisme (videocassette) (1982)
Conception Bertrand Tavernier, Jean Aurenche; Production Management Marie Dabadie; Lighting Camera Jean-François Gondre; Sound Harold Maury; Editing Luce Grunenwaldt; Music Eric Satie, Sidney Bechet, Lester young, Archie Shepp; Production Danièl Delorme for Temoins. 180 minutes.

Pays d'Octobre (1983)
Co-director Robert Parrish; Script Robert Parrish, Bertrand Tavernier; Production Management Kent Moorhead; Cinematography Pierre-William Glenn; Sound Michel Desrois; Production Yannick Bernard, Bertrand Tavernier, Robert Parrish, William Ferris, Little Bear/Odessa Films/Antenne 2/University of Mississippi. 180 minutes.

Mississippi Blues (1994)
96-minute videocassette version of *Pays d'Octobre*.

Lyon: Le Regard Interieur (television) (1988)
Script Bertrand Tavernier; Director of Photography Jean Auzer; Camera Daniel Guinand; Sound Christian Evanghelou; Musique Philippe Sarde, Antoine Duhamel, Gabriel Fauré, Bud Powell, Rodgers Hart, Ron Carter, Gerry Mulligan, Astor Piazzola; Editing Alain Robiche, Marie-France Le Bronnec; Text Gabriel Chevalier, taken from *Chemins de Solitude* and *Carrefours du Hasard*, read by Gérard Guillaumat; with the participation of René Tavernier and Pierre Merindol; Production Dominique Dreyer, FR3, Rhône-Alpes/La Sept/Cameras Continentales (for Les Chroniques de la France).

La Guerre Sans Nom (The Undeclared War) (1992)
Concept: Patrick Rotman, Bertrand Tavernier; Cinematography Alain Choquart; Sound Michel Desrois; Editing Luce Grunenwaldt; Production Manager Alexandre Déon; Assistant Director Tristan Ganne; Production Jean-Pierre Guérin, Eliane Cochi Le Studio Canal+/GMT Productions/Little Bear. 235 minutes. Witnesses: Pierre Achin; Grégoire Alonso; Robert André; Gilbert Argelès; Jacques Bec; Séraphin Berthier; Alain Boeuf; Jean Bollon; Etienne Boulanger; César Delbello; Raymond Didier; René Donazzolo; Michel Drevet; Bruno Enrietti; Gaétan Esposito; Gilbert Gardien; Ezio Goy; Bernard Loiseau; Jean Manin; Bernard Molroguier; René Perrin; Pierre Pessenti; Michel Petrone; Serge Puygrenier; François Sikirdji; Noël Trouilloud; Jean Trouilloud; Robert Zanoni.

De l'Autre Côté du Périph' (television) (1997)
Co-director Nils Tavernier; Script Bertrand Tavernier; Camera Nils Tavernier, Eric Philbert; Editing Luce Grunenwaldt. Production Frédéric Bourboulon, Denis Poncet France 2/Little Bear. First episode, 'Le Coeur de la Cité', 85 minutes; second episode, 'Le Meilleur de l'Âme', 64 minutes.

Les Grévistes de la Double Peine (television) (1999)

Other Projects

La 800e Génération (short) (1983)
Script Bertrand Tavernier, Frédéric Bourboulon; Cinematography Denis Lenoir; Sound Roger Letellier; Music Philippe Sarde, Antoine Duhamel; Editing Kadicha Barya; Production Christian Daireaux. 17 minutes.

Ciné Citron (short) 1983
Script Jean Cosmos, from an idea by Bertrand Tavernier, read by Jean Rochefort; Music Philippe Sarde; Song Ricet Barrier, Philippe Sarde, Jean-Roger Caussimon; Editing Kadicha Barya. 22 minutes.

Contre l'Oubli (1992)
Director of one of 30 segments: Aung San Suu Kyi; Narrator Anouk Grinberg; Production Béatrice Soulé, Amnesty International.

Lumières Sur Un Massacre (1997)
Director of one of ten short films, against anti-personnel land-mines; Narrator Sandrine Bonnaire; Production Frédéric Bourboulon, Bertrand Tavernier Little Bear/Handicap International.

The Lumière Brothers First Films (1996)
Collection of early shorts by Auguste and Louis Lumière. Presenter Bertrand Tavernier; Production Institut Lumière, Lyon.

LITTLE BEAR PRODUCTIONS

La Question (dir. Laurent Heynneman) 1976
Rue de Pied de Grue (dir. Jean-Jacques Grand-Jouan) 1979
La Trace (dir. Bernard Favre) 1983
Remy Duval, 28 Place des Vosges (dir. Clair Clouzot) 1986
Les Mois d'Avril Sont Meurtriers (dir. Laurent Heynneman) 1987
La Vielle Qui Marchait Dans la Mer (dir. Laurent Heynneman) 1991
Viellées d'Armes (dir. Marcel Ophuls) (television) 1994
L'Amour est Reinventé (dir. various) (television) 1996
Fred (dir. Pierre Jolivet) 1997
Restons Groupés (dir. Jean Paul Salomé) 1998
Lumières Sur Un Massacre (dir. various) (television) 1998
12 Films: Le Racism au Quotidien (dir. various) (television) 2000

BIBLIOGRAPHY

PUBLICATIONS REFERRED TO IN THE TEXT

Danièle Bion, *Bertrand Tavernier: Cinéaste de l'Émotion*, FOMA SA, Renens, 1984

Dirk Bogarde, *A Short Walk from Harrods* (diary on making *Daddy Nostalgie*) Penguin, London, 1992

John Boorman and Walter Donohue (eds), *Projections, A Forum for Film-makers*, no 2, Faber & Faber, London, 1992

Idem, *Projections, A Forum for Film-makers*, no 9, 1999

Lynda K. Bundtzen, interview with Bertrand Tavernier on *'Round Midnight*, *Film Quarterly*, vol. 40 no 3, Spring 1987

Michel Ciment, *Kubrick* (interview on *A Clockwork Orange*), Collins, London, 1982

Idem, 'Sunday in the Country with Bertrand', *American Film*, October 1984.

Jean-Luc Douin, *Tavernier*, Edilig, Paris, 1988

Idem, *Tavernier*, Editions Ramsay, Paris, 1997

Michel Euvrard, Guy Hennebelle and Monique Hennebelle, 'Spoiled Children', *Écran*, Paris, 1977

Ruth M. Goldstein, 'The Clockmaker' (review of *L'Horloger de Saint-Paul*), *Film News*, no 5, New York, 1973

William Hackman, 'A Parisian in America', *Film Comment*, vol. 2, Sep.–Oct., New York, 1986

Joseph Hurley, 'Tavernier et Noiret', *Films in Review*, vol. 34 no 3, New York, March 1983

Idem., 'Tavernier et Noiret encore', *Films in Review*, vol. 34 no 4, New York, April 1983

National Film Theatre, Programme Guide for Tavernier Retrospective, anonymous, London, August 1980

David Overbey, 'Those Obscure Objects of Desire', *The Movie*, vol. 8 issue 86, Orbis, London, 1981

Leonard Quart and Lenny Rubenstein, 'Blending the Personal with the Political', *Cinéaste*, vol. 8, no 4, Paris, 1977

Bertrand Tavernier, interview (interviewer anonymous), *Cinéma Francais*, no 1, Paris, May 1976

Idem, '*Death Watch*', *Cinéma Français*, no 31, Paris, 1979

Idem, interview on career to date (interviewer anonymous), *Cinéma Français*, no 32, Paris, 1979

Idem, 'Bertrand Tavernier talks about 'Round Midnight', *Film* (BFFS), vol. 3 no 1, London, January 1987

Idem, press release for *La Passion Béatrice*, Little Bear, Paris, 1988

Idem, '*La Guerre Sans Nom*', interview for Neuf de Coeur and l'Association des Professeurs d'Histoire-Geographie, Neuf de Couer/Little Bear, Paris, December 1991

Idem, 'Michael Powell', retrospective tribute, *Le Monde*, Paris, 12 March 1992

Idem, 'Bertrand Tavernier on *L'Appât*' (interviewer anonymous), notes from Bertrand Tavernier to Alain Choquart for the shooting of *L'Appât*, *L'Appât* press release, Little Bear, Paris 1995

Idem, production diary for *Capitaine Conan*, Little Bear/France Inter, Paris, 1996

Idem, '*Ça Commence Aujourd'hui*' (interviewer anonymous), press release for *Ça Commence Aujourd'hui*, Éditions Gilbert Salachas, Paris, 1999

David Thompson, preview on *La Vie et Rien d'Autre*, *Time Out*, no 1001, London, 25 October 1989

Dan Yakir, 'Painting Pictures', *Film Comment*, vol. 20, Sep.–Oct., New York, 1984

INDEX

Main references to films and documentaries by Tavernier are indicated by bold type.

'Academy Ratio' 65n.
action sequences
  in *Vie et Rien D'Autre, La* 137–8
actors 28
  and camera work 30–1, 78
  new talent 204
  performance 202–3, 205
Adieu Philippine (1963) 8
Adjani, Isabelle 171
Alexandre, Michel 152–3, 156, 159
Algerian War 18–20, 180, 184
Allégret, Yves 26
Alphaville (Godard, 1965) 76
Altman, Robert 9, 89, 109, 159, 176
ambiguity in
  Ça Commence Aujourd'hui 198
  Coup de Torchon 98
  Death Watch 78–9
  Des Enfants Gâtés 72
  Dimanche à la Campagne, Un 216n
  Fille de D'Artagnan, La 167
  Semaine de Vacances, Une 92, 216
America 6
  capitalist culture 77, 171
  cinema 6–7, 8, 23, 119–20, 134, 171, 172, 173
  southern states of 33–5
Amnesty International 24n
Andrea, Oswald d' 135–6, 187
anti-personnel mines 24n
anti-Semitism 60
anti-war films
  Capitaine Conan 179–87
  La Guerre Sans Nom 18, 19–20, 134, 135, 180, 184
Anzin 23, 29, 192–3
Appât, L' (Tavernier, 1995) 135, **169–77**
  close-ups in 212
  homecoming theme in 222
  moral voice in 54
  and Paris 68
Aquila Nera (Freda, 1946) 161
Aragon, Louis 5
Ardant, Fanny 139n
ARP (Association des Réalisateurs Producteurs) 23
aspect ratios 64, 135, 143, 186, 205
assistant directors 200n
Auberger, Maurice 27
Audiberti, Jacques 48, 49
audience identification
  L.627 154, 157
Aumont, Michel 68
Aung San Suu Kyi 24n
Aurenche, Jean 10, 11, 18, 26, 41, 45, 46, 67

  and *Coup de Torchon* 57, 94, 100
  and *Juge et L'Assassin, Le* 57
  Philippe Soupault et el Surréalisme 57
  and *Que La Fête Commence* 48
  written off by Truffaut 27, 133
Auriélien (Aragon) 5
Autant-Lara, Claude 26, 28, 41, 57
Autre Côté du Périph, De l' (documentary) (Tavernier, 1997) 18, 20–2, 73, 192, 222–3
Azéma, Sabine 62, 86, 131

Badlands (Malick, 1976) 176
Baiser de Judas, Le (short drama) (Tavernier, 1963), 9, 39
Bandwagon, The (Minnelli, 1953) 8
Barbie, Klaus 219, 220, 224n
Battle of Saint Pietro, The (Huston, 1945) 184–5, 188n
Baye, Nathalie 62, 84, 86, 210
Beach of Falesa, The (Stevenson) 10
Beatrice Cenci (Freda, 1956) 122, 161
Beauregard, Georges de 8, 161
Bec, Jacques 184
Becker, Jacques 27
belle époque 104, 109
Berry, Richard 172, 212
Bertrand Tavernier: Cinéaste de l'Émotion (Bion) 7
Bezace, Didier 151, 195, 212–13
Biberman, Herbert 9
big close-ups 56n, 138
Bion, Daniel 7, 28
Bird (Eastwood, 1988) 112
Birkin, Jane 62, 142, 143, 149, 204
Bogarde, Dirk 142–3, 204, 215n
Bonnaire, Sandrine 24n
Bonomi, Albert 34
Boorman, John 68
Bost, Pierre 11, 26, 41, 45, 57, 67
  Dimanche à la Campagne, Un 57, 103, 107
  written off by Truffaut 27, 133
Bourboulon, Frédéric 13, 18, 178n, 200n
  on Tavernier 31–2, 202
Brel, Jacques 10
Bresson, Robert 81
Brialy, Jean-Claude 58
Brosset, Claude 158
Bunuel, Luis 7
Burma 24n

Ça Commence Aujourd'hui (Tavernier, 1999) **189–99**
  camera work on 135, 194–5, 199, 212–13
  doubt in 223

political expression in 16, 134
portrayal of teacher in 7
on the set of 29–30, 32
spoken poetry in 92, 189, 190–1, 194, 199
Cahiers du Cinéma, Les (film journal) 10, 27
Cameron, James 29
Capitaine Conan (Tavernier, 1996) 20–1, 22, 30, 32, 135, **179–87**
  evil actions in 58
  feeling of doubt 67
  homecoming theme in 221
  political expression in 16, 134
Carabiniers, Les (1963) 8
Carné, Marcel 28
Cassavetes, John 176
Cassou, Jean 5
Catholic Church
  in *Daddy Nostalgie* 142
  in *Juge et L'Assassin, Le* 60
  in *Que La Fête Commence* 51
Caussimon, Jean-Roger 14, 30, 88
CCTV 77
César awards 202, 204
Chabrol, Claude 8, 9, 25, 130n
Chagrin et La Pitié, La (Ophuls, 1971) 19
Chambre Verte, La (Truffaut, 1978) 28, 86
Chance Explosive, Une (short drama) (Tavernier, 1964) 9, 39
characters
  and connection with past 42, 91–2, 222–3
  rebellious 132, *see also* women characters
Chateau, Denis 11
childhood fears
  in *Coup de Torchon* 97
  in *Semaine de Vacances, Une* 91
children
  in *Ça Commence Aujourd'hui* 193, 195, 198
  death of 195–7
  in *Semaine de Vacances, Une* 92
Chinatown (Polanski, 1974) 154
Choquart, Alain 30, 32, 34, 134–5, 155
  Appât, L' 176–7
  Ça Commence Aujourd'hui 194, 197
  Capitaine Conan 186–7
  on Tavernier 211–13
Christie, Julie 81, 82
Ciby 2000 production house 162
Ciment, Michel 14, 15
Cinécitta production house 161
Cinéma (film journal) 10
Cinemascope 65n, 205
cinematography **206–13**
  actor-camera dynamic 30–1, 78
  in *Appât, L'* 176–7, 212
  in *Ça Commence Aujourd'hui* 135, 194–5, 199
  camera movements 194, 195, 206–10
  in *Capitaine Conan* 186–7
  close-ups, *see* close-ups
  conventional cover 187, 188n
  in *Coup de Torchon* 98–9, 155, 195, 208

  in *Death Watch* 83
  in *Dimanche à La Campagne, Un* 108–9, 207
  distance created in *Daddy Nostalgie* 148–9
  focus-pull 42–3
  'Fordian' framings 134, 135, 136
  hand-held cameras 27, 53, 185, 186, 209
  head shots 56n
  in *L.627* 154–5, 177
  in *Passion Béatrice, La* 125
  linking people and their environment 43, 99, 109, 206–7, 209
  long-shots 134–5, 136, 185–6, 195
  medium long-shots 136, 140n
  and music 207
  panning shots 116
  reverse-angle shots 209
  in *'Round Midnight* 118–19
  Steadicam 98–9, 102n, 155, 185, 186, 187
  tracking shots 29, 36n, 39, 40, 116, 185, 186, 188n, 205, 208, 209
  two-shots 144
  'uncomposed' style 18
  wide framing 98, 129, 136–8, 143–4, 186–7, 205
city planning practices 69
Cléo de 5 à 7 (1961) 8
Clockwork Orange, A (Kubrick, 1971) 75
close-ups 56n, 89
  in *Appât, L'* 212
  big 55n, 138
  in *Ça Commence Aujourd'hui* 195
  in *Capitaine Conan* 185–6
  in *Fille de D'Artagnan, La* 167
  medium 126
  and mise-en-scène 206
  in *Passion Béatrice, La* 126
  Tavernier's wariness of 205–6
  in *Vie et Rien D'Autre, La* 135, 137–8, 212
closing sequences of
  Ça Commence Aujourd'hui 199
  Coup de Torchon 219
  Des Enfants Gâtés 72, 122
  Dimanche à la Campagne, Un 215, 216n
  Juge et L'Assassin, Le 14–15, 64–5
  Passion Béatrice, La 129
  Que La Fête Commence 14–15, 52, 55
  Vie et Rien D'Autre, La 139
Cocteau, Jean 81–2
Coin, Henri de 27
collective history 33
Comart, Jean-Paul 155
Combat (film journal) 10
Come Back To The Five and Dime, Jimmy Dean, Jimmy Dean (Altman, 1982) 109
Comédie Française, La 204
comedy
  Fille de D'Artagnan, La 162–3
comedy, black
  Coup de Torchon 96–7, 163

Compton, David 75
conflicts
  in *Capitaine Conan* 182–3
  in *Des Enfant Gâtés* 70–1
Confluences (literary magazine) 5, 219, 220
consumerism 44
Contre l'Oubli (Tavernier, 1992) 22
conventional cover 187, 188n
conversations
  in *Daddy Nostalgie* 144
  in *Dimanche à La Campagne, Un* 105
Coplan Ouvre le Feu à Mexico (Freda, 1967) 161
Coppola, Francis Ford 29
Corneau, Alain 26
Cosmos, Jean 6, 22, 87, 132–3, 138, 162, 204
  on *Capitaine Conan* 179, 180, 181
Coup de Torchon (Tavernier, 1981) **94–102**, 109
  adaptation of novel 40
  and Aurenche 57
  camera work in 98–9, 155, 195, 208
  ending of 219
  and existence of God 55
  feeling of journey and discovery 17
  hint of hope in 6
  paternal relations in 104
  pessimism in 26
  portrayal of teacher in 7
  Truffaut's admiration of 28
creativity
  in *Dimanche à La Campagne, Un* 105, 107
  in *'Round Midnight* 112–1
crime
  Appât, L' 169–77
  Horloger de Saint-Paul, L' 44, 45–6, 152
  L.627 151–60
Croix, La (Catholic journal) 60
cut-aways 127
  in *Daddy Nostalgie* 144
Cyrano de Bergerac (Rappeneau, 1990) 162

Daddy Nostalgie (Tavernier, 1991) **141–9**
  comparable with *Dimanche à la Campagne, Un* 142
  homecoming theme in 221, 223
  Paris in 68
  paternal relationship in 40, 141–9
  very little politics in 15
Danon, Raymond 11, 39
Das Blue Engel (von Sternberg, 1930) 7
Daves, Delmer 8, 10, 44
de Niro, Robert 203
de Palma, Brian 172
De Sica, Vittorio 162, 168n
death in
  Ça Commence Aujourd'hui 195–7
  Capitaine Conan 187
  Fille de D'Artagnan, La 167
Death Watch (Tavernier, 1979) 32, **75–83**, 85, 96, 156, 174

children in long-shot 195
evil actions 58
hint of hope in 6
homecoming theme in 221
interiors 218
paternal relations in 104
rapid tracking shots in 208
wide framing used in 205
Debré, Professor 5
Debré Immigration Act, Article 1 21
Delannoy, Jean 27, 41
Delbauffe, Sylvie 193
Delpy, Julie 62, 86, 87
Des Enfants Gâtés (Tavernier, 1977) 66–73, 85, 122, 218
  political expression in 14, 15–16, 17, 73
Despair (Fassbinder, 1977) 142
despair in
  Juge et L'Assassin, Le 99–100
  Passion Béatrice, La 123, 129
  'Round Midnight 118
Desplechin, d'Arnaud 21
Desprez, Nathalie 193
Desrois, Michel 'Tonton' 29, 34, 46, 47, 129
Deux Hommes Dans Manhattan (Melville, 1959) 7
Diable au Corps, Le (Autant-Lara, 1947) 57
dialogue sequences
  in *Juge et L'Assassin, Le* 58
  from old films 27
  shooting 209
  and shot sizes 53, 55n
Diary of a Country Priest, The (Bresson, 1950) 81
Didier, Bezace 87
Dieu a Besoin des Hommes (Delannoy, 1950) 27
Dimanche à la Campagne, Un (Tavernier, 1984) 22, 26, 67, **103–11**, 122, 206
  apolitical 15, 16
  and Bost 57
  camera work in 108–9, 207, 208
  Daddy Nostalgie comparable with 142
  ending of 215, 216n
  homecoming theme in 221
  humanism of 121
  lighting in 210–11
  location for 211
  paternal-filial relationship in 40, 104, 107, 114, 164
  and Tavernier's father 104–5, 141
  Truffaut's admiration of 28
  voice-over narration in 104, 106, 107, 108, 111, 213–14
distance
  in *Daddy Nostalgie* 148–9
  and wide framing 205
documentaries by Tavernier
  Autre Côté du Périph, De l' 18, 20–2, 73, 192, 222–3

Guerre Sans Nom, La 18, 19–20, 134, 135, 180, 184
Lyon: Le Regard Intérieur 5, 131, 141, 217, 218, 219–20, 223
Mississippi Blues 33–5, 103
Pays d'Octobre 33, 119–20
Philippe Soupault et el Surréalisme 18, 57, 103
Donnadieu, Bernard-Pierre 126–7
doubt, theme of 55, 67, 221, 224
  in *Ça Commence Aujourd'hui* 223
  in *Coup de Torchon* 94, 100
  in *Passion Béatrice, La* 127, 129
Doulos, Le (1961) 8
Dreyfus, Alfred 60
drugs squad 151–3, 157–60
Dubois, Abbé 48, 49, 51–2
Dubreuil, Charlotte 68
Ducreux, Louis 22, 149
Duhamel, Antoine 52, 81, 82, 149, 219, 220
Dumas, Alexandre 10, 48, 49, 161, 162
Duneton, Claude 85
Duvivier, Julien 26, 28

Eastwood, Clint 112
Edinburgh Filmhouse 112
editing
  cut-aways 127, 144
  in *Daddy Nostalgie* 144
  fades-to-black 91, 110, 111n
  inter-cutting 70–1, 110, 116
education
  cinematic portrayal of schools 7, 16, 84–92, 100, 189–99
  pleasure of learning 34
  Tavernier's unpleasant associations with 7
En Cas de Malheur (Autant-Lara, 1958) 41
Enfants Terrible, Les (Cocteau, 1950) 81
Espoir (Malraux, 1945) 7
Étrave, L' (cinema journal) 7
evil 58, 96, 101

fades-to-black
  in early film-making 111n
  on *Dimanche à La Campagne, Un* 110
  on *Semaine de Vacances, Une* 91
Falbalas (Becker 1952) 27
'false tints' 83n
family relationships
  absence of 96
  Daddy Nostalgie 142–9
  in *Dimanche à La Campagne, Un* 104, 106–7
Fassbinder, Rainer Werner 142
Faurè, Gabriel 109–10, 207
Favre, Bernard 22
Ferran, Pascale 21
50 Ans de Cinéma Américain (Tavernier co-author of) 23, 134
Figlio de D'Artagnan, Il (Freda, 1949) 161–2
Fille de D'Artagnan, La (Tavernier, 1994) 161–8

Fille du Régent, La (Dumas) 10, 48, 162
film crews
  living environment of 123
  in Romania 181
  seen in documentary *Mississippi Blues* 33–4
  working relationship with Tavernier 29–30, 32, 46–7, 68
Film Europe (France) 23
film noir 81
film scores
  Appât, L' 173
  Ça Commence Aujourd'hui 198
  Capitaine Conan 187
  Coup de Torchon 98
  Daddy Nostalgie 145, 146, 149
  Death Watch 81, 82, 219
  Dimanche à La Campagne, Un 109–10, 207
  Horloger de Saint-Paul, L' 45–6, 88, 207
  Juge et L'Assassin, Le 62–3, 88
  L.627 157
  Que La Fête Commence 51
  'Round Midnight 119
  Semaine de Vacances, Une 88, 207
  Vie et Rien D'Autre, La 135–6, 139
film stock 209
  Fuji 82
  in *Death Watch* 82–3
  in *Dimanche à La Campagne, Un* 109, 118
  in *'Round Midnight* 118
First World War 16, 179, 181, 219
flashbacks
  in *Daddy Nostalgie* 144
focus-pull 42–3
Ford, John 6, 9, 33, 89, 113, 134, 135, 203, 212
Four Friends (Penn, 1981) 81
framing **204–6**
  Appât, L' 176–7
  wide 98, 129, 136–8, 143–4, 186–7
France
  Americanisation of 171, 172
  liberation of 6
François, Guy-Claude 123, 135
Frankenheimer, John 9
Freda, Riccardo 10, 122, 161–2
Frémaux, Thierry 23
French military 134
Fuller, Samuel 9, 10
future, *Death Watch* set in near 75–83

Galabru, Michel 60, 61, 64, 87, 205
Garcia-Fogel, Cécile 153
Garfield, John 80
Gassman, Vittorio 162
GATT negotiations (1993) 23, 172
Gaumont 11
generational issues in
  Appât, L' 171–2
  Ça Commence Aujourd'hui 197
  Daddy Nostalgie 147

Des Enfants Gâtés 69–70
Fille de D'Artagnan, La 165
Horloger de Saint-Paul, L' 26, 45
Genoux d'Ariane, Les (short film) 8
Gershwin, George 214
Gillain, Marie 86, 87, 170
Glasgow 76–7
Glenn, Pierre-William 27, 30, 34, 43, 46, 64, 67, 68, 155
   and *Coup de Torchon* 98
   and *Death Watch* 82–3
   not working with Tavernier 108
   on Tavernier 209–10
   and *Semaine de Vacances, Une* 91
Go-Between, The (Losey, 1971) 81, 109
God, existence of
   in *Coup de Torchon* 102
   in *Passion Béatrice, La* 55, 101, 125, 128, 129
   in *Que La Fête Commence* 55
Godard, Jean-Luc 8, 76, 81
Goebbels, Joseph 60
Gordon, Dexter 113, 119, 192
government policy 134
Grands-Pêchers housing project, Paris 21–2, 73, 192
Grenoble 19
Grinberg, Anouk 24n
Grunenwaldt, Luce 181
Guérin, Jean-Pierre 18
Guerre Sans Nom, La (documentary) (Tavernier, 1991) 18, 19–20, 134, 135, 180, 184
Guitry, Sacha 81

Hancock, Herbie 119
hand-held cameras 27, 53, 185, 186, 209
Handicap International 24n
Hanging Tree, The (Daves, 1957) 44
Hans, Marie-Françoise 85
Hathaway, Henry 6
Haudiquet, Philippe 7
Haute Vallée de l'Aude 123
Hawks, Howard 9
head-shots 56n
Heynemann, Laurent 18, 22
hidden characteristics 191, 208
history 33, 179, 219–20
Hitchcock, Alfred 9, 27
Hollywood 35, 171, 172
homecoming theme 220–2
Honeymoon Killers (Kastle, 1970) 176
hope, hints of 6, 198
Horloger de Saint-Paul, L' (Tavernier, 1973) 11–12, 13–14, **39–47**, 96
   connections between distant and recent past 42, 91–2, 222
   crime and justice 44, 45–6, 152
   doubt as theme in 55
   film score of 45–6, 88, 207
   generational question in 26, 45

Glenn and 209
hidden characteristics in 191
humanism in 25, 45–6
Lyon used in the story 41–2, 43–4, 46
media pushing materialism in 44, 170
night and darkness theme in 39, 174
opening sequence of 39, 40, 195
paternal relationships in 40, 164
political feeling in 58
screenplay for 39–40
use of voice-over in 81
Hugo, Victor 60
human observation
   in *Des Enfants Gâtés* 72
humanism **25–35**, 45–6, 95, 121, 191–2
humour in
   Coup de Torchon 96–7, 163
   Des Enfants Gâtés 72
   Fille de D'Artagnan, La 162–3
   L.627 159
   Que La Fête Commence 50
   Semaine de Vacances, Une 87–8
Hundred Years War 122
Huppert, Isabelle 58, 61–2, 86, 203, 204
Huston, John 9, 184–5

illegal immigrants 21
insanity
   in *Coup de Torchon* 96
   in *Juge et L'Assassin, Le* 59–60
   in *Passion Béatrice, La* 125
Institut Lumière, Lyon 23
inter-cutting 110
   in *Des Enfants Gâtés* 70–1
   in *'Round Midnight* 116
interiors 218
   linked to exteriors 209
isolation theme
   in *Daddy Nostalgie* 143–4, 148
   in *Fille de D'Artagnan, La* 168
   in *'Round Midnight* 116
   in *Semaine de Vacances, Une* 96

jazz music 112–20, 214–15
Je Suis une Truie Qui Doute (Duneton) 85
Juge et L'Assassin, Le (Tavernier, 1976) **57–65**, 85, 96, 174
   despair in 99–100
   film score 62–3, 88
   first person narration in 81
   framing in 205
   negative reference to Paris in 68
   political expression in 14–15
   pseudo-parental relationship in 40
justice theme in
   Juge et L'Assassin, Le 58–9, 152
   L.627 152

Kaci, Nadia 193
Kady, Charlotte 86, 157

Kastle, Leonard 176
Kazan, Elia 9
Keitel, Harvey 75, 79–80, 204
Keyzer, Bruno de 108–9, 118, 122–3, 134, 138–9
  on Tavernier 210–11
Killer Inside Me, The (Thompson) 95
Killing, The (Kubrick, 1956) 102
Kubrick, Stanley 75, 95, 180, 185

L.627 (Tavernier, 1992) 22, 23, 25, 89, 135, 151–60, 177
  and *Ça Commence Aujourd'hui* 190, 192
  evil actions in 58
  hidden characteristics in 191
  and Lyon 221, 222
  political expression in 16
  wide framing used in 205
Lang, Fritz 7, 8, 9
Lanvin, Gérard 30, 86, 204
Last Temptation of Christ, The (Scorsese, 1988) 112
lateral tracking shots 186
Laure, Odette 142
Le Bihan, Samuel 181
Le Coq, Bernard 181
Lénaud, René 224n
Lenne, Matthieu 193
Léon Morin, Prêtre (Melville, 1961) 7–8
Lettres Françaises, Les (film journal) 10
Léviant, Michel 162
Libération 197, 200n
Lifeline (television programme) 75
lighting on
  Death Watch 82–3
  Dimanche à La Campagne, Un 210–11
  Passion Béatrice, La 125
  Que La Fête Commence 53
  'Round Midnight 115, 116, 119
  Semaine de Vacances, Une 91
Liotard, Thérèse 81
Little Bear production company 18, 22, 73, 162
Loach, Ken 192, 193, 197
locations
  Anzin 23, 29, 192–3
  Glasgow 76–7
  Haute Vallée de l'Aude 123
  importance of real 211
  Lyon 41–2, 43–4, 46, 84, 91, 217
  Paris 68, 151, 155
  Romania 180–1
  Tavernier's favourite 202
loneliness 223
  in *Coup de Torchon* 94, 95–6
  in *Daddy Nostalgie* 144
  in *Fille de D'Artagnan, La* 168
  in *Passion Béatrice, La* 125
long-shots 134–5, 136
  in *Capitaine Conan* 185–6

of children 195
  medium 136, 140n
long takes 204, 215n
Los Olvidados 7
Losey, Joseph 8, 9, 10, 44, 81, 109, 142–3
Louis XIV 48
Lumière, Louis 109
Lumières Sur un Massacre (Tavernier 1998) 22, 23
Lupino, Ida 9
Lyon 5–7, **217–24**
  compared with Glasgow 76
  in *Horloger de Saint-Paul, L'* 41–2, 43–4, 46, 217
  in *Semaine de Vacances, Une* 91
Lyon: Le Regard Intérieur (documentary) (Tavernier, 1988) 5, 6, 131, 141, 217, 218, 219–20, 223
lyricism 16, **213–15**
  in *Ça Commence Aujourd'hui* 191
  in *Death Watch* 77–8, 82
  in *Juge et L'Assassin, Le* 61, 62–3

McCarey, Leo 9
Mahler, Gustav 81
Maigret Tend un Piège (Delannoy, 1957) 41
Malick, Terence 176, 186
Malle, Louis 27
Malraux, André 7
Marceau, Sophie 162
March of Time films 82
Martin, Yves 8
Martinand, Bernard 8
M*A*S*H (Altman, 1970) 159
Mason, James 10
materialism 44, 88, 170–2
Mean Streets (Scorsese, 1973) 55
media 77–9, 197
  and materialism 44, 88, 170
medium close-ups
  in *Passion Béatrice, La* 126
medium long-shots 136, 140n
Melville, Jean-Pierre 7, 8, 9, 28, 67
memories 6, 223
Mépris, Le (Godard, 1963) 8
Mercier, Kelly 193
Miller, Claude 26
Milo, Jean-Roger 158
Minnelli, Vincente 8
mise-en-scène 11, 28
  in *Capitaine Conan* 185, 186, 187
  in *Daddy Nostalgie* 144
  and *Death Watch* 77–8
  and framing 204–5
  in *Horloger de Saint-Paul, L'* 43–4
  increasing complexity of 17
  L.627 153–4
  in *Semaine de Vacances, Une* 84, 86
  shaped around actor's performance 31, 86

stifled by cutting and close-ups 206
  in *Vie et Rien D'Autre, La* 131, 135, 137
Mississippi Blues (documentary) (Tavernier, 1983) 33–5, 103
Mitchell, Eddy 30, 88
Mizoguchi, Kenji 7
Mnich, Geneviève 68
Mois d'Avril Sont Meutriers, Les (Heynemann, 1987) 22
Monsieur Ladmiral Va Bientôt Mourir (Bost) 57, 103
Montreuil, Paris 21–2, 73, 192
Moonfleet (Lang, 1955) 8
moral voice 54, 78
  in *Capitaine Conan* 181–2
Moreau, Jacqueline 118
moving shots 194, 195, 206–9
music
  jazz 112–20, 214–15
  and political films 16
  Scottish lullaby 77
  songs 88, 145, 146, 149, 214–15, *see also* film scores

natural sounds 63, 209, 214
Neo-MacMahoniens, Les 8
New Wave 8, 9, 26
  Tavernier on 26–8
Nickel Odéon, Le (*ciné club*) 8
night theme
  Appât, L' 174–5
Nightmare on Elm Street 6 172
nihilism
  of *Coup de Torchon* 95, 102
Noiret, Philippe 11, 67, 203, 204
  Coup de Torchon 95
  Fille de D'Artagnan, La 163–4
  Horloger de Saint-Paul, L' 39, 40, 42, 46, 87
  Juge et L'Assassin, Le 57, 60, 61, 64
  Que La Fête Commence 50, 52, 53–4
  and relationship with Tavernier 113
  'Round Midnight 119
  Semaine de Vacances, Une 84, 86
  Vie et Rien D'Autre, La 131, 132, 133
non-actors 29, 192–3
non-verbal communication 117
nostalgia 40

Oeuil de Malin, L' (Chabrol, 1962) 8
old age theme in
  Dimanche à la Campagne, Un 110–11
  Fille de D'Artagnan, La 165–6
  Semaine de Vacances, Une 90–1
opening sequences of
  Capitaine Conan 185–6
  Coup de Torchon 98
  Death Watch 82
  Horloger de Saint-Paul, L' 39, 40
  Juge et L'Assassin, Le 62, 64
  Que La Fête Commence 49–50, 55

Ophuls, Marcel 19
Orléans, Philippe de 48, 99
Orwell, George 197
Ossessione Che Uddice, Le (Freda, 1980) 161

Pacino, Al 173
Panavision 65n
  lenses 89
  'panning and scanning' 93n
Paris
  Grands-Pêchers housing project 21–2, 73, 192
  as location for *L.627* 151, 155
  negative references to 68–9
  social problems in 21–2
  Tavernier at school in 7
  Tavernier's dislike of shooting in 68, 202
  urban ruination of 15–16, 69, 72
Paris Texas (Wenders) 36n
Parker, Charlie 112, 214–15
Parrish, Robert 33–5
Pascal, Christine 86
  in *Des Enfants Gâtés* 66, 68, 71–2, 78
  in *Horloger de Saint-Paul, L'* 47, 61
  in *Que La Fête Commence* 54
Passion Béatrice, La (Tavernier, 1987) 40, **121–9**, 161
  apolitical 15
  doubt in 100
  evil actions in 58
  and existence of God 55, 101, 125, 128, 129
  homecoming theme in 221
  paternal relationships in 125–8, 164
paternal relationships in
  Ça Commence Aujourd'hui 197
  Daddy Nostalgie 40, 141–9
  Dimanche à la Campagne, Un 40, 104, 107, 114, 164
  Fille de D'Artagnan, La 164–5
  Horloger de Saint-Paul, L' 40, 164
  Passion Béatrice, La 125–8, 164
  'Round Midnight 113–14
Pathé 11
Paths of Glory (Kubrick, 1957) 95, 180, 185
patriotism 5
Paudras, Francis 113
Pays d'Octobre (documentary) (Tavernier, 1983) 33, 119–20
Peeping Tom (Michael Powell, 1960) 9
Penn, Arthur 81
performance 119–20, **202–4**, 205
pessimism in
  Appât, L' 169
  Coup de Torchon 26
  Fille de D'Artagnan, La 166, 168
  Passion Béatrice, La 125
  Semaine de Vacances, Une 90
Philippe Soupault et el Surréalisme (documentary) (Tavernier, 1982) 18, 57, 103

Piccoli, Michel 66, 67, 68
piece-to-camera techniques 16
Pierrot Le Fou (Godard, 1965) 8, 81
plot 134
poetry
   Ça Commence Aujourd'hui 92, 189, 190–1, 194, 199
   Death Watch 82
Poindron, Eric 162
Polanski, Roman 154
police
   Appât, L' 177, 186
   L.627 151–60
Pollack, Sidney 75
Polonsky, Abraham 9, 143
Ponge, Francis 5
Pons, Eugène 220, 224n
Pop. 1280 (Thompson) 94
Positif (film journal) 10, 27
Powell, Bud 113
Powell, Michael 6, 9–10, 30, 89, 210
Prades film festival 104
Preminger, Otto 8
Prévert, Jacques 84
Prix Goncourt 179
Proietti, Luigi 165
Psenny, Armand 46
Putzulu, Bruno 170

Que La Fête Commence (Tavernier, 1975) 10, 25–6, **48–55**, 94–5, 96
   Fille de D'Artagnan, La and 163–4, 165
   Pierre-William Glenn and 209–10
   political expression in 14–15
   Truffaut's admiration of 28
Question, La (Heynemann, 1977) 18–19

racism 94, 100
   in *L.627* 158
radio news broadcasts
   and *Semaine de Vacances, Une* 88–9
Raoult, Eric 21–2, 73, 223
Rappeneau, Jean-Paul 162
Rayfiel, David 75, 113
Reisz, Karel 93n
Renoir, Jean 7, 25, 28, 31, 34, 109
Resnais, Alain 29
Restons Groupés (Salomé, 1998) 22
reverse-angle shots 209
reverse tracking shots 185, 188n, 205
Rich, Claude 163
Richardson, Tony 53
Rissient, Pierre 8, 10, 143, 162
Roberts, Julia 171
Rochefort, Jean 46
Roman d'un Tricheur, Le (Guitry, 1936) 81
Romance of a Horse-Thief (Polonsky, 1970) 143
Rotman, Patrick 18
'Round Midnight (Tavernier, 1986) 67, 112–20, 121, 122, 174, 192, 222
   camera work in 208
   interiors 218
   and Lyon 220–1
   very little politics in 15
   wide framing used in 205
Rozier, Jacques 8
Ruffio, Jacques 9

Sadoul, Georges 5
Salomé, Jean-Paul 22
Sampiero, Dominque 190, 195
Sarde, Alain 103, 119
Sarde, Philippe 22, 62, 98, 157
Sautet, Claude 8, 9, 67
Saving Private Ryan (Spielberg, 1998) 186
Scarface (de Palma, 1983) 172
Schatzberg, Jerry 9
Schlöndorff, Volker 7, 28, 54
Schneider, Romy 62, 75, 78, 80, 81, 210
Schoendorffer, Pierre 8
schools
   in Tavernier's films 7, 16, 84–92, 100, 189–99
Scorsese, Martin 6, 55, 112, 203
Scotland 76, 82
screenplays
   adaptation of novels 39–40, 94, 103, 179, 183
   Appât, L' 169–70
   Ça Commence Aujourd'hui 189
   Capitaine Conan 179, 180, 181
   Coup de Torchon 94
   Daddy Nostalgie 141–2, 146, 147
   Des Enfant Gâtés 67
   Dimanche à la Campagne, Un 122
   Fille de D'Artagnan, La 162
   Juge et L'Assassin, Le 57–8
   L.627 152–3
   Passion Béatrice, La 122
   Que La Fête Commence 48
   'Round Midnight 122
   Semaine de Vacances, Une 85, 122
   Vie et Rien D'Autre, La 138
Seagal, Steven 172
Second World War 94, 219
selfishness in
   Dimanche à la Campagne, Un 107
   'Round Midnight 114
Selznick, David O. 57
Semaine de Vacances, Une (Tavernier, 1980) **84–92**, 109, 174, 206, 218
   children in long-shot 195
   contrast with *Coup de Torchon* 95
   ending of 215, 216n
   feeling of journey and discovery 17
   Glenn on 210
   hidden characteristics in 191
   humanism of 121
   and Lyon 217
   moral voice in 54

optimism of 26
and schools 7, 16
sense of isolation in 96
Truffaut's admiration of 28
She Wore a Yellow Ribbon (Ford, 1949) 135
Shining, The (Kubrick) 98
shot sizes 53, 55–6n
Simenon, Georges 39, 41, 44, 45, 48, 124
Sitruk, Olivier 170, 212
Socialism 197
Sociéte des Auteurs et Compositeurs Dramatiques (SACD) 22, 132
Sociéte des Réalisateurs de Films 23
songs 88
  'These Foolish Things' 145, 146, 149, 214–15
Soupault, Philippe 18
Southerner, The (Renoir, 1945) 34
Spielberg, Steven 186
Sportès, Morgan 169
Stanton, Harry Dean 75, 79
Steadicam 98–9, 102n, 155, 185, 186, 187
Sternberg, Joseph von 7
Stevenson, Robert Louis 10
storyboards 212, 215
studio settings
  in *'Round Midnight* 112, 119
suicide 72
  in *Passion Béatrice, La* 125, 129
Sundance Festival 95
swash-buckling genre 10, 161–8
Sydow, Max von 75–6

Tainsy, Andrée 69–70
Tavernier, Bertrand
  and actors 28, 30, 61, 86–7, 202–4
  attitude to young children 195–7
  autobiographical elements in films 40, 42, 66–7, 141
  character of 13, 31, 68
  'child-gaze' of 32–3
  cinéphile 6, 23
  and comparisons with Renoir 28, 31
  critical of the Catholic Church 51–2
  directing **201–15**
  drafted into military service 18
  duality of 224
  earliest reference to cinema 6
  eclecticism of 11, 47, 48, 95, 131, 161, 168, 219
  education of 7
  and family 40–1
  fascination with people in constant motion 206–7
  fascination with time 42, 91–2, 116
  and father 5, 104–5, 141, 147, 149
  as film publicist 8
  and fine cuisine 112
  first chance at directing 8–9
  humanism of **25–35**, 45–6, 95
  insatiable curiosity for knowledge 34–5
  irritated by pigeon-holing 26
  and jazz music 112, 214–15
  and Jean-Pierre Melville 7–8
  and Ken Loach 192, 193, 197
  and Le Nickel Odéon (*ciné club*) 8
  and *L'Étrave* (cinema journal) 7
  love of swash bucklers 10, 161
  and Lyon, *see* Lyon
  and Michael Powell 9–10
  and new talent 204
  and New Wave 26–8
  optimism of 6, 26
  and Philippe Noiret 203
  and politics **13–23**, 58–61, 73, 84, 88, 133–4, 190, 197
  politics of film production 22–3
  preferred working method 194
  and preparation period 215
  promotion of cinema as art form 23
  respecting integrity of source material 164, 183
  screenwriting 10–11
  and Truffaut 27–8
  working relationship with cast and crew 29–30, 32, 46–7
  writing for film journals 10
Tavernier, Ginette (mother) 5
Tavernier, Nils (son) 21, 73, 130n, 152, 165
  interview with father 4–5
Tavernier, René (father) 5, 104–5, 141, 147, 149, 219–20, 223
Tavernier, Tiffany (daughter) 32, 34, 40–1, 190, 193, 195, 200n, 219, 224
Tavernier-O'Hagan, Colo (ex-wife) 85, 92, 122, 141–2, 146, 147
  and *Appât, L'* 169–70
teachers 7, 85, 100
  Ça Commence Aujourd'hui 189–99
  Semaine de Vacances, Une 84–92
Teboulle, Betty 195
television 83
  Death Watch 75–9
  Horloger de Saint-Paul, L' 44, 170
  Semaine de Vacances, Une 88–9
Terminator 2 172
Terreur, La 48
testimonies 18–20, 23, 33
'These Foolish Things' (Strachey-Lonk and Maschwitz) 145, 146, 149, 214–15
Thieves Like Us (Altman) 176
Thin Red Line (Malick) 186
Thompson, Jim 94, 95
317ᵉ Section, La (1964) 8
Three Women (Altman) 89
Time Without Pity (Losey, 1956) 10
Titanic (Cameron, 1997) 29
title sequences for
  Capitaine Conan 185
  Coup de Torchon 101

Des Enfants Gâtés 69, 72–3
L.627 157
Passion Béatrice, La 124
Semaine de Vacances, Une 88
Tom Jones (Richardson) 53
Torreton, Philippe 87, 155, 177, 180, 186, 193, 204, 212–13
torture
 in Algeria 18, 20
 and *Appât, L'* 169–70
 morality of filming 11
Toth, André de 162, 164n
Tourneur, Jacques 89
Trace, La (Favre, 1983) 22
tracking shots 29, 36n, 39, 40, 116, 209
 lateral 186
 rapid 208
 reverse 185, 188n, 205
Trauner, Alexandre 118
Traversée de Paris, La (1956) 11
treatments 57, 65n
Triolet, Elsa 5
Truffaut, François 9, 11, 25, 86
 cinéphile 6
 critical of Aurenche and Bost 27, 133
two-shots
 in *Daddy Nostalgie* 144

Unseeing Eye, The (Compton) 75
urbanisation 15–16, 69, 72, 76, 218–19
urgency, sense of
 Appât, L' 176
 Ça Commence Aujourd'hui 197
 Vie et Rien D'Autre, La 135, 197

'Valéria Subra' affair 169–70
Vercel, Roger 179–80, 183
Verité sur Bébé Donge, La (de Coin, 1952) 27
Vervel, Pierre 11
Vichy régime 5, 6
Vidor, King 8
Vie et Rien D'Autre, La (Tavernier, 1989) 20, 131–9, 174
 camera work on 208, 211–12
 and Jean Cosmos 22
 optimism of 6

political expression in 16, 17
portrayal of teacher in 7
urgency 135, 197
Vigne, Daniel 130n
violence
 in *Capitaine Conan* 183–4
Vitoux, Frédéric 7
voice-over narration 16, 17, 20, 213–14
 Ça Commence Aujourd'hui 189, 190–1, 194
 Daddy Nostalgie 141
 Death Watch 81
 Des Enfants Gâtés 122
 Dimanche à la Campagne, Un 104, 106, 107, 108, 111, 213–14
 Passion Béatrice, La 122
 Semaine de Vacances, Une 92
Vollmer, Jürgen 29
voyeurism 75, 83, 156, 208, *see also Death Watch*

Walsh, Raoul 8, 9
Warner Brothers 112, 118, 120
Wayne, John 135, 203, 212
Wellman, William 6
Wenders, Wim 33
wide framing 98, 129, 136–8, 143–4, 186–7, 205
wide screen format
 in *Death Watch* 82
 in *Juge et L'Assassin, Le* 64
 in *Semaine de Vacances, Une* 89–90
 in *Vie et Rien D'Autre, La* 135
wide-screen television 65n
Winkler, Irwin 112, 120
women characters 61–2, 71–2, 85–6, 210
 in *Coup de Torchon* 100
 in *Dimanche à la Campagne, Un* 105–6, 107–8
 and moral force 54, 78
work, as theme
 in *L.627* 151, 156
 in *Vie et Rien D'Autre, La* 133–5, 151, 156

Young, Lester 113, 214–15

Zola, Émile 60